The Oratory of Southern Demagogues

The Oratory of
Southern Demagogues

Edited by Cal M. Logue and Howard Dorgan

Louisiana State University Press / Baton Rouge and London

Copyright © 1981 by Louisiana State University Press
All rights reserved
Manufactured in the United States of America

Design: Patricia Douglas Crowder
Typeface: VIP Palatino
Composition: G&S Typesetters, Inc.

LIBRARY OF CONGRESS CATALOGING IN PUBLICATION DATA
Oratory of southern demagogues.

Includes index.
Contents: The demagogue / Cal M. Logue & Howard Dorgan—Jeff Davis of Arkansas / Annette Shelby—"Pitchfork Ben" Tillman and "the race problem from a southern point of view" / Howard Dorgan—James Kimble Vardaman, manipulation through myths in Mississippi / [etc.]
1. Political oratory—Southern States—Addresses, essays, lectures. 2. Southern States—Politics and government—1865-1950—Addresses, essays, lectures.
I. Logue, Calvin McLeod. II. Dorgan, Howard.
PN4193.P607   815'.09'358   81-3759
ISBN 0-8071-0792-1   AACR2

For
    Waldo W. Braden

Contents

The Oratory of Southern Demagogues

CAL M. LOGUE & HOWARD DORGAN

The Demagogue

Southern states entered the last decade of the nineteenth century in-
fected by an inflated vision of a new prosperity. Increased business
and industrial activity generated by promoters during the 1880s had
in several areas created a booming economic environment, as hundreds of textile mills were built, iron works expanded, the tobacco industry grew, transportation systems improved, and values of shipping from southern ports skyrocketed. The real benefits of this
stimulated economy, however, were monopolized by moneyed interests, industrialists, the merchant class, and the larger planters. Small
farmers, independent craftsmen, and industrial workers frequently
did not share in the New South returns. In fact, during the twenty
years prior to the turn of the century the economic status of these persons tended to worsen.[1]

Life for the small farmer had become especially hard. Before the
war cotton had been a profitable cash crop, and throughout the immediate postbellum period southerners had tried to restore this staple to its former status in their society. But a wasted soil combined
with punitive credit practices and a steady drop in cotton prices to
frustrate even the most diligent efforts of small yeoman farmers as
well as white and black sharecroppers. Each season the evils of the
crop-lien system and usurious interest rates generally left the small

1. C. Vann Woodward, *Origins of the New South* (Baton Rouge: Louisiana State
University Press, 1951), 107–41, 175–234.

farmer further in debt. As the price of cotton dropped, the actual production of the staple rose, thus ruining the market upon which southern agrarians depended.[2] By 1894 the price of cotton had slid to a low of 4.6 cents a pound, and farmers were earning less from the twenty-three million acres of cotton they planted that year than they had from the nine million acres produced in 1873.[3]

Broken by these farming conditions, many poor whites left the land and fled to the new mill villages and industrial centers. But here they encountered economic and social circumstances as oppressive as those they had left behind—long hours, unhealthy working environments, and wages so low they forced an entire family into the mill in order to produce a survival income. In town the company store took the place of the crop-lien merchant and often bound the worker in perpetual indebtedness.

Having mainly their labor to market, poor whites were jeopardized by the region's antiunion stance and by the convict lease system. Furthermore, with laborers in abundance, working whites eyed with animosity all blacks and immigrants as competitors for their jobs. Indeed, the greatest fear of the poor white class was that they would be placed on the same economic and social level as southern blacks. Abject poverty was burden enough, but to their way of thinking complete social degradation would be unbearable.

With the beginning of the twentieth century, the relative economic status of poor whites did not appreciably improve. Progress in the South continued to be advanced on the back of cheap labor, and upcountry dirt farmers and Piedmont mill workers shared the common bond of being exploited by a prospering class. Nevertheless, these poor working whites did possess the power of the ballot, a leverage that after 1880 blacks quickly lost.

This "poor white" vote was significant, and beginning with such men as Jeff Davis of Arkansas, Tom Watson of Georgia, and "Pitchfork Ben" Tillman of South Carolina a new breed of politician—soon stereotyped as the "southern demagogue"—responded to the needs,

2. Wilbur J. Cash, *The Mind of the South* (New York: Vintage-Knopf, 1941), 149, 152; Harold D. Woodman, *King Cotton and His Retainers: Financing and Marketing the Cotton Crop of the South, 1800–1925* (Lexington: University of Kentucky Press, 1968), 335.
3. Woodward, *Origins of the New South*, 185.

fears, and aspirations of lower class whites and established power bases from which they operated to sweep away most of the vestiges of the Bourbon Democrats' political control. Eventually other southern leaders such as James Kimble Vardaman and Theodore G. Bilbo of Mississippi, Cole Blease and "Cotton Ed" Smith of South Carolina, Huey Long of Louisiana, Tom Heflin of Alabama, W. Lee O'Daniel of Texas, and Eugene Talmadge of Georgia were designated members of this generic category, and the South became known as the home of the "demagogue."

I

According to Wilma Dykeman, "the term 'Southern demagogue' seems as natural a combination as cornbread and turnip greens."[4] But Dykeman also suggests that the widespread tendency to link these words inextricably may be unfair, since other regions of the nation have had their share of political leaders who fit the commonly understood demagogic mold. In fact, of the ten "demagogues" that Reinhard H. Luthin treats in his volume *American Demagogues*, only four were from the South. The remainder were from Massachusetts, Illinois, Oklahoma, New Jersey, New York, and Wisconsin.[5] Furthermore, David H. Bennett's *Demagogues in the Depression* features only one name that has been tied to the South, Gerald L. K. Smith, and Smith was, by birth, education, and much of his career, a midwesterner.[6] In addition revisionist historians such as Richard Hofstadter have frequently drawn our attention to the "demagogic" nature of midwestern populism—particularly its elements of racism, anti-Semitism, nativism, and nationalism.[7]

It should also be noted that "southern demagogues" were not all of one mind. V. O. Key, for example, explained that "the basis for the association" of Eugene Talmadge with Theodore Bilbo and Huey

4. Wilma Dykeman, "The Southern Demagogue," *Virginia Quarterly Review*, XXXIII (Winter-Autumn, 1957), 559–60.

5. Reinhard H. Luthin, *American Demagogues* (Boston: Beacon Press, 1954).

6. David H. Bennett, *Demagogues in the Depression* (New Brunswick, N.J.: Rutgers University Press, 1969).

7. Richard Hofstadter, "The Folklore of Populism," in Raymond J. Cunningham (ed.), *Populists in Historical Perspective* (Lexington, Mass.: D. C. Heath, 1968), 23–28.

Long was "little more than unruly conduct and an uninhibited tongue. Talmadge," observed Key, "had little sympathy for the heavy-taxing, free-spending ways of Huey" and "looked askance at the New Deal voting record of Bilbo." Indeed, the Georgian "was more like some northern governors, John W. Bricker, for example," than he was like "either Long or Bilbo."[8]

Dykeman does express understanding for the tendency of linking "southern" and "demagogue." "The field is not entirely ours," she says, "but we may be there 'firstest with the mostest.'"[9] But if Dykeman is correct and the South has been prominent in exhibiting this form of leadership, what precisely is the nature of this political species for which the region has become famous?

"Demagogue" is traditionally a pejorative and thus to a degree defines the political perception of the user of the term. Colorful, popular, and plebeian politicians we do not like we call "demagogues," whereas those we like we are apt to identify as "leaders of the common man" or "champions of the people." But, in addition, a part of the pejorative nature of the word is that it implies insincerity and opportunism. As Allen Louis Larson has argued, "demagogue" suggests that the recipient of the title has "made political capital out of social and/or economic discontent in order to gain influence and political power."[10] In fact, this is precisely the sentiment around which G. M. Gilbert has centered his definition of the term. "A demagogue," asserts Gilbert, "is a person who seeks notoriety and power by exploiting the fears and desires of the people, offering scapegoats and dogmatic panaceas in an unscrupulous attempt to hold himself forth as the champion of their values, needs, and institutions. His behavior is guided more by its potential effect in beguiling public opinion than by any scrupulous regard for the truth, for basic social values, or for the integrity of the individual in his person, property, livelihood, or reputation."

Gilbert's definition goes beyond a mere consideration of political technique to make a judgment about the values, honesty, integrity,

8. V. O. Key, Jr., *Southern Politics in State and Nation* (New York: Alfred A. Knopf, 1949), 117.
9. Dykeman, "The Southern Demagogue," 562.
10. Allan Louis Larson, *Southern Demagogues: A Study in Charismatic Leadership* (Ann Arbor, Mich.: University Microfilms, 1964), 85.

and ethics of the public figure to whom "demagogue" is applied. To Gilbert, demagoguery is not amoral, it is immoral, a form of political unscrupulousness packaged in a raucous and gaudy common man's style. Most of all this designation signifies treacherous insincerity, the "Big Lie," "systematic distortion of truth," "twisting of facts," "deliberative deception," "sensational and reckless" attack, and the "abuse and usurpation of authority to further . . . political strength and notoriety."[11]

Larson, however, is uncomfortable with this automatic association of sleazy political ethics with the term "demagogue." He formulates a general definition, which does not place specific boundaries around the word. For him a demagogue is simply "a political leader or public figure which operates through appeals to the passions." Furthermore, Larson specifically excludes attitudinal dishonesty from this definition, arguing that although "popular usage does ordinarily imply insincerity, it seems bad science and bad faith" to include this characteristic as a universal. Therefore, in Larson's judgment the emotions and beliefs of the demagogue may or may not be sincere.

An appeal to common passions, however, is essential to Larson's definition, for he identifies "persuasion linked to passion" as "the hallmark of the demagogue as charismatic leader." "When persuasion is linked to reason, even if couched in high rhetoric," he asserts, "we may have politics of the highest order. . . . But those who pander to passion, prejudice, bigotry and ignorance, rather than reason, fall into another category." This category, of course, is that of demagogue. "In periods of strife, economic dislocation, religious or racial turmoil," adds Larson, "men are unable to perceive the factors which are responsible for their misery and distress. Under such circumstances, they look for a leader who will deliver them from their problems."[12] Thus Larson views demagoguery as behavior resulting from an interaction of the charismatic personality of a political leader, his irrational—but perhaps honest—rhetorical methods, and the real socioeconomic needs of a moment.

Some discussions of the demagogue emphasize his style of per-

11. G. M. Gilbert, "Dictators and Demagogues," *Journal of Social Issues*, 11 (No. 3, 1955), 51–53.
12. Larson, *Southern Demagogues*, 76, 79, 85.

formance. Luthin, for example, notes the demagogue's "tricks of the ham actor," his "jokes, anecdotes, and personalized invective," "'plain folks' appeal," "profuse emotionalism," general "rusticity," "use of farmers' phraseology," and his "affectionate nicknames."[13] Dykeman mentions most of these characteristics but adds to the list the "distinctive manner of dress," the "antics and costumes," and the overall carnival-like atmosphere of the oratorical occasions.[14] From such images there emerges a picture of the demagogue as stage personality and showman—the circus barker politician, the snake oil peddler, and the used car salesman pushing his wares via the use of a straw hat, overalls, and a hillbilly band.

A final approach to the defining of demagoguery derives from a thesis advanced by Sterling Fishman. According to Fishman there are usually three steps in the psychological strategy of the demagogue: first, he intensifies a "popular crisis psychology"; next, he defines the cause of the crisis as being a single and simple abstract or concrete evil; and, finally, he provides an equally simple escape from the crisis, "a new faith, a new belief," with himself as the leader.[15] The popular crisis could be, for example, what W. J. Cash called the "rape complex,"[16] that state of mind—prevalent for a time among whites in both the North and South—that held that the greatest single weakness in a black man's character was "his innate fondness for white women and his disposition to commit the crime of rape."[17] The demagogue would first intensify this feeling before identifying its "cause"—which in this instance he might argue is the entire egalitarian movement as applied to blacks and whites. He next offers an escape from the crisis via the rejection of these libertarian ideals and personifies himself as the leader of this resistance.

13. Luthin, *American Demagogues*, 305–307.
14. Dykeman, "The Southern Demagogue," 561–62.
15. Sterling Fishman, "The Rise of Hitler as a Beer Hall Orator," *Review of Politics*, XXVI (April, 1964), 250–52.
16. Cash, *The Mind of the South*, 116–20.
17. I. A. Newby, *Jim Crow's Defense: Anti-Negro Thought in America, 1900–1930* (Baton Rouge: Louisiana State University Press, 1965), 135.

II

One finds then, a variety of perceptions concerning the demagogue, and to some degree this diversity is represented by the nine essays that comprise the remainder of this volume.

In the first essay, Annette Shelby analyzes how Jeff Davis capitalized on the plight of Arkansas' deprived citizens. In general she argues that Davis enhanced his own credibility by contrasting the dire conditions of the average Arkansan with the excessive wealth and power of persons affiliated with such institutions as trusts and state government, and by projecting himself as the symbol by which average workers could triumph.

Howard Dorgan contends that the racist views of Benjamin Ryan Tillman of South Carolina reflected the attitudes of American whites more than they caused them. Focusing upon a lecture repeated regularly by Tillman between 1901 and 1909, Dorgan demonstrates how this spokesman attempted to legitimize the oppressive authority of southern whites by deriding what he said was the ineptitude of all "colored peoples" for self-government. The author recalls the "strident" and "formless" speech Tillman employed to articulate the basic tenets of white superiority.

In his investigation of James Kimble Vardaman, William M. Strickland indicates how this Mississippian appropriated stock mythic images fostered earlier by Bourbon Democrats to defeat those political aristocrats in the 1903 gubernatorial election. Mississippi's shift from conventions to popular primaries allowed Vardaman to appeal to the passions and prejudice of the general electorate. This skillful persuader manipulated the fears of "Negro equality" and "Yankee domination," flamed the fires of class hatred, and presented himself as representing the ideals and values of the Democratic party and of the Old South. Strickland establishes Vardaman's oratory as a major reason for his rise to power in Mississippi politics.

G. Jack Gravlee studies "the first Tom Watson," before this Georgian concentrated rhetorically on racist ethnic appeals. Analyzing speeches presented by Watson in New York and St. Louis during his 1904 campaign for the presidency, and one speech delivered in Georgia after he had lost the election, Gravlee investigates how the candidate promised to rescue personal "principle" and social "justice" from business and political exploiters. Gravlee also explores why Watson's efforts to package "Jeffersonian democracy" persuasively failed to win the necessary votes and how, after losing the campaign, Watson defensively sectionalized his criteria for determining what policy was best for the country.

In 1918 Coleman L. Blease, former governor of South Carolina, found himself in an awkward position in his campaign for the United States Senate. He had previously led South Carolina's Reform Democrats in their opposition to the American declaration of war against Germany and the ensuing wartime policies of Woodrow Wilson. In attempting to extricate himself from this stance—which by 1918 was most unpopular in South Carolina—Blease employed a distinct rhetorical form, the apology. M. L. McCauley argues in his essay, however, that Blease failed as an apologist, largely because of an inability fully to assume the role.

Mary Louise Gehring suggests that it was not Ellison Durant Smith's personal convictions concerning agriculture, tariffs, immigration, states' rights, and race that returned him to the United States Senate for six terms. Indeed, his views on these topics were shared by the other major political candidates in South Carolina, and Smith offered few imaginative policies for dealing effectively with these issues. In fact, he was never noted for his prowess in senatorial debate or for any skill in legislative maneuvering. What did distinguish Smith was his effectiveness in articulating stock topics in an emotional manner and his ability to identify himself fully with rural-minded audiences.

Jerry Hendrix follows the political career of Theodore G. Bilbo from when this Mississippian was a rowdy reformer to the period when he communicated racist symbols as a means of preventing equal legal, political, and economic opportunities for blacks. Hendrix found Bilbo to be a tireless speaker who preyed upon the poverty and prejudices of white citizens.

Harold Mixon makes a detailed analysis of Huey Pierce Long's 1927–1928 gubernatorial campaign speeches, an examination seminal to an understanding of the man's political career. To win this election Long, a political outsider at the time, developed speaking strategies of "polarization" and "solidification" as means of contrasting his own reformist views with the conservative contentions of his opponents. Mixon demonstrates how in hundreds of speeches Long promised that if elected he would mobilize state agencies to serve the economic and educational needs of the average citizen of Louisiana.

Finally, Cal M. Logue examines the stock rhetorical strategies employed by Eugene Talmadge in seven Georgia elections. In studying this career of campaigning which spanned from 1926 to 1946, Logue establishes two distinctive qualities of a Talmadge campaign: the man exploited the speech scene as a means of persuasion, and his speaking was characterized by its familiarity, novelty, and professed infallibility.

III

Because the authors of these essays emphasized a variety of periods, occasions, and topics, the editors are cautious in generalizing about the nature of the public performances of "southern demagogues." The essayists here demonstrate that some of these men behaved differently in public at various stages of their careers, as did Tom Watson, for example, who as a young man stressed economic needs and only later turned to racist appeals. It becomes clear, also, that some of these legendary spellbinders failed in their persuasive efforts, demonstrating that aggressive rhetorical tactics did not guarantee success. While recognizing these differences, however, the editors suggest three qualities that generally characterized the oratory of these men.

First, these southern "demagogues" were somewhat arrogant leaders whose rhetoric often reeked with omniscience. Tenacious, haughty, and magnetic to many, they always seemed to be on the offensive, belligerent toward opponents and even subjugating to supporters. They seemed to speak with equal disdain and professed authority about blacks, trusts, political opponents, race-mixing professors, prisons, and expensive automobile tags. A central characteristic of their message was their insolent methods of persuasion. Indeed, much of their personal appeal to white workers derived from their public contempt of social, economic, and political conventions—factors the average person was made to believe held him or her captive in poverty and powerlessness. Critics perceived the "demagogues" as being dangerously authoritarian, whereas supporters felt pride in their belligerency and identified experientially with their intrepid discourse. For the first time the workers' daily drudgery and private complaints were dramatized fearlessly in public. Persons caught in a cycle of poverty concluded that they could do better by the dictations of the "demagogue" than they had done under the policies of politicians whose public behavior was usually judged as being more civil and "gentlemanly."

Next, these orators were felicitous promoters, astute in marketing themselves and their policies by manipulating messages. Although promising to rescue whites from economic poverty and political impotency, they often acted opportunistically to exploit situations profitable to them politically. Indeed, one factor that characterized the "demagogue's" performance was his tendency to propagandize ideas, issues, events, and personalities. Several of these politicians did seek significant societal changes in areas of taxation, prisons, education, agriculture, transportation, and public service, yet it often appeared that they were more interested in the seductive power of these promised reforms than in the issues themselves. Indeed the promises were sometimes merely vague verbal allusions to changes in policies relative to issues ranging from race to roads, the Confederacy to cotton, tariffs to trusts, and banks to boll weevils. Nevertheless, these promises were important to poor farmers and laborers who listened and found in the rhetoric new hope and a rekindled regional pride. Hundreds and thousands of southerners drove cars, rode horses, or walked to attend political rallies where they heard exaggerated political promises seemingly beyond the reach of both the audience and the speakers.

Finally, by their highly domineering discourse these "demagogues" created a regional climate that unfortunately was not always open to debate on social and political problems such as race relations. Here, however, it should be noted that in certain one-party states these obstinate politicians did provide the voters an option at the polls. In fact, V. O. Key maintained that "the colorful demagogue possessed of an intensely loyal personal following can introduce in the disorganized politics of one-party states elements of stability and form that are of the utmost importance," thereby remedying "an important deficiency of one-party government."[18] Still the combative stance of these men tended to stifle any constructive exchange of ideas, often clogging communicative channels with emotional platitudes and dictatorial directives, and frequently intimidating persons who possessed alternative views. The orators' efforts to control political choices came in the form of discursive strategies which ranged rhetorically from a poetic empathy with the powerless to hallucinatory harangues of self-indulgence.

This book is a sequel to the *Oratory in the Old South* and the *Oratory in the New South*, both edited by Waldo W. Braden, professor of speech at Louisiana State University from 1946 to 1979, to whom *Oratory of Southern Demagogues* is dedicated. The writers of the essays in this work express appreciation to Waldo Braden for his inspirational teaching and for his seminal research in the area of southern public address.

18. Key, *Southern Politics in State and Nation*, 106.

Davis is standing in middle of wagon, in white hat.

1 / ANNETTE SHELBY

Jeff Davis of Arkansas
"Professional Man of the People"

> In Arkansas Jeff Davis is more than a man; he is a sentiment, a
> belief, a conviction, a credo; he is a psychological fetich.[1]

Davis' friends loved him "as one of their own." His enemies hated
him with an unbridled passion. To his friends, Davis was a reformer;
he was Sampson, Lochinvar, Joshua, "a conquering Achilles," the Napoleon of Arkansas politics. To his enemies, he was "Jeff the Little," "a mental, political pigmy, a demagogue whose representations
from the stump are as 'tinkling brass or sounding symbols [sic].'"[2]
"Whence is his strength and what are the factors of his power?" veteran foe, the *Arkansas Gazette* editorially asked about this prosecuting
attorney, attorney general, three-time governor, and twice-elected
United States Senator. "We answer":

He is thoroughly democratic in speech, manner and action, and is surcharged
with personal magnetism.
He makes the people think he is persecuted for their sake and stands between them and oppression.
He appeals to the human element.
He cunningly paints things to his liking and ingeniously and unscrupulously
turns them to his advantage.
He continually does violence to the moral maxim that the suppression of
truth is the suggestion of falsehood.
He audaciously and impudently relies on the public's lack of information
about incidents in issue.

1. Rupert B. Vance, "A Karl Marx for Hill Billies: Portrait of a Southern Leader,"
Social Forces, IX (December, 1930), 180; *Arkansas Gazette* (Little Rock), August 1, 1906.
2. *Arkansas Sentinel* (Fayetteville), January 14, 1902.

He appropriates credit for about everything creditable.
He has a powerful machine.
He has not met his match.[3]

An ambitious politician who "was for the under dog in every fight," Davis reflected and capitalized upon the frustrations of Arkansas' dispossessed and in so doing forged a new political alliance that changed the face of Arkansas politics.[4] By "taking his case to the people," he gave power to the powerless and thus ensured his own political future.

The revolution Davis led was primarily rhetorical. Indeed, his own actions as well as those he demanded of his followers were largely symbolic. Privilege would be destroyed, he argued, when the "men of the hills touch hands with the men of the valleys."[5] The action called for was implicit: vote for Jeff Davis. The rhetoric—a key factor in any assessment of Davis as demagogue—may be examined by analyzing these factors: conditions crucial to the rise of the "one gallus democracy"; Davis the man; issues; rhetorical strategies; persuasive techniques; and finally, effect.

Roots of Davisism

Davisism, that peculiar brand of neopopulism that captured the imagination of the people and effectively ruled Arkansas politics for more than four decades, grew out of festering agrarian discontent met by an unresponsive political power structure that promised no remedy of economic, social, political, and cultural grievances.[6] Undergirding

3. *Arkansas Gazette*, August 1, 1906.
4. Jeff Davis, "The Suppression of Pools, Trusts and Combinations in Trade," U.S. Senate speech, December 11, 1907, in L. S. Dunaway (ed.), *Jeff Davis: His Life and Speeches* (Little Rock: Democrat Printing and Lithograph, 1913), 101–21. In this celebrated "Cobweb" speech, Davis broke precedent by speaking on an important issue only nine days after he entered the Senate. He delivered a second speech on the suppression of trusts May 1, 1908. Daniel M. Robison, "From Tillman to Long: Some Striking Leaders of the Rural South," *Journal of Southern History*, III (August, 1937), 303–304.
5. This epigram appears in practically every stump speech Davis ever made.
6. See V. O. Key, Jr., *Southern Politics in State and Nation* (New York: Alfred A. Knopf, 1949), 184; Morton Harrison Fry II, "Jeff Davis of Arkansas: A Study of Neo-Populism and Economic Democracy" (Senior thesis, Princeton University, 1968), 74–81; Reinhard H. Luthin, *American Demagogues* (Boston: Beacon Press, 1954), 11–12; Richard B. Dixon, "Press Opinion Toward the Populist Party in Arkansas, 1890–1896" (M.A. thesis, University of Arkansas, 1953), 59–61; George James Stevenson, "The Political

this confrontation were a persistent antiintellectualism, particularly among the hill folk, and a reassertion by the mountain men of their traditional rugged individualism. Conditions were ripe for a change in Arkansas politics.

Although certainly more than a vestige of the agrarian movement that had swept the country in the 1870s, 1880s, and 1890s, Davisism reflected the same kind of discontent with insensitive government as had the farm organizations and political parties of the preceding decades. Arkansans were particularly strapped by the declining cotton economy. And, though industrialization came rather slowly to the state, dispossessed farmers laid the blame for their vicious cycle of poverty squarely on the shoulders of the great combinations and monopolies. The grievances persisted, and so did the commonly alleged "cause"—the creditor classes, most notably the trusts. The battle lines were thus drawn: dispossessed farmers against the symbols of northern capital. This special interest politics was fertile ground for agitation.

The grievances were real. At stake were economic survival, political participation, and status. The instability of the cotton economy; problems of inequitable land distribution that resulted in tenancy; a credit system that effectively dispossessed many yeoman farmers of their land; low prices for farm products, both in terms of dollars and in comparison with industrial price levels; worn-out land; droughts— these pushed many into a hand-to-mouth existence. Not only did farmers lose ground economically; they also lost political clout. Although Arkansas was still predominately an agricultural state, cotton was no longer king. Agrarian interests, represented by the Bourbon planters in the Old South, had been replaced in the state capitol by industrial interests favorable to "foreign" investors. The accommodation of moneyed interests by the conservative Democrats resulted in discriminatory legislation including a system of mortgages advantageous to the creditor class, burdensome taxation that put the onus on those least able to pay, and differential freight rates that penalized southern producers. Finally, along with their economic and political debarment, agrarians lost social status, being ridiculed as hillbillies

Career of Jeff Davis: An Example of the Southern Protest" (M.A. thesis, University of Arkansas, 1949), 5–20.

and red-necks. The results were predictable—resentment, anger, frustration, and when all doors of relief were seemingly closed, malaise.[7]

Disillusioned in the belief that the entrenched power structure would remedy the prevailing situation, agrarians were ready for a radical shift in power. The shift came, however, not in a repudiation of the Democratic party, that "confraternity"—as Wilbur Cash called it—that had ruled Arkansas since Reconstruction, but within the party itself. In 1892, the Democratic platform in Arkansas incorporated significant Populist demands. And the 1896 election of Dan W. Jones as governor effectively ended conservatism's grip on the state. That election "paved the way for Jeff Davis' even more progressive measures." Davis in turn was precursor for the southern demagogues who followed, including Huey Long who "listened with rapt attention" to his speeches.[8]

Davis the Man

The first in the "procession of twentieth-century Southern demagogues," Davis was no political accident. This "political prodigy," as the *Arkansas Gazette* called him, was a product of his times; he was also "peculiarly a product of Arkansas."[9] Born in secession, reared in civil war and Reconstruction, this son of a former Baptist minister and county and probate judge lived most of his early life in the heart of the Arkansas hill country. As the poet-historian John Gould Fletcher observed, "It was the mountain people who had produced Jeff Davis; from the beginning of his career to its end, he was their spokesman and their champion." In the hill country Davis developed the fierce independence, the unshakable willpower, the "almost unerring judg-

7. Leo Lowenthal and Norbert Guterman, "Portrait of the American Agitator," *Public Opinion Quarterly*, XII (Fall, 1948), 426.

8. Stevenson, "The Political Career of Jeff Davis," 24; Thomas S. Staples and David Y. Thomas, "The Rise of the One Gallus Democracy," in David Yancey Thomas (ed.), *Arkansas and Its People: A History, 1541–1930* (4 vols.; New York: American Historical Society, 1930), I, 259; T. Harry Williams, *Huey Long* (New York: Alfred A. Knopf, 1969), 69.

9. Francis Butler Simkins, *A History of the South* (New York: Alfred A. Knopf, 1965), 541; *Arkansas Gazette* (Little Rock), August 1, 1906; *Senate Documents*, Henderson M. Jacoway, *Jeff Davis: Memorial Addresses Delivered in the Senate and the House of Representatives of the United States*, 62nd Cong., 3rd Sess., No. 1146, p. 67.

ment of men," the unswerving loyalty toward his friends, and the reverence for human dignity that were to influence and characterize his subsequent political and personal actions. In the hill country he shaped his own politics against a background of resistance to Republican tactics, repudiation of populism, and a persistent "undercover radicalism" that permeated the prevailing political philosophy of the mountaineers.[10] He adopted the pervasive antiintellectualism of the region, though as his Senate colleague James P. Clarke noted in a memorial address, "he was a more powerful intellectual force than casual observers . . . believed."[11] In the hill country Davis learned to enjoy a good fight. He embraced the crude humor of the frontier and excelled at sarcasm, ridicule, namecalling, and practical jokes. Furthermore, Davis never forgot his hill country "raising."

Sociologist Rupert Vance suggested that "luck made Jeff."[12] And perhaps it did. No doubt Davis' boyish good looks and magnetic personality accounted in some measure for his success. But it was a series of fortuitous circumstances that thrust him into the mainstream of political affairs. Initially, Davis had wanted to be a soldier. Failing to gain a scholarship to West Point, he pursued, instead, a degree in law. And he used his position at the bar and as prosecuting attorney for the 5th Judicial Circuit to hone his rhetorical skills. Relying primarily on his memory rather than on notes, he "marshalled the evidence . . . in a careful and analytical manner." His cross examination was skillful and forceful, and "it was difficult to get an acquittal when Jeff Davis made the last appeal to the jurors." Charles Jacobson, his long-time private secretary, thought there was "no question" that Davis' experiences "materially qualified him for his future conquests. He acquired confidence in himself, ability to meet opposition, legal experience, and acquaintance throughout his district. . . . He received favorable comment over the state, all of which combined to implant within him seeds of political ambition."[13]

10. John Gould Fletcher, *Arkansas* (Chapel Hill: University of North Carolina Press, 1947), 280, 315; *Senate Documents*, William Shields Goodwin, *Jeff Davis: Memorial Addresses*, 62nd Cong., 3rd Sess., No. 1146, p. 73.
11. *Senate Documents*, James P. Clarke, *Jeff Davis: Memorial Addresses*, 62nd Cong., 3rd Sess., No. 1146, p. 23.
12. Vance, "A Karl Marx for Hill Billies," 182.
13. Charles Jacobson, *The Life Story of Jeff Davis: The Stormy Petrel of Arkansas Politics* (Little Rock: Parke-Harper, 1925), 21–23.

Davis' political aspirations, thwarted by his certain defeat and subsequent withdrawal from the 1896 congressional race, reasserted themselves in 1898 when he ran statewide for attorney general. The campaign was a near fiasco, as Davis suffered a minor paralytic stroke that prevented his actively campaigning. In fact, he made only one speech, which he read while seated in a chair, and the Eureka Springs audience responded politely but unenthusiastically. Discouraged by the sure victory of his opponent, Frank M. Goar, Davis prepared to move his family to Oklahoma. Fate again intervened. Goar died in the final weeks of the campaign, and Davis was elected attorney general. His tenure in office effectively allied him with "the people" against the trusts. That posture—most probably influenced by close study of William Jennings Bryan's speeches—thrust him into the governorship for three terms (1901–1906) and then into the U.S. Senate (1907–1913) where he served until his death. The man and the milieu had met.

Although his political enemies accused him of "inordinate and selfish ambition," Davis countered that he worked only for the welfare of the people—or, as his successor in the U.S. Senate William M. Kavanaugh phrased it, "to serve the great common people . . . and to restore the affairs of government to the simplicity and democracy of the forefathers." [14] Without a doubt Davis was politically ambitious and satisfied his own aspirations through wedding himself to the common people and becoming their champion. Yet, his motives do not appear to have been solely selfish. His genuine sympathy for the common man was unquestionable. J. V. Bourland, a contemporary, thought him "Jacksonian" and believed that "his political career was largely shaped by a natural passion for equality and exact justice. He stood for right; believed in government by the people, not by a favored class." Jeptha Evans agreed: "He was not very well suited to try a cause for a rich citizen against a common citizen. . . . His great delight was to champion in court and vindicate the rights of the poor and weak against the rich and strong. His feelings and sympathies were always intensely human." Further, political ally Congressman John C. Floyd, who judged Davis to be "honest and sincere but often

14. *Senate Documents*, William M. Kavanaugh, *Jeff Davis: Memorial Addresses*, 62nd Cong., 3rd Sess., No. 1146, p. 33.

misunderstood," believed "he would have gone down to defeat rather than to have surrendered the principles for which he stood." [15]

Although consistent in his principles—particularly the rights of the common man against institutionalized power—Davis felt no compunction to maintain continuous political alliances. For example, he incorporated many Populist demands into his own political platform. Explaining this philosophical shift to a Bentonville audience, he chortled: "Populists—why, I used to hate them; but I did not know as much then as I do now; I did not have as much sense then as I have now. Those old Populists twenty years ago saw what we are seeing today." [16] Numerous political realignments found his former friends enemies and his former enemies friends. Toward the end of Davis' career, his personal secretary, Jacobson, became one of his most caustic critics. Davis never "broke" with the people, however. Nor did they desert him.

The Issues

Davis once confided to Jacobson his belief that "the public was not interested in men, but in issues, and no man could make a successful campaign unless he had a popular issue behind his race." [17] Issues were for Davis both a vehicle for political advancement and an identification of ills to be remedied by his own election. In the ideology of Davisism, issues were the "they" (or the evidences of the "they") —the "enemy." Davis neither created the issues nor initiated public discussion of them. But he did give them currency, visibility, and animation.

Five major issues emerged as paramount in Davis' rhetoric: the trusts, the state capitol, "the penitentiary gang," Davis himself, and race. By passing an antitrust law and providing for the building of a new state capitol, the legislature provided the young attorney general

15. J. V. Bourland, introduction to Dunaway (ed.), *Jeff Davis*, 8, and Jeptha Evans' January 5, 1913, "Eulogy," p. 29 of the same work; *Senate Documents*, John Charles Floyd, *Jeff Davis: Memorial Addresses*, 62nd Cong., 3rd Sess., No. 1146, p. 45.

16. Speech at Bentonville, December 2, 1905, segments in Dunaway (ed.), *Jeff Davis*, 81–100.

17. Jacobson, *The Life Story of Jeff Davis*, 43; Stevenson, "The Political Career of Jeff Davis," 39.

the two particulars that secured for him an undisputed place in Arkansas politics. Davis capitalized on these points of contention, referring to them as the "foreign trust conspiracy" and the state capitol "steal." During his first term as governor, he added "the penitentiary gang" to his roster. And, though other concerns surfaced during the reign of Davisism, these three themes continued to dominate. Ultimately, the central issue became Davis himself, and undergirding the entire superstructure was the sometimes latent, sometimes lively topic of race.

Trusts

The identification of the trusts as villain was firmly rooted in populism and in the platforms of Davis' predecessors, most notably that of Governor Dan W. Jones. During Jones's tenure as governor the legislature had passed the controversial Rector Anti-Trust Act, which provided that any corporation doing business in Arkansas that conspired to fix prices would be judged guilty of conspiracy in restraint of trade. A corporate howl went up, insurance companies protesting especially loudly. Newspapers, politicians, and the man on the street all took sides. Davis had his central issue, and he was never to veer far from it.

As attorney general Davis set out to enforce the anti-trust law, declaring, "The fight is on; it is between the trusts and the corporations and the people."[18] Painting the corporations as inhuman, "without a soul to damn, a body to punish—mere creatures of the law," he argued for control of the trusts. His "fight"—involving 125 test suits against insurance and other companies—was primarily a rhetorical ploy, however, for, as Davis scholar George Stevenson observed, "Whether Davis won or lost on the legal issues involved, he would certainly win before his supporters on the emotional issue, and practically speaking, he would achieve more by posing his cases than winning."[19]

Davis lost the legal battle. The circuit court reversed his interpretation of the law and the supreme court affirmed the lower court's ruling. But he won before the people. The trusts, symbolic of—if not

18. Dunaway (ed.), *Jeff Davis,* 42; speech at Center Point, February 12, 1900, in Dunaway (ed.), *Jeff Davis,* 46–70; *Arkansas Gazette* (Little Rock), February 14, 1900.
19. Stevenson, "The Political Career of Jeff Davis," 103, 26–27.

synonymous with—privilege, provided an explanation for people's suffering. Davis dared tangle with these corporate giants, taking action, symbolically, by suing "everything that looked like a trust." He would look for vindication from the people. He promised "at the proper time" to "go before the people and submit my cause to them for their final determination in justification of what I think is right in the premises."[20] An antitrust conference in St. Louis supported his legal position, and the following year (1900), the people of Arkansas spoke by electing Davis their governor.

The trusts remained a central issue during Davis' gubernatorial and senatorial careers. In his first speech before the Congress, he reaffirmed his uncompromising stand "against the established interests and in the interests of the common man." The Cotton Exchange, that "gambling device by which men are permitted to gamble in the products of the soil," ultimately became the object of his ire.[21] But the central argument remained: privilege is bleeding the people of Arkansas; therefore, destroy privilege.

The State Capitol

The legislature provided the young attorney general a second issue around which to rally support, the construction of a new state capitol. The enabling legislative act appointed a board of commissioners to make plans for the new edifice, appropriated fifty thousand dollars for construction, and authorized the Penitentiary Board to obtain lands to build a new prison facility since the new capitol was to be built on the site of the existing penitentiary. Calling the act "the most infamous steal ever perpetrated against the people of Arkansas," Davis challenged its constitutionality and instituted legal proceedings against the State Capitol Commission.[22] The courts upheld the legislation, and Davis took his case to the people. Raising the prospect of graft, Davis argued that even if no graft were involved the project was wasteful, "imposing . . . grievous burdens of taxation on the peo-

20. *Arkansas Gazette* (Little Rock), May 28, 1899.
21. Cited in Stevenson, "The Political Career of Jeff Davis," 87–89; Davis' positions on the trusts likely hampered industrialization in a state that badly needed economic stimulus; Paige E. Mulhollan, "The Issues of the Davis-Berry Senatorial Campaign in 1906," *Arkansas Historical Quarterly*, XX (Summer, 1961), 118–25.
22. *Arkansas Gazette* (Little Rock), July 5, 1899.

ple." "Did any of you ever see the State Capitol building?" he asked a Bentonville audience. "It covers eight acres of floor space. You could put every man, woman and child in Arkansas, stand them up . . . inside this building, and then leave plenty of room for me to beat Senator Berry for the Senate."[23] Realizing, as governor, that abandonment of the project was unrealistic, he called for close supervision of the construction and fueled the controversy by continuing to attack the rising construction costs.

The Penitentiary Board

Davis identified the penitentiary board as a third "enemy of the people," though the larger issue was penal reform. He saw the prison system as a fertile field for corruption, another example of privilege tyrannizing the disadvantaged, for prison inmates were a decided economic asset under the prevailing system. Further, since the prison population was largely poor, Davis cast himself as friend to the dispossessed. In his first inaugural address as governor in 1901, he called for measures to establish a reform school and to repeal the law providing for use of convict labor in building state railroads. In office, he surveyed prison conditions, annulled the controversial Dickson convict lease agreement, appointed a political ally to the superintendency of the penitentiary, and granted large numbers of pardons.[24]

Under severe attack during his second term as governor, Davis sought to shift public attention by directing vituperative attacks against the penitentiary board and its members.[25] Since the board was "a unitary body, much more easily personalized for propaganda purposes," Davis found it convenient rhetorically and potent politically to censure this "penitentiary crowd" of "leeches" and "bloodsuckers" for abuses in the system. He opposed the board's purchase—in compliance with the Capitol Construction Act—of property for a new convict farm. He called for former governor Eagle's resignation from the board and forced the resignation of several other board members. Board member George Murphy, the attorney general, rented a local

23. Jefferson Davis, "Message," *Arkansas Public Documents*, 1902, p. 4; speech at Bentonville, December 2, 1905.

24. Jacobson, *The Life Story of Jeff Davis*, 86–88.

25. Thomas S. Staples and David Y. Thomas, "The Triumph of the One Gallus Statesman," in Thomas (ed.), *Arkansas and Its People*, I, 274–75.

theatre and publicly responded to Davis' accusations, calling for the governor's impeachment.[26] Ultimately, a joint legislative committee upheld the property purchase agreement, but it failed to institute impeachment proceedings against the governor. Although he had vowed not to seek a third gubernatorial term, Davis' confrontation with the prison board, the impeachment attempt, and the legislature's failure to pass his legislative program prompted him—or at least gave him the excuse—to run again. To the precedent argument of not seeking a third term, Davis replied, "George Washington . . . never had an Arkansas legislature to deal with." "Had they acquitted me before that body," he explained, "I should have not asked you for re-election as Governor."[27] The people gave Davis their vote of confidence by electing him for a third term (1905–1906).

Davis as the Issue

By identifying the issues with his own political success or failure, Davis made himself the central issue—at least from his second term as governor onward. Indeed, during his third gubernatorial campaign the *Gazette* observed, "Davis is the issue."[28] His personal habits, integrity, motives, methods, and record were hotly debated on the stump and in the newspapers in both the second and third campaigns. When his opponents accused him of theft, bribery, and drunkenness, charged him with putting blacks in office, and opposed his wholesale granting of pardons, Davis countered that "his enemies were trying to ruin an honest servant of the people." Always defending himself and his record, he told the voters in his second campaign for governor, "If you don't like my record, vote for Rector. He's a gentleman."[29] Davis responded to the theft and bribery charges by citing the lack of evidence in the impeachment inquiry. He answered the drunkenness argument with humor, calling his detractors "quart Baptists" and himself only a "pint Baptist." But he was more sensitive to

26. Stevenson, "The Political Career of Jeff Davis," 57–59.
27. Speech at Bentonville, reported in *Arkansas Gazette* (Little Rock), December 15, May 17, 1903.
28. *Arkansas Gazette* cited in Staples and Thomas, "The Triumph of the One Gallus Statesman," I, 276; Stevenson, "The Political Career of Jeff Davis," 36.
29. Staples and Thomas, "The Triumph of the One Gallus Statesman," 267–68, 272.

indictments on the issues of race and his pardon record. To his opponent Judge Wood's claim that he appointed blacks to office, Davis replied that he "never . . . *knowingly* appointed a negro to any office" and boasted, "no man could be appointed to office under my administration unless he was a white man, a Democrat and a Jeff Davis man." But Wood, he charged, had appointed black jury commissioners to secure the black vote.[30]

Davis was most vulnerable on his pardon record, particularly pardons of blacks. One widely publicized incident involving the pardon of a black man convicted of assaulting a white girl led Davis to defend himself as "a Southern man, imbibing all the traditions and sentiments of the Southern people." Questioning the pardoned man's guilt, he explained to his Eureka Springs audience, "In our country when we have no doubt about a negro's guilt we do not give him a trial; we mob him, and that ends it." However, he argued, "the mere fact that this negro got a trial is evidence that there was some doubt of his guilt." To the larger issue of wholesale pardons (especially pardons of liquor law violators), the single most damaging charge brought against him in his gubernatorial campaign and a particular source of conflict between the governor and the church, Davis asserted that "the law ought to be administered in mercy."[31] For him, a pardon was a "deed of charity," an "act of kindness." "I am always glad to reach down and pull a boy out of hell and give him back to his mother," he said. "I am always glad to pull a poor fallen man from this cesspool of filth and corruption, the Arkansas penitentiary, and start him out again on the road of right living." Besides, he argued, "I never pardon a man unless the best citizens of the county send me a petition." But, though Davis promised to "run the pardon mill fair and impartial," he reminded his followers that "none but my friends need come around me begging for pardons."[32]

30. Speech at Eureka Springs, November 5, 1903, in Dunaway (ed.), *Jeff Davis,* 71–80; *Arkansas Gazette* (Little Rock), November 6, 1903.

31. Speeches at Eureka Springs, November 5, 1903, and Center Point, February 12, 1900.

32. Speeches at Bentonville, December 2, 1905, and at Eureka Springs, November 5, 1903; Dunaway (ed.), *Jeff Davis,* 44.

The Race Issue

Although Davis has been accused of exploiting the issue of race, of roaring "against the 'nigger' across the Ozark mountains," of "larruping the specter of the black man up and down the hills of Arkansas,"[33] judged in terms of his time and place in history, he was no radical on this point. Rhetorically, the black man was a stock issue, an image, a stereotype, a figure of speech—though admittedly the symbolism was disparaging to the race. Davis capitalized on that image. "I have whipped the squirrel-headed editors . . . until you couldn't convict a negro for stealing on the testimony of half a dozen of these squirrel heads," he told his delighted rural white audiences. Yet, such boasts as "I can eat more 'possums and yellow yam potatoes than any negro out of jail" were probably more to reaffirm his own hill country roots than to deprecate the black man.[34] Davis was not above trading on white supremacy, however, when it was advantageous to do so. "I stand for the Caucasian race in government," he assured his followers, "and I say that 'nigger' dominion will never prevail in this beautiful Southland of ours, as long as shotguns and rifles lie around loose, and we are able to pull the trigger."[35] Although he condemned lynching, Davis believed it the inevitable answer to the attack of the black man on white womanhood. Pushed against the wall on the race issue during his third campaign for governor, Davis reassured the legislature of his loyalties. "I have come to the conclusion," he stated, "that any effort upon the part of Arkansas or the Southland to further divide her blessings with this degenerate and improvident race is futile. A negro is not susceptible of higher education . . . [or] higher moral culture. He is born and bred to be a servant."[36] But for Davis, race was not a central concern; to him the issue was simply a necessary evil to be dragged out when the occasion demanded it.

33. Luthin, *American Demagogues*, 106; Wilbur J. Cash, *The Mind of the South* (New York: Vintage-Knopf, 1941), 248; Stevenson, "The Political Career of Jeff Davis," 122; see Billy Travis Booth, "An Analysis of the Myths in Selected Speeches of Jeff Davis of Arkansas, 1899–1911" (Ph.D. dissertation, Louisiana State University, 1977).
34. Cited in Dunaway (ed.), *Jeff Davis*, 36–37.
35. *Arkansas Gazette* (Little Rock), August 5, 30, 1904.
36. Jefferson Davis, "Message," *Arkansas Public Documents*, 1905–1906, pp. 35–36.

Rhetorical Strategies

These issues—the trusts, the State Capitol Commission, the penitentiary gang, race, and Davis himself—easily translated into traditional
agitational themes.[37] The rhetoric essentially set the "plutocrats"
(those of privilege, especially the "foreign" corporations) in opposition to Davis and the people. Davis painted government, a partner in
the "conspiracy" to deprive the common folk of their rightful share in
life, as being pernicious, not because of its basic structure but because
of domination by the "Little Rock gang." The "silk-stocking" crowd
reaped the benefits of that government. But the "woolhat brigade"
need forebear no longer; through exercising its latent power, the vote,
this "new elite" would "gain one more victory for good government."
The hillbillies and the red-necks would "join hands" and, with "Jeff"
as their leader, clean house. Davis' rhetoric was carefully orchestrated
to articulate the masses' discontent, to personalize the "causes" of
dissatisfaction by identifying the perpetrators of felt inequities, and to
promise to thwart—if not punish—the privileged. The people need
only give him the mandate to lead the battle against oppression. To
these ends, he employed strategies of polarization, identification, and
confrontation.

Essential to Davis' rhetoric was naming the enemy and setting
him in direct opposition to the people. Since Arkansas had no aristocracy against whom the dispossessed poor whites might vent their
frustrations, the most obvious target was the trusts, "the terror of the
90's." Davis played to the theme, painting the trusts as sinister, vil-
lainous creatures, dedicated to keeping the masses in bondage. Further, he sought to discredit his opponents by identifying them with
the trusts. He used this tactic, for example, to attack his opposition
while defending his own pardon record. "I pardoned *people*," he
boasted, "while Judge Wood pardoned the *railroads*."[38] Davis' protests
against monopoly were symptomatic and, to a degree, symbolic of a
larger concern—"predatory wealth," economic power vested in a

37. For analysis of agitational themes, see Leo Lowenthal and Norbert Guterman, *Prophets of Deceit: A Study of the Techniques of the American Agitator* (New York:
Harper and Brothers, 1949).
38. Speech at Eureka Springs, November 5, 1903.

privileged few. At one time or another, Davis tilted with all forms of institutionalized authority, including the Little Rock Baptist Church. He tangled not only with the utilities, the oil and tobacco companies, and every trust or combination he could find, with banks, railroads, and other corporations; but he also took on the newspapers, the courts, and the "Little Rock gang." It was "us" (Davis and the people) against "them" (whomever Davis should choose to so label).

Whether Davis instigated "class war" by polarizing country and city was an issue in his own time and has remained a subject of scholarly dispute. Vance interpreted Davis' crusade as essentially a "class struggle": "For Jeff Davis divided in order to rule and stirred up strife that victory might light on his banner."[39] Numerically, class divisiveness would have appeared a logical strategy, for Arkansas was predominately rural. But Davis categorically denied that he was "trying to array the country against Little Rock." "There are many noble men and women living there," he countered, "lots of them. God bless them. But there is a gang down there that needs cleaning out." Davis promised a purge comparable to running the Red River through the state capitol.[40] Both L. S. Dunaway and Charles Jacobson, Davis' associates and biographers, also took exception to the claim that Davis perpetrated class war, Jacobson arguing that "he was simply appealing to those who were in the majority and were amenable to his method of campaigning." Stevenson, on the other hand, concluded that "by accepting the already marked differences in social and political beliefs between the country folk and the city 'slickers,' Davis unified the yeomanry and poor whites to promote his own interests as the interests of those whose support he sought." As Davis himself put it, "If the boys in the hills will only touch hands with the boys in the valley, we will win one more victory for good government, and in the meantime whip these yankees out on dry land and let them stink themselves to death."[41]

39. Vance, "A Karl Marx for Hill Billies," 180–81; Arthur S. Link, "The Progressive Movement in the South, 1870–1914," *North Carolina Historical Review*, XXIII (April, 1946), 194.

40. Speech at Center Point, February 12, 1900; *Arkansas Gazette* (Little Rock), June 20, 1903.

41. Dunaway (ed.), *Jeff Davis*, 20, 32; Jacobson, *The Life Story of Jeff Davis*, 63; Stevenson, "The Political Career of Jeff Davis," 20; Allan Louis Larson, *Southern Dema-*

If Davis' aim was to forego city votes in favor of country ones, his strategy was notably unsuccessful. An analysis of his gubernatorial campaigns showed that he averaged 61 percent of the vote in the county seats and over 71 percent in the 185 "principal incorporated towns in the state." Dunaway analyzed the situation and concluded:

While it is true that the so-called "red-necks" and "hillbillies" (terms coined by him) were lined up with Senator Davis, it is also true that the leading business and professional men in the largest towns and cities of the State were often his staunchest supporters. He classed among his closest friends some of the leading citizens and wealthiest men of the State; men who stood high in social, business and intellectual circles.[42]

What accounts for the apparent contradiction? The key is that Davis did not direct his raillery against the *people* from the city; the objects of his ridicule were "the *gang* in Little Rock," "yankees" (an epithet Davis used for all who opposed him), "the silk stocking crowd," "high collared roosters," "plutocrats," and "squirrel-headed editors" —metaphors Davis used for the entrenched political structure that undergirded monopoly and privilege.[43]

Although Davis initially had worked within the prevailing power structure of the Democratic party, he lacked support of party regulars as early as his statewide campaign for attorney general in 1898. Further, by challenging the trusts he threatened the political "rings" that had compromised with the northern industrialists.[44] And his election as governor "literally wrecked all the organized political plans and systems that had grown up in the State for half a century." Ostracized by the party hierarchy that effectively controlled the election machinery, Davis bypassed the "courthouse crowd" and took his case directly to the people. Ultimately he built through appointments and pardons his own political organization, which was so rigidly controlled that the *Gazette* caustically compared it to "the ancient Persian

---

gogues: A Study in Charismatic Leadership (Ann Arbor, Mich.: University Microfilms, 1964), 366–67.

42. Dunaway (ed.), *Jeff Davis*, 20.

43. Davis' running battle with the press began in the 1896 campaign in which Davis labeled the *Arkansas Gazette* a "goldbug paper." Subsequently he referred to the paper as "that old red harlot" and its editor as president of a "'nigger' club." Much of the rural press supported Davis, however.

44. Fletcher, *Arkansas*, 286.

Empire or . . . China of today."[45] But he never let up his "almost ceaseless canvass before the people." From start to finish it was Davis and the people against privilege and "predatory wealth." He would not abandon the common folk in the face of adversity. Neither would they repudiate their "Savior."

Essential to Davis' strategy of polarization was a sense of community, an "acting-together," a collaboration between himself and the people. The rhetorical figure was a joining of hands. Davis reinforced this complicity through making common cause with "the average perspiring, honest yeoman."[46] He often began speeches with the phrase, "My fellow citizens." "I'm one of you," he told the common folk. And he proved it by identifying with their background, lifestyle, and value system. The press strengthened the bond—though probably inadvertently—through its disparaging characterizations of Davis. The Helena *World*, for example, dismissed him as a "carrot-haired, red-faced, loud-mouthed, strong-limbed ox driving mountaineer lawyer . . . a friend to the fellow that brews forty-rod bug-juice back in the mountains."[47] Davis delighted in quoting that characterization to his backwoods audiences.

Davis' background was rural and probably poor, though it is unlikely he ever had to "cry for bacon" as he claimed to his hillbilly audiences. No doubt he had "picked cotton, 'possum-hunted and raised great big old yellow yam potatoes and pumpkins." He understood the aspirations, frustrations, and hopelessness of those constrained by lack of education, capital, and status. In short, he empathized with the plight of Arkansas' dispossessed. Comfortable with a "one gallus democracy," Davis straightforwardly identified with his followers' lifestyle, particularly their clothes and food. "My opponents wear silk socks," he told his rural audiences, "but I wear the same kind you

45. *Senate Documents*, James P. Clarke, *Jeff Davis: Memorial Addresses*, 62nd Cong., 3rd Sess., No. 1146, pp. 15–16; editorial, *Arkansas Gazette* (Little Rock), April 1, 1906; Davis' strategy was exceptional. Most southern demagogues came to terms with the existing political machinery in their states; editorial, *Arkansas Gazette*, August 1, 1906.

46. Editorial, *Arkansas Gazette* (Little Rock), October 17, 1905; Atkins (Ark.) *Chronicle*, April 25, 1902; Jacobson, *The Life Story of Jeff Davis*, 38; Lowenthal and Guterman, *Prophets of Deceit*, 5; Kenneth Burke, *A Rhetoric of Motives* (New York: Prentice-Hall, 1950), 21.

47. Helena (Ark.) *Weekly World*, May 3, 1899.

farmers wear, and if you farmers will stay with me we will whip this silk-stocking crowd one more time." Pointing to a supporter in a crowd, Davis said: "Just look at Uncle Jim Bettis here with his home-spun clothes, with his home-knit socks. These are my kind of folks—fellows that chew hill-side navy, smoke a cob pipe and sing in the choir." Again and again, he reaffirmed his preference for country food—fried country ham, hot biscuits "with pimples on them," gravy, turnip greens, hog jowl, cornbread, buttermilk, and possum. And, whenever possible on the campaign trail, he would spurn hotel food to eat "home cooking." While governor, Davis reassured his constituents that he had not taken up city ways and invited them to visit him in Little Rock. "The word 'Welcome' is written on the outside of the door for my friends," he told them. "If I am not at home tell my wife who you are; tell her you are my friend and that you belong to the sun-burned sons of toil. Tell her to give you some hog jowl and turnip greens. She may be busy making soap, but that will be all right." [48] On occasion, Davis staked a mule to graze on the lawn of the governor's mansion. While Governor, he snubbed society, including the president of the United States, whose banquet he refused to attend on the grounds he would not sit at table with Arkansas' Reconstruction governor, Republican Powell Clayton. [49]

Davis also identified with the value system of the "wool hat brigade." Although no "bible toting politician," he liberally seasoned his speeches with the potent religious imagery loved by his backwoods, fundamentalist audiences. Further, he reasserted the frontier virtues of courage, loyalty, and devotion to family. His own courage was undisputable; he dared to battle the trusts. He was loyal—to a fault. "My friends are always right to me," he boasted, and his actions proved it. He constantly reaffirmed to his audiences his devotion to his wife, a "good and brave . . . little Southern woman," his twelve children (four dead), his mother, his Confederate father, and his nine "pointer dogs." Moreover, particularly before audiences of war veterans, Davis played to the myth of the Confederacy. "When I see you," he told the "battle-worn, gray-headed veterans" in his audi-

48. Dunaway (ed.), *Jeff Davis, passim*; Stevenson "The Political Career of Jeff Davis," 75.
49. Speech at Bentonville, December 2, 1905.

ence, "I always want to take off my hat to you. I always want to do honor to you, especially when I see you with an empty sleeve and an empty boot leg." But though he sympathized with the veterans, Davis had no war scars with which to make common cause. His argument that his Baptist minister father "laid down his Bible and picked up his rifle," bearing it "as gallantly as any soldier" did not provide a reciprocal bond: the facts of the situation were widely disputed in the papers, Davis' father having been conscripted as a chaplain.[50]

Lacking a substantive basis for identification with the Lost Cause, Davis relied on symbolic or rhetorical means. He capitalized on his famous name, wore a Prince Albert grey cutaway which, with the "Baptist" string tie and slouch Stetson hat, resembled a Confederate uniform, and expressed a deep devotion to the cause. The image was effective. One veteran, confusing him with Jefferson Davis, president of the Confederacy, remarked, "I fought for him in the sixties and I'm going to go on voting for him if he lives forever. He is the greatest and longest lived man that ever was."[51]

Although identifying himself as one of the people, Davis also set himself apart as their leader. As historian T. Harry Williams noted, Davis became "one of them and yet somehow above them."[52] As leader, he also became martyr. In his maiden speech for governor at Hardy, Arkansas, Davis alleged a conspiracy to raise his hotel rent, refuse him telephone service, and deny him the right to cash his personal checks—all because of his stand on the trusts. In a subsequent speech at Conway, he further developed the theme and identified himself as the only friend of the people.[53] The *Gazette* recounted an alleged incident that indicated Davis' penchant for martyrdom—or at least his recognition of its rhetorical value:

In one of Jeff Davis's campaigns his opponent arose and fiercely denounced Davis in unmeasured terms for his alleged misrepresentations. Did Davis fight, cut, stab or shoot—either bullets or epithets? No. He simply said to the audience that his opponent had been put in the race to kill him; that he knew

50. Dunaway (ed.), *Jeff Davis*, 44; editorial, *Arkansas Gazette* (Little Rock), August 1, 1906.
51. Cited in Vance, "A Karl Marx for Hill Billies," 190.
52. Williams, *Huey Long*, 69; Lowenthal and Guterman, *Prophets of Deceit*, 119.
53. Speech at Hardy, July 4, 1899, in *Arkansas Gazette* (Little Rock), July 5, 1899; speech at Conway, July 13, 1899, in *ibid.*, July 16, 1899.

his opponent would take his life before the race was over. "But . . . [said Davis] all I ask is that when I am dead, you bury me in the old graveyard and write on my headstone the words: 'He died a martyr to the common people.'"

"And," the *Gazette* editorialized, he "never cracked a smile." Davis was crusader, savior, and more—he was the sacrificial lamb. When criticized by the press for his motley following, he countered, "Jesus Christ . . . went to the humble and lowly."[54] The martyr metaphor was complete.

By identifying with the common people and polarizing "us" (Davis and the people) and "them" (the trusts and the entrenched political structure), Davis set the stage for confrontation. Rhetorically, confrontation provided entertainment for his audiences. Further, it dramatized the struggle between the weak and the poor and the strong and the rich. Finally, it gave Davis a vehicle to gain the advantage in or prescribe the boundaries and ground rules of a dispute. By employing the strategy, he gained credibility for himself and the issues he supported.

Davis' audiences delighted in the frontier-style, head-on combat that characterized his stump oratory. His campaigns, more challenging than his administrative duties, were "hot, to the boiling point." Davis reveled in the role of challenger, and his was no guerrilla warfare. He preferred to fight in the open, for, as he explained it, "I don't want to get shot in the back. If I die I want to die with my face to the rising sun, with my windows open toward Jerusalem."[55] Davis took no quarter and gave none. He loved the thrill of combat. His physical encounters with opponents made headlines, particularly incidents in which he rapped the heads of his adversaries with his walking cane. His verbal encounters were no less restrained. Clearly the resulting sensationalism gained visibility for the issues he espoused and ultimately forced the spotlight on Davis himself. It also gained him free publicity in the press.

Davis used confrontation to dramatize the "struggle" between "us" and "them." Not content during his second term as governor to veto over three hundred bills *after* the legislature had adjourned, he

54. Editorial, in *ibid.*, August 1, 1906; speech at Center Point, February 12, 1900.
55. Bourland, introduction to Dunaway (ed.), *Jeff Davis*, 8; speech at Center Point, February 12, 1900.

had the bills loaded in a wheelbarrow and dumped ceremonially in the secretary of state's office. Davis' confrontation was most often symbolic, with war the prevailing metaphor. Again and again, the words *fighter, tactics, battle,* and *warrior* emerged in his speeches. In the opening sally of his first gubernatorial campaign, for example, he declared, "The war is on." For him the altercation was "not a battle between my opponents and me—they are gentlemen—but the war is on. It is knife to knife, hilt to hilt, foot to foot, knee to knee, between the corporations of Arkansas and the people."[56] On other occasions, Davis declared the battle to be against newspaper editors, the prevailing political power structure, or the Republican legacy of Powell Clayton.

Through confrontation, Davis set the parameters of a dispute and thereby gained the advantage. Pitting "us" against "them," he focused campaign debate on the trusts and the "Little Rock Crowd." Painting himself as martyr, he made himself an issue in the campaign. In short, he used confrontation to seize the initiative. As Fred W. Allsopp observed, he "seemed to court the antagonism of the newspapers and then to seek to turn their adverse criticisms to his advantage . . . by a hue and cry about a so-called subsidized press."[57] Indeed, when the polarity between "us" and "them" was not clearcut, Davis forced a choosing of sides by personalizing the conflict. If you're not for me, he challenged, you're against me. And when he had no burning issue of his own or was not himself the source of controversy, he provoked strife through *ad hominem* argument and through meddling in others' races. Both tactics helped to solidify his own political position.

Once the ground rules were set, Davis usually maintained the offensive, a strategy Senator Kavanaugh thought the secret of his political success. Davis countered the charge that he instigated strife by claiming to "purify" politics by turning the "sunlight of truth" on every public transaction. The governor explained the purifying process to a Bentonville audience:

56. Speech at Center Point, February 12, 1900.
57. Davis temporarily lost the offensive in the third gubernatorial campaign when opponent Wood used Davis' own weapons. Fred W. Allsopp, *Twenty Years in a Newspaper Office* (Little Rock: Central Printing, 1907), 186; "Jeff Davis and the 'Red-Necks,'" *Literary Digest,* XLVI (January 25, 1913), 194.

How do you ladies in this audience make butter? Do you make it by setting your churn in the yard and letting it set there all day? No; you take the dasher and stir, and stir, and stir; then you get golden, yellow butter. How does God purify the atmosphere? By lightening. This is the only remedy He has provided. It may kill some men, but that is the only remedy. . . . The Master . . . said . . . "Agitate, stir." [58]

When accused of public drunkenness, Davis asked all those fellows who ever took a drink to vote for him, whereas "all those who haven't may vote for Judge Wood." Dismissed from membership in the Little Rock Baptist Church for "declaring non-fellowship, using the press for notoriety and scandalizing the Church and disturbing its peace, harmony and prosperity," he lambasted the hypocrisy of the "quart Baptists" and was "restored" at a church in Russellville. According to his own account, over one hundred people came to witness that event. The *Gazette* contended that the number was closer to a dozen, several of whom were relatives. [59]

Persuasive Techniques

Davis' method of campaigning was revolutionary in Arkansas politics. Heretofore, candidates for statewide office had depended primarily on local politicos to "deliver the vote." Customarily, candidates would seek commitments from the local county courthouse "ring" and perhaps a few prominent citizens of the county seat and then return home. Davis, on the other hand, liked long, personal campaigns and—much to the chagrin of his opponents—had the stamina for them. During the six or seven months prior to an election he would stump the state, making essentially the same speech two to five times a day to crowds as large as five thousand. These "campaigns of education," as Jacobson called them, "taught" the common folk the issues—or at least the issues as Davis chose to view them. [60] Braving all kinds of weather and difficult travel conditions, he sometimes made a

58. Speech at Bentonville, December 2, 1905.
59. Nevin Neal, "Jeff Davis and the Reform Movement in Arkansas, 1898–1907" (M.A. thesis, Vanderbilt University, 1939), 70; editorial, *Arkansas Gazette* (Little Rock), August 1, 1906.
60. Jacobson, *The Life Story of Jeff Davis*, 184. For a summary of the campaign itinerary, see John Richard Johnson, "The Campaign Speaking of Jeff Davis of Arkansas, 1899–1904" (M.A. thesis, Louisiana State University, 1974).

joint canvass with his opponents. Often he went alone—to the branch heads and the hollows, to hamlets where people had never seen a "big-time" politician, to county fairs, "all day singings," and local political rallies. Davis went to the people.

As a prelude to his platform performance, Davis mingled with the crowd, eating chicken, kissing babies, shaking hands, "asking after the family," and commiserating with the farmers over the state of the crops. By the time the formal festivities began, he often had already won the hillbillies and red-necks to his side and usually had "planted" his supporters strategically in the crowd to ensure an enthusiastic response. And once he got the floor, he held it as long as he pleased. For example, having been invited to introduce Socialist Eugene Debs at a Labor Day rally in Fort Smith, Davis took charge of the platform and spoke himself for two hours before making the introduction.

Amidst stifling effluvia in crowded rooms or in the open air, in courtrooms, churches, circus and evangelist tents, brush arbors, and public meeting halls, "Jeff" took off his coat, proudly displayed his one gallus, and got down to the business of haranguing the crowd. He attacked his opponents, their records, and their motives, defending his own record and asking his hillbilly and red-neck audiences for their backing. After his own speech—which through careful maneuvering was likely to be first on the program—Davis would often leave the gathering, taking his supporters with him. On other occasions, he would stay to heckle his opponents.

Davis not only made stump oratory the standard in Arkansas politics, he also added to Arkansas campaigning the wholesale distribution of printed campaign speeches. Not trusting the newspapers to print accurate accounts of his oratory and/or finding such a charge politically potent, Davis hired stenographers to transcribe speeches, which he then published. When coming to town, he would "flood" the area with these printed pamphlets, thereby reaching an even larger audience. By the third gubernatorial campaign, both Davis and his opponents had added satirical cartooning to their media storehouses.

Essentially irrational, Davis' rhetoric employed emotional appeals to sharpen the contrast between the haves and the have-nots and to discredit as villains those who opposed him. His speeches teemed with stories of bedraggled wives, ragged, barefoot children, prison inmates "almost whipped to death, starved to death, eaten up with lice, sores all over their bodies." [61] By flaunting such emotionally potent images, he stirred excitement in his audiences and augmented and sharpened their dissatisfaction. Further, a pervasive appeal to deity—with graphic representations of God in his heaven, Christ the Savior and Master, and angels in glory—allied Davis, the people, and their "righteous cause" with the Almighty and, in so doing, legitimized Davis' claim to leadership. Still, at root the conclusion to the arguments never varied: vote for Jeff Davis.

Although characteristically his rhetoric was more of the heart than of the intellect, Davis did not exclude logical appeals from his speeches. His campaign valise bulged with sworn statements, "certified copies," affidavits, and the like, which, incidentally, he sometimes misrepresented or did not always have "time" to read. He also depended on examples, analogies, and maxims to carry his points—though his proofs reflected the grass-roots antiintellectualism of his audiences. Examples, likely hypothetical and most often drawn with vivid, emotion-laden and religiously symbolic language, personalized the causes of the masses' dissatisfaction and intensified antagonism toward the "enemy." Homespun analogies simplified complex issues: the trusts, Davis argued, were a "more loathsome disease . . . to the body politic than smallpox is to the human body"; and, on the issue of whether the state was liable for payment of bonds issued to build a railroad, he compared the contract relationship to that of an agent hiring "a one-eyed 'nigger.'" Particularly noteworthy was Davis' penchant for using classical allusion with his hillbilly audiences. The Trojan horse analogy was typical: "Now, I want to say to the Farmers' Union . . . that the ringsters and tricksters . . . of Arkansas have left poor old George Donaghey [a Davis opponent] standing solitary and alone just outside the Farmers' Union gates, hoping that curiosity may lead you to carry him into your fold and into the Governor's office." In addition, maxims drawn from the experience of his audience were employed as a kind of "shorthand" logic: "What is sauce for the

61. Speech at Bentonville, December 2, 1905.

goose is sauce for the gander," he reminded a Eureka Springs gather-ing.[62] Davis' listeners were able to complete the argument: the com-mon people have the same rights as the privileged.

Davis' premises were the premises of his Populist-minded au-dience. His unique contribution lay in the particulars he provided and the satisfying, if not always logical, conclusions he drew. His fol-lowers cared little that his arguments were often patently fallacious. Neither were they affronted that Davis was sometimes careless with the facts, regularly misquoting the public records of his adversaries, or that his appeals were typically *ad hominem*. His *word* was sufficient for the common folk. They trusted him and believed whatever he told them.

Davis' power as a stump speaker derived neither from argumen-tative powers nor polished prose, but from his "skill in vitalizing—in humanizing" an event through simple, direct, and vivid language. Jacobson noted that Davis "spoke to the rank and file in a language with which they were familiar." Further, he "couched" his widely cir-culated written speeches "in terms that the most illiterate might un-derstand."[63] Davis defended his pardon record, for example, with simple, though compelling word pictures of the downtrodden. De-scribing a petitioner from Pike County as "footsore and tired: her shoes . . . worn and her dress bedraggled," her children "ragged and barefooted," Davis touched his Bentonville audience as Mrs. Har-ris' "pathetic story [had] 'totched'" both the governor and—Davis avowed—"the great White Throne of God." "I believe," he said, "that the Recording Angel of God dipped his wing in a fount of eternal gold and wrote to my credit that deed of charity, that act of kindness."[64]

Davis freely used clichés, epigrams, and stereotypes to simplify and personalize complex issues. He indicted the board of exchange, for example, as a "gambling house" and juxtaposed little children along the White River, "thinly clad on a cold, frosty morning . . . picking the cotton, pulling it from the bolls, their little hands almost frozen" against "the gamblers of Wall street . . . gambling, not only

62. Speech at Center Point, February 12, 1900; speech at Ozark, February 18, 1908, in Dunaway (ed.), *Jeff Davis*, 122–35; speech at Eureka Springs, November 5, 1903.
63. Editorial, *Arkansas Gazette* (Little Rock), August 1, 1906; Jacobson, *The Life Story of Jeff Davis*, 64.
64. Speech at Bentonville, December 2, 1905.

in the products of the soil of the South, but gambling in the flesh and blood and bone of the children of the South." Davis shared with his audiences his own response to these "leeches" who had never seen a cotton field "ripening under a Southern sun." "My heart cried aloud: 'My God! Is there no help in Israel? Is there no help for the children of the South?'" Any time the spectre of Republicanism was raised, Davis played to the stereotype, Powell Clayton. Graphically recounting the horrors visited on the Davises by that "one-armed villain" and his "hell-hounds," he rekindled in his audiences the hatred engendered by Reconstruction. "Many a night has my mother laid out with me, a baby, in the woods, to escape the ravages of these demons," he accused. "He [Clayton] murdered our citizens, he pillaged our homes, he depleted our treasury, and my mother would have no respect for me if I should sit down and eat with him. The food would sour on my stomach."[65]

Often the charges Davis leveled against his opponents were not nearly so damaging as the vituperative, biting language he used to describe their dealings. Protesting the price paid for fifteen acres of land for the new state capitol, he railed, "That land is so poor that two drunken men could not raise a difficulty upon it. It is so poor you could not raise an umbrella upon it. It is so poor you have to manure it to make brick out of it."[66] "Vindictive, severe, and often merciless in debate," Davis minimized his opposition through denunciation, ridicule, stinging sarcasm, and insinuation. He indicted, for example, as "five jackasses" members of the supreme court who had resisted him; he labeled political opponent Judge Wood as the "singing candidate" and likened his "racket singing in the choir in Little Rock" to farmers calling hogs. "I am going to put knee breeches on Judge Wood and run him for page when the Legislature meets," Davis taunted. "I will also try to get Vandeventer [a Davis challenger] some kind of a job, even if I have to have him put in as chambermaid around the Statehouse." He called his bachelor opponent Judge Bryant to come up on the platform "where the ladies can see you." "I want to show you the color of one man's hair that never hugged a woman in his life," he told the delighted spectators. "Look at the Judge's bald head. I can shave

65. *Ibid.*
66. Speech at Center Point, February 12, 1900.

one of these eighteen-year-old boys, put an old dress on him and run Judge Bryant out of town."[67] Davis disparaged his opponents with nicknames, calling them "Shug," "Jubert," "Aunt Puss," "Sister Hine-mon," "Horace Greely," "Aunt Julie," and "Aunt Jennie." He lost some of the biting sarcasm and vindictiveness in his declining years, however, his Senate colleagues noticing an "increasing absence of that intemperate form of expression which usually characterized his comment on official matters." Finally, admitting a measure of responsibility for "personal" and "abusive" tactics in earlier campaigns, Davis preferred in his 1912 senatorial race to go his own way rather than meet his opponent in debate. As the Pocahontas *Star-Herald* noted in that campaign, the senator "failed to arouse any enthusiasm in his audience," a reaction the editors correlated with loss of prestige. Davis' supporters seemed to prefer the "old Jeff Davis" style.[68]

Clearly Davis' style was typical of the pattern of southern demagoguery described by Cash—"full of the swaggering, hell-for-leather bluster that the South demanded in its heroes and champions," a "quizzical, broad, clowning humor, and a capacity for taking on the common touch." C. Vann Woodward thought the manner burlesque.[69] A great practical joker, Davis once hid a bottle of whiskey in his prohibition opponent's grip and, on another occasion, a pistol in a foe's pocket—only to reveal both on speaking platforms amidst great hilarity. When his opponent Colonel Rector teased him about his affinity for Wizard Oil, Davis "doctored" Rector's glass of water with the patent tonic and sent his opponent into a coughing, sputtering spasm. The Walnut Grove audience heartily approved the governor's "cute trick," which undercut Rector's solemn address.[70]

Davis delighted in showmanship and on the stump had "few equals and no superior." He usually spoke extemporaneously, and his physical gestures reinforced his vivid images. As Dunaway observed,

67. *Senate Documents*, John Charles Floyd, *Jeff Davis: Memorial Addresses*, 62nd Cong., 3rd Sess., No. 1146, p. 45; Dunaway (ed.), *Jeff Davis*, 8, 37, 39.
68. Stevenson, "The Political Career of Jeff Davis," 111; *Senate Documents*, James P. Clarke, *Jeff Davis: Memorial Addresses*, 62nd Cong., 3rd Sess., No. 1146, p. 22. Fletcher, in *Arkansas*, 313, suggested that Davis' final speeches were probably written for him by others; Pocahontas *Star-Herald*, cited in Jacobson, *The Life Story of Jeff Davis*, 147.
69. Cash, *The Mind of the South*, 284. C. Vann Woodward, *Origins of the New South* (Baton Rouge: Louisiana State University Press, 1951), 376.
70. Jacobson, *The Life Story of Jeff Davis*, 160–61.

"when reaching a climax, he would stamp his feet and clap his hands together in a remarkably quick and fascinating manner that would seem to inspire enthusiasm in the crowd." In his study of Davis, Nevin Neal suggested that "even in prejudiced audiences he had them cheering him before he left." "There was a gusto about Davis," Vance concluded. "He played the demagogue but he liked it. It was not a distasteful business to him; it was glorious fun. Nor did he despise the people with whom he played the game. If the common people heard him gladly, let it be said he offered himself for their amusement—and his profit—gladly."[71]

Effect

Davisism represented a genuine concern by Arkansans for more democratic government. Historians Thomas S. Staples and David Y. Thomas characterized the "legislative temper" of the period as "clearly plebeian," the Arkansas legislature struggling "to curb through statutes every form of rapacious big business."[72] Responding to authentic social and economic problems, Davis offered the common people participation in that fight. He gave them simple, believable explanations for their economic plight and proposed a remedy—limitation of entrenched power. The implicit message of Davis' rhetoric was the *challenge* to *act*—to throw off the shackles imposed by privilege and to impose a new political and economic order. Davis gave his disciples the authority and the permission to act and identified for them a simple, specific means of wielding force—voting for him. The appeal of his Center Point speech was typical: "All that I am, all that I expect to be, I commit into your hands and into your keeping, knowing that if I deserve your confidence I will receive it. If I do not merit it you will withhold it." He echoed the theme at Bentonville: "If the people of this State believe that I will make them a good and faithful officer in that position, I ask your suffrage and support; if not, then it is your duty as good citizens to support my adversary."[73]

71. Dunaway (ed.), *Jeff Davis*, 21; Neal, "Jeff Davis and the Reform Movement in Arkansas," 55; Vance, "A Karl Marx for Hill Billies," 184.
72. Staples and Thomas, "The Rise of the One Gallus Democracy," 260.
73. Speech at Center Point, February 12, 1900; speech at Bentonville, December 2, 1905.

By casting himself as savior, Davis not only ensured his own political future but left an indelible mark on Arkansas politics. When asked during his third campaign for governor what he had accomplished as an elected official, Davis replied, "It is not so much what I have done as what I have kept the other fellow from doing."[74] Yet, through restraining the forces of privilege, he influenced the passage of important reform legislation, gave status to Arkansas' dispossessed, and forged a new political alliance that changed the face of Arkansas politics. In so doing, the man became a myth.

Davis never articulated a comprehensive reform program. Nor, as Vance observed, did he need to do so, for "to have solved the ills of the body politic would have left Jeff without a mission and the hillbillies without their safety valve." In any case, many of Davis' listeners cared more about having "voice given to their conscious dissatisfaction" than about the "feasibility of any suggested remedy."[75] Nonetheless, Davis' contribution to reform legislation was greater than is commonly imagined. Although the majority of the constructive legislation enacted during his tenure as governor related to "railroads, trusts, corporations not chartered in the State, the insurance business, State lands, problems affecting agriculture, and the State debt," Davis' program included a number of progressive measures beyond the regulation of trusts. In his first inaugural address, the new governor called for employment safety laws, repeal of the act providing for state construction of railroads with convict labor, and establishment of a reform school. The 1901 legislature obliged him by repealing the state construction of railroads act and, during his second term as governor, it limited working hours on railroads, authorized county boards of health, and expanded the inheritance tax. In his gubernatorial address to the assembly at the beginning of his third term, Davis challenged that body to provide for a reform school and to correct abuses in the penitentiary system. Not only did the legislature establish a reform school for the "discipline, employment, education, and reformation" of boys under eighteen, but it also set a legal day's work in the lumber mills, changed the management of the pen-

74. Speech at Eureka Springs, November 5, 1903.
75. Vance, "A Karl Marx for Hill Billies," 185; *Senate Documents*, James P. Clarke, *Jeff Davis: Memorial Addresses*, 62nd Cong., 3rd Sess., No. 1146, p. 20.

itentiary, fixed the state rate tax, and insured protection of labor unions.[76] Such social reforms helped bring government closer to the people. Davis was less successful in the United States Senate where, Senator Clark suggested, he was "not satisfied with his career." Neither did Davis' militant agrarianism long survive him in Arkansas, for as V. O. Key noted, "the great upthrust of organized business killed off the loud but feeble agrarian protest." Davis' war against the corporations thus was ultimately futile, and his legacy on behalf of Arkansas' dispossessed lay rather in the penal, health, education, and labor law reforms he championed.[77]

In addition to instigating some much-needed social reforms, Davis returned to the common folk the status deprived them by economic change and political realignments. Specifically, he conferred status on the masses by cirumventing traditional strongholds of authority and seeking political power directly from the common people. He simplified complex issues and called on his uneducated audiences to construe legal statutes. He assured his hearers that it didn't take a lawyer to figure out the Rector Anti-Trust Act. Interpreting that legislation line by line, he explained: The law says, "Mr. Corporation, if you are a member of ANY, a–n–y pool or trust you can not do business in Arkansas."[78] Why are the courts having such difficulty, Davis queried, when the people know exactly what the act means? Davis also gave status to the laboring class when he put the farmer, the mechanic, the brickman, the wood-hauler, the red-necks, and the patched britches brigade "in charge" of his campaign. In one celebrated incident, he juxtaposed his opponent Judge Wood's campaign manager, "a little two-by-four upstart lawyer . . . who hasn't got sense enough to bound Pulaski county," against his own campaign manager, "just the farmers of Arkansas."[79] What higher compliment could Davis have paid the common folk?

In sympathy not "with the aristocracy of wealth, but with the aristocracy of worth," Davis did not measure the nobility of people "by

76. Staples and Thomas, "The Rise of the One Gallus Democracy," 260; Neal, "Jeff Davis and the Reform Movement in Arkansas," 76.

77. *Senate Documents*, James P. Clarke, *Jeff Davis: Memorial Addresses*, 62 Cong., 3rd Sess., No. 1146, p. 20; Key, *Southern Politics in State and Nation*, 184–85.

78. Speech at Center Point, February 12, 1900.

79. Cited in Jacobson, *The Life Story of Jeff Davis*, 235.

their social position, but by their true and real worth." Thus, he increased his followers' self-esteem by identifying them with the commonly held virtues of humility, loyalty, bravery, gentleness, and nobility. The common people were "the best, truest, noblest Democrats" Davis ever met. Arkansans were "as noble, as brave, as generous, as gentle a race of people as ever sunned themselves in the smile of Omnipotent God." And to the charge that no one would vote for him "except the fellow who wears patched breeches and one gallus and lives up the forks of the creek, and don't pay anything except his poll tax," Davis countered: "There is no great reformation that originated on the earth that did not come from the ranks of the humble and lowly of the land."[80]

Davis made such pejoratives as *red-neck, hillbilly, hayseed,* and *yokel* terms of esteem, almost of endearment. His followers were "sun-burned sons of toil," and they had nothing of which to be ashamed. Indeed, he assured his audiences that he was a hillbilly too. And, through redefining wood-haulers, farmers, and laborers as "business men," he elevated them to a par with people of traditionally higher prestige. The rhetoric was Bryanesque:

The farmer at his plow is a business man, the blacksmith at his anvil is a business man, the carpenter in his shop is a business man, the railroad employee at his hazardous task is a business man, the lawyer with his client, the minister in the pulpit, the merchant behind his counter, are all business men. We are all united by a community of interests binding us together, that comes down to us from the great White Throne of God himself. We are all business men.[81]

In Davis' rhetoric, the "wool hat brigade"—not the "silk stocking crowd"—was the Old Guard, and in the face of adversity, they were not impotent but powerful. The people believed him.

Finally, by snubbing entrenched political power and taking his case directly to the people, Davis forged a new alliance in Arkansas politics. He tapped "the still-unused and long-wasted human ability of the Ozarks" and bound the mountaineer to the flatlands farmer.[82]

80. *Senate Documents*, Thomas U. Sisson, *Jeff Davis; Memorial Addresses*, 62nd Cong., 3rd Sess., No. 1146, p. 79; *Arkansas Gazette* (Little Rock), July 16, 1899; speech at Center Point, February 12, 1900.

81. Speech at Eureka Springs, November 5, 1903.

82. Fletcher, *Arkansas*, 314.

Successful in identifying the discontent of the one with that of the other, he laid the foundations for a political machine that was to dominate Arkansas politics long after his own demise. The coalition, agrarian in philosophy, tied the hillbillies to the red-necks; it also linked the dispossessed from the country to the "outsiders" from the towns. More importantly, it inextricably bound Davis to the people. The alliance, Davis argued, could provide relief for the disfranchised—though, significantly, the solution was symbolic. "The fellow at the other end of the line is controlling prices," Davis challenged. "Are you going to dally with it; are you in earnest about this matter? Then, shut them out; don't let them come here."[83] The people took action—they "joined hands" and voted for "Jeff."

Davis always felt the public pulse and responded to its erratic beat. Indeed, that ability was the secret of his success. The *Arkansas Gazette* said it best: "He puts his hand in the public hand and gives it a grip that makes a firm and feeling bond between. Thousands of people, men and women, look on him as their champion, their guardian, their safety, and their hope. He makes his wounds and injuries theirs, and they would avenge them as they would their own." Davis was indeed the "stormy petrel" of Arkansas politics.[84] To his enemies, he was a harbinger of trouble, but in the eyes of Arkansas' oppressed, Jeff Davis could truly "walk on water."

83. Speech at Center Point, February 12, 1900.
84. *Arkansas Gazette* (Little Rock), March 31, 1912; *Senate Documents*, William M. Kavanaugh, *Jeff Davis: Memorial Addresses*, 62nd Cong., 3rd Sess., No. 1146, p. 32; Jacobson, *The Life Story of Jeff Davis*, subtitle of book.

TILLMAN

SOUTH CAROLINA'S SENATOR

This photograph is obviously the portrait to the
left superimposed onto the wagon.

"Pitchfork Ben" Tillman and

"The Race Problem from a Southern Point

of View"

On July 20, 1898, Benjamin Ryan Tillman was addressing an audience in Lexington, South Carolina, when he created for himself an image that lasted the rest of his speaking career. At the time, Tillman was campaigning for a seat in the United States Senate, having just served two stormy terms as governor of the Palmetto state. After touching on several agrarian issues of the day, Tillman addressed one of his favorite topics, the alleged unfitness for office of President Grover Cleveland. "When Judas betrayed Christ," shouted the orator, "his heart was not blacker than this scoundrel, Cleveland. . . . He is an old bag of beef and I am going to Washington with a pitchfork and prod him in his old fat ribs." [1]

It is not the purpose of this essay to provide a detailed analysis of "Pitchfork Ben" Tillman's speaking career. Such an overview already has been provided by Lindsay S. Perkins.[2] Instead, the essay will concentrate on a lecture the orator delivered many times between 1901 and 1909 on Chautauqua and lyceum circuits and will examine (1) Tillman's ideological background relevant to the lecture, (2) the occasions for the address, (3) the speech's content and development, (4) audience reactions, (5) the Tillmanesque style, and (6) the lecture's rhetoric and the American mind at the turn of the century.

1. Charleston (S.C.) *News and Courier*, July 23, 1894.
2. Lindsay S. Perkins, "The Oratory of Benjamin Ryan Tillman" (Ph.D. dissertation, Northwestern University, 1945). Also see Lindsay Perkins, "The Oratory of Benjamin Ryan Tillman," *Speech Monographs*, XV (1948), 1–18.

I

By 1900 Tillman had become known as the most outspoken advocate
of white supremacy in the Senate. The circumstances that cast him in
this role arose out of the debates over Cuba, the Philippines, and Hawaii, parts of the nation's newly acquired territorial empire. During
these deliberations Tillman developed a position that allowed him to
harass Senate Republicans who were eager to annex Hawaii. His position ironically contained elements of both a liberal foreign policy and
a racist domestic one; for he argued, somewhat contradictorily, that it
was wrong for one nation of people, without due cause, to subjugate
another, particularly after allegedly fighting a war to liberate them;
that the annexation of Hawaii and the Philippines would weaken
America by introducing additional hordes of "colored peoples"; and
that annexation would necessitate granting to those "colored peoples" the protections of the Fourteenth and Fifteenth amendments,
an action that, according to Tillman, would perpetuate a wrong already committed in the South.[3]

Tillman freely admitted his own disdain for the self-governing capabilities of all "colored peoples." "A small handful of white men," he
argued, "are owners and rulers of these islands [Hawaii] simply because they are a superior race, possessing the superiority of manhood
and intellect which distinguishes one people from another." He was
able to place his Republican colleagues on the horns of a dilemma:
annex Hawaii and withhold the franchise from most of the native
population, thus seeming to repudiate the spirit of the Fourteenth
and Fifteenth amendments; or anger the powerful group of whites
who controlled the islands by granting to the native Hawaiians the
same rights granted to former slaves in the South. "Under the fifteenth amendment," argued Tillman, "the moment the islands are annexed their inhabitants become citizens of the United States. Under
the same fifteenth amendment, you can not deny them the right to
vote unless you deny it to the white men in those islands."[4]

In these debates Tillman also assumed those more traditional

3. *Congressional Record*, 55th Cong., 2nd Sess., 6530–35; 56th Cong., 1st Sess.,
2243; 57th Cong., 1st Sess., 5100–5101.
4. *Ibid.*, 55th Cong., 1st Sess., 6533, 2nd Sess., 6535.

southern racial postures. "We" of the South, he argued, "have been confronted by the condition of a large, ignorant, debased vote, thrust upon us by the fourteenth and fifteenth amendments. . . . That vote stands as a menace to the freedom, to the purity of the ballot box, to the purity and honesty of elections, to the decency of government, and it is there forever until there is a constitutional provision made here which will relieve us from it." Members of the "colored races" were "unfit for suffrage," even when they had been "educated to a limited degree," because such people did not "possess that moral character and moral fiber . . . necessary to good citizenship." "We of the South," he proclaimed, "have never recognized the right of the negro to govern white men, and we never will. We have never believed him to be equal to the white men, and we will not submit to his gratifying his lust on our wives and daughters without lynching him. I would to God the last one of them was in Africa and that none of them had ever been brought to our shores."[5]

II

Such strident expressions soon placed Tillman in great demand as a speaker on "The Race Problem from a Southern Point of View."[6] Between July 1, 1901, and November 15, 1909, the senator presented his lecture to over three hundred Chautauqua or lyceum audiences in thirty-eight states. His busiest years were 1906 and 1907, with one six-month period—March through August, 1907—devoted to 101 lectures in one hundred cities in thirty states.[7] In January, 1908, before the South Carolina House of Representatives, he offered this analysis of his lecturing activities: "I have talked in the last eighteen months to some 250 audiences in the northern states. I have been at Chautauquas, at theatres, lyceums, been out in the open, and in tents, occasionally have spoken in a grove, as I am accustomed to do here in the summer time, and once in a while in a church. I have told these peo-

5. *Ibid.*, 56th Cong., 1st Sess., 2245, 3224.
6. Apparently Tillman delivered his first public lecture on this topic at the University of Michigan in 1898: Augusta (Ga.) *Chronicle*, September 17, 1903; Little Rock *Democrat*, October 10, 1906.
7. For the dates and places of most of these lectures see Perkins, "The Oratory of Benjamin Ryan Tillman," 450–63.

ple to their teeth of their mistakes and errors and crimes—and I have actually rubbed it in."[8]

The Chautauqua and lyceum audiences loved to hear Tillman "rub it in." They came as supporters, as would-be detractors, or just as curious observers—but they came. "Senator Tillman tomorrow!" announced the Columbia, Missouri, *Daily Tribune*. "That means a tremendous crowd at the Chautauqua grounds. Boone County has long been anxious to hear the great South Carolina senator, and the opportunity has at last come."[9] "It will be a big day," declared the *Daily Camera* of Boulder, Colorado. "There will be a big crowd. There will be a big speaker. The fur will fly where the pitchfork strikes. No mincing of words when Ben Tillman talks, and he will talk tomorrow. . . . His audience will be a record breaker and all should plan to be on time." The *Daily Eagle*, in Marinette, Wisconsin, reported, "One of the largest audiences that has visited the Assembly this year was in attendance . . . to listen to the thundering of Pitchfork Tillman." And in Fond du Lac, Wisconsin, the *Daily Commonwealth* observed that "Senator Benjamin Ryan Tillman, the 'pitchfork' statesman from South Carolina, was at his best . . . when he addressed a large audience . . . on the subject of 'The Race Question in the South.' . . . He went at the question from the Southerner's standpoint, and without gloves, and the way he pitched out thoughts sizzling hot made his listeners sit up and take notice from the very beginning." Finally, in Spokane, Washington, the *Spokesman Review* headed its coverage of the lecture with "TILLMAN RANTS AT NEGRO RACE. . . . HEARD BY 1400." "Fiery denunciations of the negro race, hurled almost in hisses through clenched teeth, vitriolic scathings of anti-slavery leaders, and carpetbaggers before and after the Civil War, and even severe arraignment of the Northern political leaders of to-day for their attitude toward the South," continued the *Spokesman Review*, "met with vigorous applause . . . when Senator Benjamin Ryan Tillman of South Carolina spoke on the race problem for two and a half hours."[10]

From 1901 through 1903 Tillman concentrated his Chautauqua

8. *Address, "The Negro Problem and Immigration," by B. R. Tillman, Delivered by Invitation before the South Carolina House of Representatives, January 24, 1908* (Columbia, S.C.: Gonzales and Bryan, 1908), 18–19.
9. Columbia (Mo.) *Daily Tribune*, August 17, 1906.
10. Boulder (Colo.) *Daily Camera*, July 26, 1907; Marinette (Wis.) *Daily Eagle*, Au-

and lyceum activities in the South and the Midwest, delivering 66 lectures. Then during 1904 and 1905 his lecturing almost stopped. Perkins found evidence of only five bookings for these years, one in Nebraska and the other four in the South. But in 1906 the orator delivered 90 lectures throughout the Midwest, South, and border states, moving as far west as Montana. In 1907 he accelerated this pace to 154 lectures in thirty-five states extending from Mississippi to Massachusetts and from the Carolinas to California. The only sections of the country not covered that year were the far Southwest, where centers of population in 1907 were probably too scattered to make bookings feasible, and upper New England, where he may not have been in as great demand as apparently he was in other areas, particularly the Midwest.[11]

"Pitchfork Ben" was on the circuit so much in 1907 that some of the homestate folks began to wonder if he were not shirking his senatorial duties. His response to such criticism was to claim a kind of mission. "We need to educate the North along the line I have been trying to," he told the South Carolina House of Representatives. "All we need is to send the best speakers in the South up there, and . . . teach them the fundamental truth . . . that the white race is the superior race, and that the white man has the God-given right to govern this country." "I have at a Chautauqua in Iowa . . . in Michigan, and in other states," he said, "talked three hours, and they have clamored for more; and have preached the gospel of white supremacy straight from the shoulder and had them applaud ten times as much as you have tonight. . . . I have told them to their teeth that they didn't believe that the negro was equal to the white man; that they were hypocrites and liars when they said it."[12] When South Carolina citizens heard how their senator had "educated" the errant North, they may not have minded that he spent nine months of 1907—March through November—on the circuit receiving as much as six hundred dollars for each lecture.[13]

---

gust 5, 1901; Fond du Lac (Wis.) *Daily Commonwealth*, November 30, 1906; Spokane (Wash.) *Spokesman Review*, October 2, 1907.

11. Throughout this eight-year period Tillman avoided much of New England, lecturing only fourteen times in the state of New York and twice in Massachusettes.

12. Tillman, *"The Negro Problem and Immigration,"* 9, 12, 20–22.

13. Six hundred dollars was Tillman's regular fee, although he sometimes took

After 1907 Tillman's lecture travels quickly came to an end.[14] In March of that year the orator suffered a stroke that left him partially paralyzed and temporarily impaired in speech. Then in 1910 and 1911 a cerebral hemorrhage and other serious health problems kept him from ever returning to the nation's lecture circuit.[15] The last time he delivered this speech was on November 15, 1909, in Charleston, West Virginia.[16]

III

Tillman's lecture was, to a large degree, a formless one. According to the orator, it was never written down.[17] In addition, it varied in basic format from one delivery to another,[18] being built around a set of modular components—colorful anecdotes, a few basic arguments, spirited proclamations, vitriolic denunciations, and dire predictions —which could be arranged in a multitude of patterns. This looseness in structure allowed Tillman to speak from one to three hours, depending upon such limitations as a tight train schedule to his next booking.[19]

Even though the lecture did not always follow the same organizational pattern and did not always contain precisely the same supportive materials, there were basic topics that gave a consistency to the presentation. In fact, five divisions of thought surfaced repeatedly: universal racism and northern ignorance of racial factors, harmful northern policies, present and past, general unfitness of the black

less if a church sponsored his lecture: Spokane (Wash.) *Spokesman Review*, October 3, 1907. By another account he earned twenty-five thousand dollars lecturing the summer of 1906: "Men We Are Watching," *Independent*, LXI (December 13, 1906), 1429. Another source said this sum rose to forty thousand dollars for the summer of 1907: Boulder (Colo.) *Daily Camera*, July 29, 1907.

14. Perkins, in "The Oratory of Benjamin Ryan Tillman," records only three bookings in 1908 and one in 1909.

15. Francis Butler Simkins, *Pitchfork Ben Tillman, South Carolinian* (Baton Rouge: Louisiana State University Press, 1944), 461–69.

16. Perkins, "The Oratory of Benjamin Ryan Tillman," 463.

17. Omaha *World-Herald*, May 15, 1907.

18. For examples of this variance, see Pittsburgh *Post*, April 25, 1907; Mansfield (Ohio) *Daily Shield*, August 29, 1906; Spokane (Wash.) *Spokesman Review*, October 2, 1907.

19. Missoula (Mont.) *Daily Missoulian*, October 10, 1907.

man, solutions to the race problems, and predictions of a race war if those solutions were not adopted.

Universal Racism and Northern Ignorance

Tillman wanted to make his audiences aware of what he called a "universal racism." This "sentiment of caste," reflected in a dislike for blacks, was, he charged, "lurking somewhere in every human breast." "There is a feeling of antipathy between all different races," said Tillman, and "this feeling was planted there by God for some good purpose . . . to keep the races from crossing." Northerners should recognize, he argued, that they, too, are prejudiced, that they do not relish social and political equality with the black man any more than do their southern brothers.[20]

Northern audiences usually applauded such sentiments, and Tillman would report to the South that white men were united "on the proposition that this is a white man's country, and that white men must and will rule." Northerners, he announced in South Carolina, "have no more use for the negro at close quarters than you have, and have got very little [use] for him at any kind of quarters. They only want his vote."[21]

"Ninety per cent of the people of the North," Tillman told a Salt Lake City audience, "were ignorant of the race problem, knowing nothing about it but falsehood put out by fanatics and politicians." He told his Pittsburgh listerners that they were "as ignorant of this problem as anybody in the world." And in Waterloo, Iowa, he began his lecture by announcing bluntly: "I have decided this afternoon to talk upon a subject of which I know something and of which you know absolutely nothing." "It has been left to you smart alecks," he said in Chicago, "to discover that the African is the equal of the Caucasian and the Anglo-Saxon. I know a colored man, and whatever brains and character he has he got from his white father." "Most of you from your cradles," he announced in Montana, "have heard nothing but

---

20. Madison (Wis.) *Democrat*, March 20, 1903; Fond du Lac (Wis.) *Daily Commonwealth*, November 30, 1906; Milwaukee *Sentinel*, July 28, 1903; Salt Lake *Tribune*, May 27, 1907.
21. Little Rock *Democrat*, October 10, 1906; Tillman, "*The Negro Problem and Immigration*," 19.

talk about black abolition sentimentalism, about the fatherhood of God and the universal brotherhood of man, and all that rot." In Idaho he said baldly, "You have been pitiable in your ignorance of this matter, and I have come to enlighten you."[22]

Harmful Northern Policies

Operating in this state of ignorance, argued Tillman, northerners instituted national policies that severely injured southern political and social institutions. As a conquerer, the North had turned southern states over to "carpetbaggers, the nigger, and Southern scalawags and scoundrels" who governed through "eight dismal years when the sun of hope never shone." It was a period, he charged, marked by "robbery and anarchy," by the "black man's lust," and by a general debauchment of southern systems.[23]

Political ghouls infested the South and South Carolina went under a cloud and for eight years negroes and carpetbaggers ruled and ruined the fair name of the state, its bonds depreciated until worth nothing, our lands were devastated, and do you blame us for hating the source of our misery and disgrace? We did hate you.

Negro militiamen lorded it over us, all puffed up, claiming that Massa Grant had put the bottom rail on top, and these devils would tell our children that they would kill the white man, take his wife and make the white children work for them as they had worked for their daddies.

Had we known that such would be the terms of our surrender we would have fought until now. Life was not worth living.[24]

One of the greatest injuries supposedly was done to the black man himself. "You planted this sting of the scorpion in the negro," he told Wisconsin people, "by imparting the doctrine of equality in the black man's mind. You marched them to the polls to go through the farce of voting. What has been the result? Pick up a newspaper almost

22. Salt Lake *Tribune*, May 27, 1907; Pittsburgh *Post*, April 25, 1907; Waterloo (Iowa) *Daily Courier*, September 8, 1906; Chicago *Tribune*, November 28, 1906; Missoula (Mont.) *Daily Missoulian*, October 10, 1907; Nampa (Idaho) *Leader-Herald*, October 8, 1907.

23. Marinette (Wis.) *Daily Eagle*, August 5, 1901; Mansfield (Ohio) *Daily Shield*, August 29, 1906; Boseman (Mont.) *Courier*, November 16, 1906; Bloomington (Ill.) *Daily Pantagraph*, August 5, 1901.

24. Urbana (Ill.) *Courier-Herald*, August 24, 1906.

any day and read . . . of the outrages that our white women of the South have been made to suffer." [25]

This alleged cause-and-effect relationship between the enfranchisement of blacks and the rape of southern women was one of Tillman's most persistent charges: "The association of white men with negroes often times starts the demon in the negro, which ends in an assault upon a white woman. The negro is led to believe that he is as good as a white man and if as good as a white man why not as good as a white woman?" [26] "Negro equality in politics," he reasoned, "means . . . social equality, mongrelization, hell-fire and damnation." [27]

According to Tillman, the black man had not always been this "bestial" in character. Prior to emancipation, he argued, "the wives and daughters of the Confederate soldiers were left unprotected at home, at the mercy of the negroes. . . . Had the blacks been so minded, they could have begun to pillage, burn and ravish. But in spite of this opportunity . . . the records show that during the four years of the war not a solitary white woman was harmed." From this behavior he concluded that "the negro was more Christianized and civilized" before the war than he became after emancipation. Although Tillman claimed not to advocate a return to slavery, he frequently asserted that the institution had done "more for the negro than anything else" and that the "best negroes" were former slaves. [28]

In addition to representing a threat to southern white women, the liberated and "equalized" black man constituted, according to Tillman, a profound threat to the southern political system. First, the black man was unfit totally for civilized self-government; next, this unfitness was established clearly by the experience of 1865–1876; and, finally, the South was able to save herself only by political "subterfuges" recognized as illegal and injurious to the American political system—"stuffed ballot boxes" and "the disfranchisement of the ne-

25. Fond du Lac (Wis.) *Daily Commonwealth*, November 30, 1906.
26. Little Rock *Democrat*, October 10, 1906. Tillman was not the only racist of the period to suggest that this association existed. See I. A. Newby, *Jim Crow's Defense: Anti-Negro Thought in America, 1900–1930* (Baton Rouge: Louisiana State University Press, 1965), 135–40.
27. Madison (Wis.) *Democrat*, March 20, 1903.
28. Fond du Lac (Wis.) *Daily Commonwealth*, November 30, 1906; Milwaukee *Sentinel*, July 28, 1903; Madison (Wis.) *Democrat*, March 20, 1903.

groes by property and educational qualification." "We have had to shoot many of the niggers . . . [to] take the government from them," Tillman bragged. "This is white man's country," he declared with finality, "and shall be governed by white men." [29]

General Unfitness of the Black Man

Tillman devoted a considerable portion of his lecture to an expression of his basic attitude toward blacks: "The negro is the tail end of creation and first cousin to the baboon." "You can't make a white man out of a nigger even if you do send him to college," he told his Missoula, Montana, audience, "even if you do elevate him, even if you do encourage him, even if you do give him the liberty to govern." In fact, education usually was detrimental to blacks, charged the orator. "A negro can be educated, but only educated as an underling, as God made him so. When you educate a man above his station he becomes an insidious snake that some time or other will harm you." "About one in a thousand," he added, "is the average which can successfully be educated to the place of equality with the white man." "It has been said," he told a Mansfield, Ohio, crowd, "that in educating a negro you spoil a good field hand and at once make him a candidate for the three P's—preaching, politics, or penitentiary." "Ten thousand negroes," he said, "and only one Booker Washington, with him half white." [30]

But the main weaknesses in black character, according to Tillman, were the race's general immorality and its inability to create and sustain civilized societies. [31] "The African . . . for forty or fifty centuries has done what?" he asked. "He has never been enlightened enough to create a written manuscript or even to invent an alphabet;

29. Fond du Lac (Wis.) *Daily Commonwealth*, November 30, 1906; Bowling Green (Ohio) *Sentinel-Tribune*, December 21, 1906; Milwaukee *Sentinel*, July 28, 1903; Missoula (Mont.) *Daily Missoulian*, October 10, 1907; Beatrice (Neb.) *Daily Express*, July 5, 1901; Minneota (Minn.) *Mascot*, September 21, 1906.

30. Salt Lake *Tribune* May 27, 1907; Missoula (Mont.) *Daily Missoulian*, October 10, 1907; Pittsburgh *Post*, April 25, 1907; San Francisco *Chronicle*, September 19, 1907; Mansfield (Ohio) *News*, August 29, 1906; Nampa (Idaho) *Leader-Herald*, October 8, 1907. In some accounts of Tillman's lecture the term "nigger" is used, while "negro" is used in others. Which term did Tillman actually employ? According to the Pittsburgh *Post*, April 25, 1907, he "referred to the blacks as 'niggers'" throughout the lecture.

31. San Francisco *Chronicle*, September 19, 1907.

he has never built a city of stone, or brick, or wood, or even of mud, and such habitations as he had were of bamboo or cane." He "had no government except a tribal government, in no way developed the resources of the country, had no religion, no laws, no morals, nothing." Tillman further argued that it would be ludicrous "to say that the negro, by virtue of foolish legislation which gave him the ballot, is an equal to the white man, and capable of exercising the duties of citizenship." "We are ready to swap you to-day," he told the people of Nebraska, "three niggers for one white man, and we don't care what kind of a white man he is." "I hope you will encourage the migration of negroes to Iowa," he announced in that state. "We can spare about 200,000 of them and you will receive a lesson from them which will do some of you good." [32]

Solutions to the Race Problem

During Senate debates over the annexation of Hawaii, Tillman argued for a Supreme Court reinterpretation of the Fourteenth and Fifteenth amendments that would allow the enfranchisement of only the islands' white population. [33] He hoped for a judicial sanction for de facto disfranchisement measures southern states already were taking. [34] On the lecture circuit, however, he argued bluntly for the repeal of these amendments and warned that failure to do so would lead to "one of the greatest and bloodiest struggles in the history of the country." [35]

This struggle would come, he reasoned, because more and more blacks eventually would meet the education requirements for franchisement. Thus, disfranchisement of blacks by "indirection and evasion of the Federal constitution was only a temporary relief." "It will soon come to the place that they will be in a position to contest the government with us, unless something is done." [36]

32. Fond du Lac (Wis.) *Daily Commonwealth*, November 30, 1906; Nampa (Idaho) *Leader-Herald*, October 8, 1907; Beatrice (Neb.) *Daily Express*, July 5, 1901; Waterloo (Iowa) *Daily Courier*, September 8, 1906.

33. *Congressional Record*, 55th Cong., 2nd Sess., 6534–35.

34. For a discussion of southern actions to disfranchise blacks see C. Vann Woodward, *Origins of the New South* (Baton Rouge: Louisiana State University Press, 1951), 321–49; and C. Vann Woodward, *The Strange Career of Jim Crow* (New York: Oxford University Press, 1955), 54–56.

35. Nampa (Idaho) *Leader-Herald*, October 8, 1907.

36. Salt Lake *Tribune*, May 27, 1907; Little Rock *Democrat*, October 10, 1906.

Predictions of a Race War

Many of Tillman's critics charged that he advocated violence.[37] Certainly his lecture was loaded with violent assertions. "The sword of Damocles, threatening negro domination, is hanging over our heads," he said, "and woe upon him who would sever the sword." "The time is coming," he predicted, "when thousands will be killed just on account of the 5 per cent of the negroes who are bad."[38] Furthermore, Tillman consistently argued that a race war would occur if federal legislation allowed black political dominance to develop in the South. "He and his brethren were ready to down their shotguns again." "We will have to butcher the negroes some day," he said, "and when the struggle comes . . . it will be a horrible one."[39]

Tillman and his brethren also stood ready to lynch any black man accused of rape: "I say never let the law drag a woman into court to tell of her own disgrace—worse than death itself. When a woman says 'that is the man,' that is all I want. Up he goes." "Southern men," he declared, "would not crucify their women by making them appear in court but, instead, constituted the injured woman as judge, jury, and prosecutor and lynched the man whom she pointed out as her assailant." "I have justified lynch law for one crime, that is all," he announced. "Unless this ravishing of white women stops I predict bloodshed both in the North and the South." The *Daily Pantagraph* of Bloomington, Illinois, observed that Tillman's "reference to the sanctity of . . . Southern women and remarks on lynching were heartily applauded."[40]

37. See resolution passed by the Boston Literary and Historical Society, Chicago *Tribune*, November 27, 1906, and resolution passed by Sacramento black citizens, Sacramento *Evening Bee*, September 18, 1907.

38. Waterloo (Iowa) *Daily Courier*, September 7, 1906; Little Rock *Democrat*, October 10, 1906.

39. Bloomington (Ill.) *Daily Pantagraph*, August 5, 1901; Nampa (Idaho) *Leader-Herald*, October 8, 1907.

40. Little Rock *Democrat*, October 10, 1906; Salt Lake *Tribune*, May 27, 1907; Chicago *Tribune*, November 28, 1906; Bloomington (Ill.) *Daily Pantagraph*, August 5, 1901.

IV

The audience response observed by the *Daily Pantagraph* apparently was typical. Most lecture crowds—particularly in the Midwest—vigorously applauded Tillman, even when he was voicing racist or antinorthern ideas. "A significant feature of the occasion," reported the Minneapolis *Journal*, "was the earnest applause everytime the speaker asserted that the white man must rule in the South and will not permit the black man to rule." The Omaha *World-Herald* noted that "frequently during the stirring periods of his discussion of the race question the great audience . . . was clamorous in its applause." The *Daily Shield* of Mansfield, Ohio, also mentioned the "frequent bursts of applause," reporting that such audience response often occurred when Tillman "told the deepest truths regarding people in the North." "Although his sarcasm cut and slashed the North and the ideas the northern people have long held dear," observed the *Daily Commonwealth* of Fond du Lac, Wisconsin, "the audience scarcely winched, but when it cut deepest, cheered and shouted for more." [41]

Many of these auditors apparently were expressing approval of Tillman's ideology. But the Minneapolis *Journal* suggested that some applause simply demonstrated appreciation for the speaker's showmanship: "It was so out of the usual for a man to be so fiercely emphatic in addressing what might be supposed to be a hostile audience, that the audience spontaneously assumed the attitude of a man at a good entertainment, who puts prejudice aside and goes in for appreciation. Senator Tillman's fiercest thrusts at the northern point of view were received in the best of humor and always with applause." [42]

In his lecture introductions Tillman was fond of claiming to be a straight-forward, hold-nothing-back, avoid-no-sensitive-fact, absolutely honest person. "I think I am right," he announced in Salt Lake City. "I know I am honest. I'm going to tell the truth, the whole truth and nothing but the truth, so help me God. If you don't like it, I can't

41. Minneapolis *Journal*, March 21, 1903; Omaha *World-Herald*, May 15, 1907; Mansfield (Ohio) *Daily Shield*, August 29, 1906; Fond du Lac (Wis.) *Daily Commonwealth*, November 30, 1906.

42. Minneapolis *Journal*, March 21, 1903.

help it, and I don't care." [43] "I do not believe in beating about the bush," he declared in Missoula, Montana. "I will say what I know and will speak the truth. Whatever else can be said of me, no one can say that I have lied." [44]

All these professions of honesty apparently worked, for the dominant view of Tillman, as expressed by white reporters, was that he was precisely what he claimed to be. One observer even glowingly described him as a "sober, serious, clean, wholesome, pure, upright, decent man in every sense of the word: brusque, abrupt, outspoken, candid, [and] brutally frank. His word is his bond, and your word must be yours." And there were others who agreed, saying he was "ruggedly honest," that he possessed "honesty of purpose and indomitable courage," that he was "earnest and honest in every one of his convictions," and that no one hearing his speech "could for a moment question his absolute sincerity or doubt for an instant that he was "perfectly honest." [45]

These same reporters also noted that crowds generally responded enthusiastically to practically everything the South Carolinian said, particularly when he discussed rape and white supremacy. [46] There was, however, a persistent and vocal minority, composed of black community leaders and a few white intellectuals, who vehemently opposed Tillman's racial remarks and who thus questioned the speaker's general character and intelligence. These dissonant voices usually were confined to the larger cities such as Chicago, Minneapolis, Pittsburgh, Sacramento, and San Francisco, where in each instance Tillman encountered an organized protest.

In Chicago black community leaders convinced the mayor that he should not introduce Tillman and also raised five thousand dollars in an unsuccessful attempt to persuade the sponsoring organization—a ladies guild of the Chicago Union Hospital—to accept an in-lieu-of-

43. Salt Lake *Tribune*, May 27, 1907.
44. Missoula (Mont.) *Daily Missoulian*, October 10, 1907.
45. W. A. Lewis, "The Tillman of the Armchair," *Success*, IX (1906), 396; "The Cornfield Lawyer," *Outlook*, CXIX (July 17, 1918), 442; "Men We Are Watching," *Independent*, LXI (December 13, 1906), 1430; Marinette (Wis.) *Daily Eagle*, August 5, 1901; Mansfield (Ohio) *News*, August 29, 1906.
46. Omaha *World-Herald*, May 15, 1907; Minot (N.D.) *Daily Optic*, November 10, 1906; Shelbyville (Ill.) *Democrat*, August 13, 1903.

lecture contribution.[47] James Wallace, president of Macalester College, tried in vain to convince the First Baptist Church of Minneapolis to close its doors to Tillman's lecture.[48] San Franciscan black clergymen "called on Mayor Taylor, asking him not to countenance nor to attend officially the [Tillman] meeting." Taylor did not attend, but three thousand other citizens did.[49] Finally, in Pittsburgh some blacks organized to heckle Tillman, but the rest of the audience—a decided majority—shouted down the dissidents and rushed the stage following the lecture to shake hands with the orator.[50]

One organized protest was moderately successful. In Sacramento, Tillman's appearance was being sponsored by the local Y.M.C.A. and was to be held in the Congregational church. But three days before the event a black group formulated the following protest resolution:

> Whereas, a notorious and unscrupulous negro-hater—Senator Tillman—is to deliver a lecture in this city in the near future, vilifying the negro race, and on an invitation from the Y.M.C.A. in a so-called Christian church; therefore, be it
>
> Resolved, that we the undersigned colored people in mass-meeting assembled, do declare that if the sentiments expressed by the Senator voice the views held by the ministry and the churches of this city, that their God is a myth, their Bible a lie, Christianity a fraud, and the teachings of the clergy a travesty on the ethics of moral philosophy.

The black group also threatened a bloc vote against a pending city ordinance excluding saloons from the residential sections of the city, an action favored by white church leaders. This threat, plus the resolution, pressured the Sacramento Y.M.C.A. into asking Tillman not to speak on "The Race Problem from a Southern Point of View," but to speak instead on an alternate topic. Nevertheless, a portion of the audience clamored for the famous "negro-hating" speech. Therefore, the president of the local Y.M.C.A. faced a hostile crowd when he announced that the South Carolinian's pitchfork would be jabbed not into the black man but into tariff policies and railroad rates.[51]

47. Chicago *Tribune*, November 27, 1906.
48. Minneapolis *Journal*, March 20, 1903.
49. San Francisco *Chronicle*, September 18, 19, 1907.
50. Pittsburgh *Post*, April 25, 1907.
51. Sacramento *Evening Bee*, September 21, 1907.

V

When Tillman himself faced hostile audiences he invariably emerged as the crowd favorite. In fact, his explosive and vitriolic responses to hecklers—and sometimes even to inane supporters—became a standard feature of the Tillmanesque style. He was a "put down" artist and seemed to relish all opportunities for verbal battles with speakers of lesser forensic talent. And after such encounters the audience invariably burst into instant applause or laughter, while the would-be heckler retreated into silent anonymity or left the hall.

In Chicago, for example, Tillman asked his audience what the North had done for the black man in granting him the franchise.

"Everything," shouted a man in the gallery. Quick as a flash the speaker turned and faced the man who interrupted.

"Sure you have," he shouted, shaking his fist in the air. "You have made him a ravisher of women."

This outburst of passion on the part of the senator was followed by a tremendous demonstration of approval by the audience. The crowd yelled, shouted, whistled, applauded, and laughed, the noise continuing for several minutes, while Senator Tillman stood in characteristic attitude with arms folded across his breast.

During the same lecture Tillman bellowed impatiently at another heckler: "Oh, shut your mouth. You don't know the A, B, C of this thing; I have forgotten fifty years ago more than you ever knew."[52] To a white minister in Urbana, Illinois, he screamed, "You pretend to love the negro, you hypocrite! We [of the South] do not pretend to."[53] In Omaha, Nebraska, Tillman even insulted an overly enthusiastic supporter who applauded a prosaic expression. Tillman stopped, stared at the auditor, and declared, "I'd like to know—honestly I would—I'd like to know what mental process led you to applaude that."[54] Similar exchanges occurred with hecklers in such places as Salt Lake City, Pittsburgh, and Fond du Lac, Wisconsin, and in each

52. Chicago *Tribune*, November 28, 1906.
53. Urbana (Ill.) *Courier-Herald*, August 24, 1906.
54. Omaha *World-Herald*, May 15, 1907.

of these instances the audience supported Tillman with laughter and applause.[55]

Tillman seemed to act on the supposition that Providence had granted him license to attack anything and anyone, at any time and in any way, and with the most unrestrained verbal imagery and physical demeanor imaginable. "I drew a sword and threw the scabbard away," he once said, "and I have never looked for it since. I have attacked friend or foe, whoever or whatever got in the way, and with truth and right as my guiding stars, I shall move straight onward til I reach my goal."[56]

On the lecture circuit that goal often was to assault his opponents with thoroughly offensive rhetoric. "He is the most vindictive speaker we have ever listened to," noted the Minneota, Minnesota, *Mascot*.[57] "His heavy square jaws snapped like a steel trap," observed the *Daily Courier* of Waterloo, Iowa. "He swung his pitchfork and prodded his helpless victims until the tines ran blood. Then he would withdraw the instrument from the quivering wound, hold it up to display for a moment and then jab it in again."[58]

Tillman's pitchfork style became most pronounced when he fell prey to what Wilbur J. Cash has called the "rape complex."[59] This state of mind held that the foremost weakness in a black man's character was "his innate fondness for white women and his disposition to commit the crime of rape."[60] Tillman's imagery was never more vivid, his physical demeanor never more vigorous, than when he was discussing this issue. "If an innocent, sweet girl of sixteen was going along a country road skirted on either side by a thick wood, and there should be lurking on one side a wild tiger . . . and on the other a brutal negro with fiendish intent, and it was her fate to be delivered up to one or the other" Tillman would rather "a thousand times" that the

55. Salt Lake *Tribune*, May 27, 1907; Pittsburgh *Post*, April 25, 1907; Fond du Lac (Wis.) *Daily Commonwealth*, November 30, 1907.
56. Charleston (S.C.) *News and Courier*, April 20, 1886.
57. Minneota (Minn.) *Mascot*, September 21, 1906.
58. Waterloo (Iowa) *Daily Courier*, Setember 8, 1906.
59. Wilbur J. Cash, *The Mind of the South* (New York: Vintage-Knopf, 1941), 116–20.
60. Newby, *Jim Crow's Defense*, 135.

girl "become food for the tiger." [61] "When the speaker approached the subject of sex in connection with the race problem," noted the Chicago *Daily Tribune*, "he emphasized his points by waving his arms, slapping his hands, and shouting at the top of his voice." [62]

VI

Several students of North/South states of mind, including Woodward, Cash, I. A. Newby, and Donald Brown, have noted the permissive attitudes that prevailed in the North at the turn of the century relative to racism in general and to black disfranchisement in particular. [63] Woodward argues that the northern retreat on the race issue began as early as 1877, that the Tilden-Hayes compromise of that year "left the freedman to the custody of the conservative Redeemers upon their pledge that they would protect him in his constitutional rights." But, "as these pledges were forgotten or violated and the South moved toward proscription and extremism, Northern opinion shifted to the right, keeping pace with the South, conceding point after point, so that at no time were the sections very far apart on race policy." Woodward also observes that America's imperialistic adventures in Cuba, Hawaii, Philippines, and Samoa sped up this retreat. "As America shouldered the White Man's Burden," argues Woodward, "she took up at the same time many Southern attitudes on the subject of race." [64] Newby also supports this position, observing that during this period the "force-bill psychology, endorsing federal action to protect the Negro, was replaced by an exaggerated emphasis on nationalism, reunion, and the superior ability of Southerners to understand and solve their own problems." Cash agrees by noting the prevalence of southern racist themes in popular culture in the 1890s and early 1900s. Brown simply concludes that "by 1895 the liberal attitude [relative to blacks] was a thing of scorn; moderation was dead

61. Augusta (Ga.) *Chronicle*, September 17, 1903.
62. Chicago *Tribune*, November 28, 1906.
63. Woodward, *The Strange Career of Jim Crow*, 67–74; Woodward, *Origins of the New South*, 352–54; Cash, *The Mind of the South*, 201; Newby, *Jim Crow's Defense*, 13–14; Donald Norton Brown, "Southern Attitudes Toward Negro Voting in the Bourbon Period, 1877–1890" (Ph.D. dissertation, University of Oklahoma, 1960), 268–69.
64. Woodward, *The Strange Career of Jim Crow*, 69–70, 72.

and the traditional antagonists of the Negro were in political control." [65]

Brown's thesis could explain the response of Tillman's 1901–1909 lecture-goers. Seemingly, these audiences were in basic agreement with much that the South Carolinian had to say, particularly his judgments of black character and of black competence to function in a democratic system. In addition, newspaper coverage of the lecture often supported Tillman's major arguments. For example, after the Nampa, Idaho, *Leader-Herald* reviewed Tillman's remarks relative to the "evils" of Reconstruction, it went on to argue that "every honest man both of north and south is agreed that the wrongs of that time were many." "It is also agreed," continued the *Leader-Herald*, "that the people of the south were justified in resorting to heroic means to get out of the awful condition." The *Daily Shield* of Mansfield, Ohio, also took special note of the "injustice the [Reconstruction] South suffered"; and the Boulder, Colorado, *Daily Camera* argued that "everyone is now willing to admit that giving the vote to the negro slave was a mistake unless it was based on a property qualification. It was a bit of fanaticism due to the hatred engendered by the war and is regretted by the descendants of Charles Sumner himself." Finally, the Minneapolis *Journal* stated succinctly that "sentiment is now widespread in the North that the South should be left to settle its own race problem." Such supportive responses encouraged Tillman to say to a Spokane, Washington, audience, "At every place where I have spoken in your state, and in fact everywhere in the North, I have found the people to be sympathetic with my views." [66]

Therefore, this pitchfork orator was not as radical to his age as one might initially surmise. Indeed, his racist rhetoric came very close to being the mainstream of American thought at the beginning of the twentieth century. And though Tillman may have been somewhat intemperate in expressing his racism, he did not deviate sharply from what had become, at the close of the gilded age, the American position on black/white relations.

---

65. Newby, *Jim Crow's Defense*, 15; Cash, *The Mind of the South*, 128, 201; Brown, "Southern Attitudes Toward Negro Voting," 269.

66. Nampa (Idaho), *Leader-Herald*, October 8, 1907; Mansfield (Ohio) *Daily Shield*, August 29, 1906; Boulder (Colo.) *Daily Camera*, July 29, 1907; Minneapolis *Journal*, March 21, 1903; Spokane (Wash.) *Spokesman Review*, September 30, 1907.

James Kimble Vardaman
Manipulation Through Myths in Mississippi

In 1902 Mississippi adopted a law that changed the method of nominating gubernatorial candidates from a convention system to a popular primary. This new law shifted the power from the hands of a few political bosses to the white people of Mississippi and thus affected the whole nature of campaigning for party nominations in the state. This change not only had a far-reaching effect on Mississippi politics, but it also gave rise to the career of the southern demagogue James Kimble Vardaman of Greenwood, Mississippi. This labeling of Vardaman as a demagogue probably would be used by almost anyone who could picture this showman dressed in a white Prince Albert suit, white boots, and black Stetson, wearing his long hair brushed back from his forehead while delivering a fiery speech denouncing blacks and "Yankees." A speech by Vardaman was like a circus: people often went to be entertained by the spectacle as well as by the oratory.

Before Vardaman captured the state with his oratory he had been an unsuccessful lawyer, a successful newspaper editor, and a mediocre state legislator. Twice he had been defeated for the Democratic gubernatorial nomination under the old primary system which had allowed the Bourbon wing of the party (agrarian aristocrats) to maintain tight control over party policies. But the popular primary allowed him to take his case for social reform and repression of blacks directly to the white voters and to win the 1903 Democratic nomination for governor. In the one-party state of Mississippi, this nomination was equivalent to election.

Immediately after the Democratic primary, James Garner pointed out that the primary method of nomination allowed demagoguery to win for Vardaman. Garner wrote, "He is a most violent negro-hater, and has taken advantage of the passions and prejudices of the ignorant white population to arouse their hostility to the blacks, and by this means to ride into office. He is an open advocate of lynch law (when negroes are involved), and I dare say he has done more to arouse a spirit of lawlessness and mob rule throughout the state than all other causes combined."[1]

Vardaman answered this attack in his 1904 inaugural address by speaking of the wisdom of placing political power in the hands of the people and thus eliminating the danger of demagoguery: "There is no danger in falsehood—false doctrines, conscienceless and irresponsible error are harmless, the poisonous tongue of the sanctimonious, mercenary and sectarian partisan, the machinations of the artful demagogue, the cunning of the diplomatic office seeker, all are absolutely impotent and inocuous [sic], just so long as truth is untrammeled and the source of all political power rests with and is vouchsafed by law in the hands of the white people of Mississippi."[2]

The question of whether Vardaman was the champion of the common man or a "nigger-baiting demagogue" has been answered both ways. To A. S. Coody, the answer was simple. Coody concluded his *Biographical Sketches of James Kimble Vardaman* by saying, "Such men as James K. Vardaman are the flower of modern civilization and of the Anglo-Saxon race." William A. Percy, however, expressed a different view in *Lanterns on the Levee* when he described the Great White Chief as a "vain demagogue unable to think. He stood for the poor white against the 'nigger'—those were his qualifications as a statesman."[3] An apparently more accurate view was made by William F. Holmes in his definitive biography *The White Chief: James Kimble Vardaman*: "In Vardaman's career ran strains that affected southern politics throughout the twentieth century. On the one side there was the master dem-

1. James Wilford Garner, "A Mississippian on Vardaman," *Outlook*, LXXV (September 12, 1903), 139.
2. *Mississippi Senate Journal*, 1904, p. 116.
3. A. S. Coody, *Biographical Sketches of James Kimble Vardaman* (Jackson: A. S. Coody, 1922), 195; William A. Percy, *Lanterns on the Levee* (New York: Alfred A. Knopf, 1941), 143–44.

agogue who fanned the flames of racial hatred. On the other side there was the dedicated reformer who worked for programs he believed benefited small white farmers, laborers, and businessmen. In Vardaman the white masses of Mississippi found a spokesman and champion. His career, combining racism and reform, appeared to many baffling and paradoxical and it was. It also affords insight into the history of the South." [4]

Vardaman's 1903 gubernatorial campaign also affords insight into the history of southern oratory, for it represents significant changes in campaign rhetoric. [5] The first and most obvious change in campaigning was the need to speak directly to the public on state issues. Between 1865 and 1900 many speeches were given mainly for entertainment; during Reconstruction decisions were made by federal authorities or northern supported state and local governments, and after Redemption decisions were made in party caucuses or conventions. Thus, there was little need to persuade voters that one candidate was superior to another or that a policy option was correct or incorrect. Speeches concentrated on mending the defeated South's shattered ego, maintaining one-party Democratic control, and placating the common man with visions of progress. In his excellent article, "'Repining Over an Irrevocable Past': The Ceremonial Orator in a Defeated South, 1865–1900," Waldo Braden explains how the Bourbon Democrats manipulated thought and maintained control by the use of rhetorical myths. Braden emphasizes the importance of myths created to control a defeated population that enjoyed little direct participation in government. The people were told that they were superior because they had the great virtues of the Old South and fought valiantly in a war in which they were doomed to defeat. Mississippi communities were assured that the South's defeat in the Civil War was not a result of any southern failure. The people were encouraged to present a solid Democratic stand against the insidious coalition of "Negroes" and "Yankees"; by so doing, they could be a part of the

4. William F. Holmes, *The White Chief: James Kimble Vardaman* (Baton Rouge: Louisiana State University Press, 1970), xii.

5. For an excellent traditional rhetorical analysis of this campaign see Eugene E. White, "Anti-Racial Agitation in Politics: James Kimble Vardaman in the Mississippi Gubernatorial Campaign of 1903," *Journal of Mississippi History*, VII (January, 1945), 91–110.

progressive spirit of the New South. Soon such myths became so thoroughly accepted that they defied rational analysis, challenge, or opposition. Indeed, they helped maintain the status quo by destroying any challenger's credibility, smothering an opposing argument, driving underground a counter thought, and stifling reform.[6] "Myths," according to Paul Gaston, "are not polite euphemisms for falsehoods, but are combinations of images and symbols that reflect a people's way of perceiving truth."[7] Employed by southern speakers over a thirty-five year period, these myths helped develop images and symbols that determined attitudes and sentiments, still extremely important when political power was given directly to the people. The shift of rhetoric from ceremonial situations to the stump in no way diminished their appeal. Indeed, the success of James K. Vardaman can be largely attributed to his ability to use myths in the new deliberative speech setting, and his 1903 gubernatorial campaign is a vivid illustration of astute political manipulation of these myths.

The first, and in some ways the most important, myth in the 1903 campaign was that of the "Solid Democratic South." Speakers had repeatedly told their audiences that the only political party to represent the true interests of the South was the Democratic party. To support another party, they insisted, would create division in the region which would ultimately lead to northern or black control.[8] They emphasized that the Democratic party had redeemed the South from "Yankee" control. And to defeat populism, the Bourbon Democrats used this mind vision of a splintered party system falling victim to "Yankee" and/or black control. Vardaman, however, offered a different challenge to the conservative Bourbons, for he was a Populist who had not split from the Democratic party. As pointed out by the Starkville *News*, the 1903 primary was unique when compared with past elections when the people had no direct choice in the nominating process. "The campaign now in progress," observed the paper, "is distinct and apart in character, from any other made in the state for

6. Waldo Braden, "'Repining Over an Irrevocable Past': The Ceremonial Orator in a Defeated Society, 1865–1900," in Harold Barrett (ed.) *Rhetoric of the People* (Amsterdam: Rodopi N.V., 1974), 300.

7. Paul Gaston, *The New South Creed: A Study in Southern Mythmaking* (New York: Alfred A. Knopf, 1970), 9.

8. Braden, "'Repining Over an Irrevocable Past,'" 287.

more than a quarter of a century. Since the overthrow of 'scalawag' and negro rule and the righteous restoration of authority to the hands of the white people the only question at issue between Democratic candidates has been one of personal fitness, of capacity to adequately discharge the duties of the official positions aspired to. In this canvass, however, we have a war of sentiment and a well defined conflict of principle between men who have, heretofore, stood together in unity of spirit and community of interest."[9] Thus, the Democratic party was not solid in 1903, and identifying the party's true representative then became an important issue. In a state whose electorate was so disposed to vote Democratic, this issue was no small question. Each of the candidates' campaign rhetoric expressed the idea that he was more Democratic than his opponents. In fact, when candidates spoke of themselves as Democrats, they often inserted before the term such adjectives as "real," "true," "oldest," or "faithful." Ultimately it was left to Mississippians to evaluate the conflicting claims: (1) that Vardaman represented the true principles of the Democracy, and (2) the assertions of his two major opponents—Frank A. Critz and Edmund F. Noel—that it was Vardaman who was outside the party mainstream.

Critz and Noel, both from the Bourbon wing of the party, generally focused their rhetoric on demonstrating that Vardaman was not part of the old Democratic party. In a speech in support of Judge Critz, R. N. Miller tried to exclude Vardaman from the majority party because Vardaman did not support the policies of its prominent leaders. Miller said it "was effrontery on the part of Vardaman to try to undo what the wisdom of Wiley P. Harris, W. C. Wilkerson, J. Z. George, Judge Calhoun, Judge Mayes and many other of our best men had done in the way of forming our constitution." The White Chief was branded forthwith by his opponents as a radical who was abandoning the wisdom of the conservative philosophy of the Democratic party. The campaign rhetoric of Noel and Critz was summed up by the Jackson *Weekly Clarion-Ledger*: "Stated in broad terms the issue is between conservatism on the one hand and radicalism on the other." Noel was eliminated in the first primary and issued a state-

9. Starkville (Miss.) *News*, July 24, 1903.

ment defending his conservative principles and giving his support to Critz in the runoff. "I stand," he said, "for precisely the same principles I did during my canvass for Governor and believing that those principles are more nearly represented by Judge Critz, I shall vote for him." [10] Critz used this statement in the closing days of the runoff as evidence for his claim of being more Democratic than Vardaman.

Vardaman and his supporters, of course, claimed that he was the true representative of the Democratic party and charged that Critz and Noel were the ones who had abandoned its tenets. The controversy was explained by B. F. Ward: "The Republican cohorts marshalling under the leadership of Roosevelt, Booker Washington, Edgar S. Wilson and Andrew H. Longino, have already invaded the State and are moving stealthily, but steadily, against our defenses. Over against this towering and gigantic form stands James K. Vardaman, the young David of the Old Democracy, with his sling in his hand and his pocket full of rocks, selected from the perennial brook of Anglo-Saxon Supremacy." [11]

Vardaman's claim of representing the principles of the old Democracy was counterfeit in comparison to those of his conservative opponents because he advocated such reforms as equality of taxation and property assessment, reduction in interest rates, fire insurance regulations, welfare for the indigent, the outlawing of nepotism, and the abolition of the Mississippi River Levee Board of Control, all of which were opposed by the old Bourbon Democrats. However, his support of reforms did not in the minds of most voters exclude him from the mainstream of the party, for issues were not the basis of solidarity. Issues had not been openly discussed in the days of the convention system, and voters had not been asked to support a Democratic candidate on the basis of his positions on the issues. [12] Instead they had made their decision on the basis that he was the Democratic nominee, and that to vote for another party's candidate would split the solid Democratic party. Such a split, it was reasoned, would en-

10. Jackson *Weekly Clarion-Ledger*, August 20, 1903.
11. Starkville (Miss.) *News*, July 24, 1903.
12. Albert D. Kirwan, *Revolt of the Rednecks: Mississippi Politics, 1876–1925* (Lexington: University of Kentucky Press, 1951), 16–161; Heber Ladner, "James Kimble Vardaman, Governor of Mississippi, 1904–1908," *Journal of Mississippi History*, II (October, 1940), 175–205.

danger the state and offer less protection from the "Yankees" and blacks. Indeed, the people had such a limited basis for determining the true representative of the party that they made their selection for governor for other reasons. None of the candidates controlled the myth of a "Solid Democratic South," but Vardaman's assertions that he was the true Democrat neutralized an argument that could have led to his defeat.

The White Chief was also successful at exploiting the most important myth of the electorate: "White Supremacy," the cement of the solid South. Since emancipation southern speakers had dwelt on the dangers of blacks. They had exploited the terror of blacks felt by the majority of white Mississippians and, at the same time, had lifted the egos of the poor dirt farmer by assuring him that no matter how intolerable his conditions he could always consider himself superior to the black.

No one in Mississippi was more rabid in his opposition to blacks than was James K. Vardaman; he was, indeed, the candidate for white supremacy, including in every campaign speech an attack on blacks. A few selected quotations from his remarks at Crystal Springs show how he viewed the race: "The Negro was designed for a burden-bearer." "Six thousand years ago the Negro was the same in his native jungle as he is today." "The only effect of negro education is to spoil a good field hand and make an insolent cook." "If I were the sheriff and a Negro fiend fell into my hands I would run him out of this county. If I were governor and asked for troops to protect him I would send them, but if I were a private citizen I would head the mob to string the brute up, and I haven't much respect for a white man who wouldn't." [13]

In his attacks on blacks, Vardaman often made reference to the "unmentionable crime" of rape, vividly describing the heinous act of a "negro brute" attacking a white woman. His fear appeals concerning rape can be seen in an editorial he wrote for his newspaper, the Greenwood *Commonwealth* on the burning of a black rapist:

I sometimes think that one could look upon a scene of that kind and suffer no more moral deterioration than he would by looking upon the burning of an

13. Jackson *Weekly Clarion-Ledger*, July 30, 1903.

Orangoutang that had stolen a baby or a viper that had stung an unsuspecting child to death. He ceases to be regarded as a human being, and is only looked upon as a two legged monster. When one of these devils commits such deeds as this nigger did, somebody must kill him and I am in favor of doing it promptly. In this case I only regret the brute did not have ten thousand lives to pay for his atrocious deed. An eternity in hell will not be adequate punishment for it.[14]

Vardaman also wrote that the whites of Mississippi "would be justified in slaughtering every Ethiop on the earth to preserve unsullied the honor of one Caucasian home."[15]

Vardaman was the first candidate to enter the campaign and thus preempted the extreme position on the race issue. It is doubtful that the other candidates, even if willing, could have found a stance more antiblack than his. Vardaman's position on race allowed the Starkville News to write: "Will you vote for Vardaman and maintain white supremacy, Anglo Saxon rule and the protection of the noble and true womanhood of our state, or will you vote for Critz and place in power an administration . . . whose policy is to reap rewards thro' Roosevelt's administration at Washington. Shall it be Vardaman, and the best thought of the State in Control, or Critz who says we are powerless and can do nothing to avert the calamities lurking in the smooth and specious pleading of conservatism and industrial progress. It is 'nigger' or white, which will you serve."[16]

Vardaman proposed controlling blacks by repealing the Fourteenth and Fifteenth amendments to the U.S. Constitution and by distributing the school tax revenue according to the percent contributed by each race. The school tax plan would have provided, therefore, only about 5 percent of the school funds for black schools. Vardaman often chided his audiences for spending "thousands of dollars in 1890 to disenfranchise the Negro," and then spending millions on negro education "to qualify him and bring him back."[17]

Critz and Noel were placed on the defensive in relation to the myth of white supremacy. The antiblack statements they made were

14. Greenwood (Miss.) *Commonwealth*, October 10, 1902, quoted in Holmes, *The White Chief*, 88–89.
15. Kirwan, *Revolt of the Rednecks*, 146–47.
16. Starkville (Miss.) *News*, August 14, 1903.
17. Jackson *Weekly Clarion-Ledger*, July 30, 1903.

drawn from them as a defense against Vardaman's earlier and more vicious statements, and their major response was that white supremacy was not an issue. The Natchez *Daily Democrat* made the point: "The efforts of the Vardamanites to link the waning fortune of their leader with the cause of white supremacy is pitiable in the extreme. All the white Democrats of Mississippi believe in the supremacy of the white man." Critz and Noel argued that the race issue was solved by the Mississippi Constitution of 1890. Critz declared in a speech at Crenshaw: "We are living in peace with the negro." Noel in a speech in Jackson stated that the new constitution "dropped from the voting lists about 40,000 white men and more than four times that many negroes, leaving the white electors in a majority of over 100,000. Since then, no negro has held, or sought, any state or county office."[18] Because orators for thirty-five years had convinced the white people of the great danger from and "problems" created by blacks, this strategy of minimizing the race issue rather than controlling and using the myth of white supremacy was ineffective. The majority of the white public could not be persuaded that this was not an issue and that Vardaman was thus not on the right side.

Another theme Vardaman exploited was that of "Yankee Domination," the fear of northern interference in southern policies, particularly in race relations. In this election Vardaman constantly talked of the great threat from President Theodore Roosevelt and the Republican party, who supported racial equality and were opposed to the sacred creed of white supremacy. Many of Roosevelt's actions made him an easy target for such attacks. For example, he had invited blacks to a White House reception. The Starkville *News* wrote of the reception: "It is said that the very air of the executive mansion was warm and heavy with the incense of the Roosevelt devotion to humanity regardless of race, and that the 'strange invisible perfume' arrested and puzzled wayfarers passing on the avenue." This reception was given as evidence that Roosevelt was "genuinely agreeable to negro equality." In a colorful style popular with whites, Vardaman commented on blacks as guests in the White House: "Let Teddy take

18. Natchez *Daily Democrat*, August 21, 1903; Memphis *Commercial Appeal*, July 29, 1903, quoted in Ladner, "James Kimble Vardaman," 178; Jackson *Weekly Clarion-Ledger*, April 9, 1903.

'coons' to the White House. I should not care if the walls of the ancient edifice should become so saturated with the effluvia from the rancid carcasses that a Chinch bug would have to crawl upon the dome to avoid asphyxiation." [19]

The major action of Roosevelt that ignited "negrophobia" in Mississippi was his closing of the Indianola post office in retaliation for the white boycott that caused the black postmistress to resign. [20] Vardaman responded to the closing with his most vicious attack against Roosevelt:

He had the power—not the right under law—but the power, and like the spectacular lion masquerading ass that he is, dared to prostitute that power. It is said that men follow the bent of their genius, and that prenatal influences are often patent in shaping thoughts and ideas of after life. Probably old lady Roosevelt during the period of gestation was frightened by a dog and that fact may account for the qualities of the male pup which are so prominent in Teddy. I would not do her an injustice but I am disposed to apologize to the dog for mentioning it. [21]

Vardaman consistently attacked Roosevelt as the "coon-flavored miscegenationist," and he once advertised in the *Commonwealth* that "sixteen big, fat, mellow rancid 'coons'" were needed to "sleep with Roosevelt when he comes" to Mississippi to hunt bear. Also, in a personal statement entitled "To White Democrats of Mississippi," Vardaman stressed the importance of the Roosevelt issue in the campaign: "My election will mean, and will be taken by the aspiring, trouble-breeding, ambitious negro as a condemnation by the white people of Mississippi of Roosevelt's criminal policy of social and political equality. It will have a most salutary restraining influence upon them. My defeat will, on the other hand, encourage these same negroes to aspire to the unattainable, and trouble, discord and demoralization will follow. That is the real issue." [22]

Critz and Noel could only argue that Roosevelt's policies were not issues for a governor's race, an argument that did little to refute the years of speeches decrying the dangers resulting from northern-

19. Starkville (Miss.) *News*, January 30, 1903.
20. Holmes, *The White Chief*, 105.
21. Greenwood (Miss.) *Commonwealth*, January 10, 1903.
22. *Ibid.*, October 31, 1902; Starkville (Miss.) *News* August 14, 1903.

ers' interfering with southern race relations. Vardaman was thus able to exploit one of the very attitudes that the Bourbon Democrats had fostered to control Mississippi politics. The Starkville *News* concluded that "Vardaman's election is chiefly due to the desire on the part of the people of Mississippi to repudiate any suggestion of a toleration of the methods of Theodore Roosevelt in dealing with the race question. Mr. Vardaman's eloquent and scathing denunciation of Roosevelt's pernicious intermeddling in the affairs of the South made him the conspicuous opponent of the most noted policy of the rough rider. The race questions became an issue and Vardaman was the positive force which afforded the people an opportunity for registering an unmistakable repudiation of Roosevelt's despicable negrophilism."[23]

Another myth employed in the campaign was "The Myth of the Lost Cause." It provided "escape from guilt feelings" and restored "self-respect and self confidence" to the defeated South, and it contained the themes of "heroism of the ex-soldiers and the self-sacrifice of the home folks."[24] Vardaman presented this myth in the same way as the speakers from 1865–1900 had done, as entertainment. The White Chief usually included in his speeches a section of high praise for the Confederate veteran. In Meridian, for example, he declared that "The six hundred thousand poor equipped [Confederate] soldiers simply wore themselves out against the 2,800,000 soldiers of the north."[25] Eugene White has recorded the reports of Vardaman's Lost Cause eulogies:

The Waynesboro *Beacon* reported that in Vardaman's address at the Waynesboro court house "his word painting of the departing and returning confederate soldiers . . . [was] the grandest and most touching speech ever delivered." In Popularville, according to that town's *Free Press*, "old gray-haired veterans wept like children when, with heart sincere, sublime, he told of his love for these grand old heroes." The *Okolona Sun* said that his tribute to the . . . "remnant of that brave and gallant army of confederate soldiers . . . as well as the flowery eulogy passed upon women, brought the grand and tender endowments of the noble man to a pinnacle."[26]

23. Starkville (Miss.) *News*, September 4, 1903.
24. Braden, "'Repining Over an Irrevocable Past,'" 282–83.
25. Meridian *Evening Star*, May 18, 1903.
26. White, "Anti-Racial Agitation in Politics," 104.

Although Noel made limited reference to the Lost Cause myth himself, he tried to reduce the effectiveness of Vardaman's use of it by questioning his opponent's sincerity. In a Jackson speech Noel asked how Vardaman could care so much about Confederate veterans when "nothing was done by the legislature of which Major Vardaman was a member towards establishing a soldiers' home." [27]

The most often repeated and most effective attack on Vardaman's Lost Cause oratory was in relation to his statement concerning Roosevelt's mother being frightened by a dog. He was accused of not being chivalrous, gentlemanly, or noble. Typical of this attack was the following statement in the *Daily Democrat* of Natchez: "The southern women are the sweetest and gentlest in the world, They have long been noted for their courtly graces. During the dark days of the war and after, they made for themselves a place in history. No Spartan mother ever earned for herself a higher place in history than the southern woman. It is one of these women about whom Maj. Vardaman wrote. A fair daughter of Georgia, she had one brother in the Confederate navy. All her people were true to the South." [28]

Critz, Vardaman's runoff opponent, in one way symbolized the myth of the Lost Cause, for "he was a gallant Confederate soldier, one of Forest's trusted men." The *Clarion-Ledger* summed up Critz's embodiment of the Lost Cause myth: "It is a bit inconsistent for an old Confederate soldier who wears his cross of honor, to throw over a brave soldier like Critz and vote for Vardaman, who was born after the war began, just because he cusses the negro and orates." This argument was countered by the Vardaman press which labeled their candidate "the orphan boy of a gallant confederate soldier." [29] But though Vardaman was not a Confederate soldier, he made much more use of the myth of the Lost Cause than did his opponents. His eulogies to the soldiers and their brave women at home moved crowds the way this myth had faithfully moved them since the Civil War. Indeed, his enthusiasm for the Lost Cause was such that the questioning of his sincerity apparently did not hurt his appeal.

27. Jackson *Weekly Clarion-Ledger*, April 9, 1903.
28. Starkville (Miss.) *News*, July 24, 1903.
29. Jackson *Weekly Clarion-Ledger*, August 27, 1903; Starkville (Miss.) *News*, July 31, 1903.

The White Chief often invoked another myth which was not bound solely to the southern region and which in many ways ran counter to the legend of old plantations, pretty ladies, and happy "darkies"; it was the "Agrarian Myth" of the Populist movement. This myth created visions of the poor but honest farmer or laborer as exemplifying the highest values of America. Vardaman thus appealed to the group his opponents called "hillbillies," "white trash," or "rednecks." He attacked the wealthy and praised the poor. Typical of his remarks are the following from a speech given in Meridian: "Real kings are men who produce wealth." "Capital has no conscience." "A country that allows small children to be worked in the factories can not hope for glory from the generations to come." "I don't believe a man ever made a million honestly."[30] In his inaugural address Vardaman gave a clear statement of his campaign position in relation to the agrarian appeal. In words reminiscent of William Jennings Bryan's Cross of Gold speech he stated:

In later day political parlance the term "business man" describes anybody except the man who toils. The important fact is overlooked absolutely that the only real wealth is the labor of man. The mountains might be of solid gold, and the rocks of refined silver, and yet the world would starve without the products of human toil. Therefore, instead of the little creature, swollen with luxury, the possessor of gold "coined from the ruddy drops that visit the sad heart" of the patient toiler, the keenness of whose spiritual sense has been blunted with narrow schemings, instead of him being the "business man," it is rather the honest laborer, who in the sweat of his face, in time of peace, maintains the commerce of the nation, and in time of war fights its battles.[31]

Vardaman's appeal to the agrarian sentiment was successful. Campaigning mainly in the piney woods and backwoods sections of the state, he received most of his support "not from the intelligent and cultured planters of the Yazoo Delta, not from the professional and business men of the towns and cities, but from the small farmers of the hill counties."[32] Indeed, he carried nineteen of the twenty-three counties in which the Populist candidates had polled significant votes when they were active.

30. Meridian *Evening Star*, May 18, 1903.
31. *Mississippi Senate Journal*, 1904, p. 118.
32. John M. Mecklin, "Vardamanism," *Independent*, LXXI (August 31, 1911), 461.

The one myth Vardaman's opponents employed most effectively was that of the New South. Both Noel and Critz spoke of the great agricultural and industrial progress of Mississippi since the Civil War. In a Jackson address Noel claimed, "The last United States census reports proved that factories and their products are more than doubling in our state every ten years; and agricultural labor is so improving in efficiency that its products are increasing at the rate of four per cent a year." Thus the major attack on Vardaman by Noel, Critz, and their supporters was that he would hamper the great progress of Mississippi with his radical policies. Three central reasons were usually offered for the danger Vardaman would cause the economy. The first was that he would discourage northern investment. The *Weekly Clarion-Ledger* maintained that a Vardaman victory "would wrench from" Mississippi "that good name and high integrity the state today enjoys at the north and east among financiers and manufacturers. It would be the signal for capitalists to withhold investment from the state." The second accusation was put forth in the same newspaper—a claim that Mississippi would lose large members of her black population who "would not hesitate to move out of the state. Herein lies the great danger from the present appeals to race hatred and prejudice. For Mississippi is dependent upon the negro as a laborer." [33] The final reason was that he would create racial strife. The Jackson *Evening News* asserted that "the endorsement of such a platform" by Vardaman "would tend to create strife between the two races that are living harmoniously together now." [34] The great irony of these charges is that they run directly counter to the anti-Yankee, and antiblack rhetoric the Bourbons had used to maintain one-party control. Neither Critz nor Noel, by any enlightened standards, could be described as friends of the North or blacks. The charges thus carried little persuasive power.

Vardaman did not manipulate the New South myth to any great extent. He did, however, devote considerable space in his speeches to the charge that he would hurt industrial growth: "I have heard the thing so much that it produces a mental nausea. Now, every patriotic Mississippian wants to see the state grow industrially. But I want to

33. Jackson *Weekly Clarion-Ledger*, August 9, 20, 22, 1903.
34. Jackson *Evening News*, June 15, 1903.

see that growth based on the eternal rock of equality and justice." To the class to whom he primarily appealed, Vardaman's Populist-styled attack on wealth and large industries refuted the notion of progress of the South. Indeed, he sometimes argued against the ultimate value of industrial growth, exploiting prejudices against the North, especially against Massachusetts. He avowed, "This spirit of commercialism usually points to Massachusetts as a state worthy of emulation. With all of her wealth, there is more sin in Boston in one night than there is in Mississippi in twenty-four months. Massachusetts beats the world on shoes, but Mississippi beats it in raising folks." [35] Thus, although the most damaging attack on Vardaman was developed around the myth of the New South, it did not persuade the lower class to abandon him, since they had been excluded from the little industrial growth that had taken place.

Another sentimental image that aided Vardaman in winning the governorship was the "Southern Orator Myth." Southern speakers from 1865 to 1900 had "resorted to stylistic flourishes, commonality in tone, and expansive delivery." [36] They helped develop the stereotype of the "Southern Orator" whose qualities came to be considered a great virtue. It was extremely high praise when an editorial stated, "As an orator and debater Vardaman's enemies admit that he has few equals since the day of Prentiss"; the praise was so high in fact that an opposition paper felt compelled to write: "Vardaman a rival of Sargent S. Prentiss! No wonder the heavens have been weeping for the past two weeks." [37] Noel made Vardaman's oratory a campaign issue. In a joint debate between the two candidates, he slyly maintained, "I am not seeking an office where oratory has a place. A governor who attends to his business has no time or opportunity to compile speeches from poems and novels. When God was looking for a leader in Israel, he first called Moses. Moses demurred, saying he was slow of speech and his brother, Aaron, was more skillful than he. What did Aaron do with his oratorical talents? He led them off from common sense and worship of a true God to bow down to a golden calf." [38] Vardaman's

---

35. Jackson *Weekly Clarion-Ledger*, July 30, 1903.
36. Braden, "'Repining Over An Irrevocable Past,'" 301.
37. Starkville (Miss.) *News*, July 31, 1903; Natchez *Daily Democrat*, July 29, 1903.
38. Jackson *Weekly Clarion-Ledger*, July 30, 1903.

addresses resembled epideictic or ceremonial speeches rather than campaign or deliberative speeches, as whenever possible he avoided debate and used very little argumentation. In other words, Vardaman delivered a ceremonial address in a deliberative speech setting. Furthermore, his commitment to oratory can be seen by the frequency of his speeches—over seven hundred of them during the fourteen months he campaigned for the governorship. Vardaman's biographer, William F. Holmes, believes that "Vardaman's personal magnetism and ability to sway crowds with his oratory contributed heavily to his success."[39] The Starksville *News*, sixty-seven years earlier, came to the same conclusion:

We are from time to time advised that oratory is a thing of the past, but there is little doubt that Mr. Vardaman's splendid gifts as a public speaker materially contributed to his elevation, and he has the satisfaction demonstrated that ooratory [*sic*] is not dead, at least in Mississippi. He has strong convictions and is fearless and forceful in expressing them. Added to his courage and sincerity are an impressive personality, a charming voice, a graceful delivery and that intangible, indefinable something called magnetism, which is the soul of oratory. These are mental and physical qualifications which drew many of the voters to the gallant Major.[40]

The fact that Vardaman's speeches were notably lacking in logical content did not seem to harm him with an audience of unlettered rural whites, for he spoke in the style employed by southern speakers for the previous thirty-five years, during which time arguments were largely undeveloped. His election was in great part due to his ability to present himself as the representative of the old Democracy, exploit the racial fears of white Mississippians, exploit the fears of Yankee domination, entertain his audience with stories of the "Lost Cause," refute the myth of the "New South" with class and sectional prejudice, flatter rural Mississippians with the "Agrarian Myth," and entertain his audiences with his oratorical style. The ironic element in this election is that the Bourbon Democrats were defeated because of their inability to make effective use of the myths they themselves had developed to entrench their own leadership.

39. Holmes, *The White Chief*, 108–15.
40. Starkville (Miss.) *News*, September 4, 1903.

Tom Watson

Disciple of "Jeffersonian Democracy"

In his successful 1890 campaign for Congress, Tom Watson chided the incumbent for placing on record an undelivered phantom speech:

It took him ten days to compose the speech after he was said to have made it in Congress! . . .

This reminds me of a story I once heard about a man who went to a museum. The showman said to him, on showing him a rusty sword, "This is the very sword that Balaam had when he met the angel." The countryman was pretty well up with the Bible as countrymen generally are. He said that Balaam did not have a sword but that he wished he had one. "Ah, yes," said the showman, "this is the identical sword that he wished he had."[1]

Although such stories made him a perennial spellbinder on the stump, after 1890 Thomas E. Watson did not win another election until the 1920 U.S. Senate race in Georgia. In those three intervening decades, from the 52nd to the 67th Congresses, he debated numerous opponents, conducted national speaking tours, attended Populist and Democratic party conventions, continued a brilliant and profitable legal career, changed political parties twice, organized publishing companies, edited newspapers and magazines, authored several historical volumes and one novel, rejected an offer to join the Hearst newspaper empire, escaped conviction for an alleged postal law violation, was jailed for a campaign disturbance, opposed the U.S. Army

---

1. William Brewton, *The Life of Thomas E. Watson* (Atlanta: Published by the author, 1926), 217.

for World War I action, and managed to lose a total of seven elections during the years 1892, 1894, 1895, 1896, 1904, 1908, and 1918.

With a persistent, yet perplexing, plea for "Jeffersonian democracy," Tom Watson led at least two divergent rhetorical careers. The first, ending about 1906, featured emotional support for the downtrodden irrespective of race or religion. The second, ranging from about 1907 until his death in 1922, fostered those racist and anti-Catholic sentiments for which Watson unfortunately is now remembered. In order to explain the emergence of the latter, it is necessary to understand those reverses that stalked the former. The 1904 campaign for president, his last attempt at biracial politics, formed something of a Watson transition from populism to sectionalism. Therefore, this study will concentrate on his 1904 campaign by reviewing his personal background, clarifying campaign issues, analyzing critically two campaign speeches and one post-campaign address, and summarizing some potential effects of his rhetorical efforts.

I

Thomas E. Watson, born near Thomson, Georgia, in 1856, was "raised under the influence of Robert Toombs and Alexander H. Stephens, who were frequent guests in his father's house." He grew up during bitter Reconstruction when the family fortune was "lost to creditors" in "an economic system rigged to favor the capitalist." Thus, he was a "poor southern farm boy" who had to face "almost insuperable odds" in combating degradation, ignorance, despair. But he attended two years at Mercer College, taught school, read law, was admitted to the bar, and acquired both fame and fortune "as a criminal lawyer whose oratory jurors found irresistible."[2]

Spartan existence in an economically and intellectually depressed area pushed Watson toward his role as spokesman for laborer, sharecropper, tenant, miner, millhand, unemployed—both black and white. As a successful criminal lawyer, he grew to learn the language of rural juries, to gauge their needs, and to read the vibrations of the

2. Harold H. Martin, *Georgia: A Bicentennial History* (New York: W. W. Norton, 1977), 133; John D. Hicks, *The Populist Revolt* (Minneapolis: University of Minnesota Press, 1931), 176.

occasion. As a teenager he absorbed the stump speeches of Howell Cobb, Rance Wright, John B. Gordon, Robert Toombs, Benjamin H. Hill, and he later practiced these skills as "a fiery orator before local Temperance societies." But this same environment made him suspicious, combative, temperamental. Oratory was war. An opponent's position automatically lacked truth and justice. To oppose Watson was to create an instant enemy who never isolated issue from personality. "With me it is a fight for principle, it is a fight until somebody gets whipped, and I don't congratulate the fellow that whips me either." Such methods "inspired in his adherents an intense, almost fanatical, devotion, and in his opponents, who regarded him as a demagogue, an equally violent hatred."[3]

Watson's physical appearance and delivery characteristics matched his speaking personality. His presence was impressive— lean, redheaded, clean-shaven, square-jawed, suntanned. He was a vehement speaker who at times was unable to control his temper. But, during the era of the two-hour oration, he could command extended attention with a combination of historical narrative, poetic charm, wry humor, biting invective, gross exaggeration, and histrionic showmanship. When pressing an idea, he had a habit of "gesturing with whirling arms, swaying body, and tossing head that loosed a lock of hair which 'punctuated his periods with a loppy emphasis.' Some noticed a 'hawkish tendency' in his manner, and in his 'shrill, raspy voice, the power of strong, high flight, the pinion, the talon, the beak, and withal the swoop of the hawk.'"[4]

Watson's desire to see his ideas in print led to his ownership and editing of, and prolific writing in, such Populist publications as *Peo-*

3. Martin, *Georgia*, 134; Speech typescript, Thomson, Georgia, Nov. 19, 1904, p. 22, in Thomas Edward Watson Papers, Southern Historical Collection, University of North Carolina Library, Chapel Hill, hereinafter cited as Watson Papers, with subsequent reference to this speech cited as Thomson Address. The author is indebted to Richard A. Shrader, reference archivist, and the staff for their assistance in using the Southern Historical Collection at the Wilson Library of the University of North Carolina, Chapel Hill, and to Tom Watson Brown and family, Atlanta, Georgia, for their permission to publish pertinent excerpts from the Thomas E. Watson papers in the Southern Historical Collection. Work Projects Administration, *Georgia: A Guide to Its Towns and Countryside* (Athens: University of Georgia Press, 1940), 411.
4. C. Vann Woodward quoting from clippings in the Watson Scrapbooks, "The Political and Literary Career of Thomas E. Watson" (Ph.D. dissertation, University of North Carolina, 1937), 349.

ple's Party Paper, Daily Press, Tom Watson's Magazine, Jeffersonian, and *Watson's Jeffersonian Magazine.* From an early age he was an avid reader of fiction and nonfiction as well as a composer of poetry. William Brewton reproduces Watson's "list of books read up to 1872" and concludes that he was "the best read 15-year-old boy of whom we have any record." Later, especially in the period immediately prior to the 1904 campaign, Watson published historical narrative, biography, and fiction. In reviewing Watson as an historian, Woodward found him lacking in objectivity, primary sources, and sound theories, while dwelling excessively on violence, militarism, and imperialism. His writing was "popular history, history for the common man, history with a purpose," though often Watson as historical writer seemed to sanction that which he condemned as a Populist speaker. Napoleon was a hero to be praised, but contemporary political bullies who possessed Napoleonic characteristics were to be destroyed. Nevertheless, during "a day when the tradition of the statesman as historian flourished," his efforts do "not suffer in comparison with other products of that tradition." By contrast, his only novel, *Bethany,* was "a hodge-podge of historical and political essays intermixed with a sentimental love story and some autobiography." [5]

Watson achieved monetary success and a degree of fame with his writing, for his books sold impressively and he "commanded considerable awe in a community where a man of letters was a rarity." His library contained over ten thousand volumes which he claimed was "the largest personal library in the South." Literary success coincided with increased speaker popularity on the paying lecture circuit. For example, his carefully itemized "Lecture Receipts" for fifty-three presentations during 1902 and 1903 resulted in a total income of $6,675, or almost $126 per appearance, no small figure for the turn of the century. His most popular presentations included "The Mission of Democracy," "The South," and "Is the South Glad It Lost?" In Atlanta he drew larger audiences than either Henry Ward Beecher or Robert Ingersoll, two giants of the lecture platform. Watson's writing probably

5. Brewton, *The Life of Thomas E. Watson,* 31–44, 53; Woodward, "The Political and Literary Career of Thomas E. Watson," 380–88, 394–95, reviews of Watson's *The Story of France* (1899), *Napoleon* (1902), *The Life and Times of Thomas Jefferson* (1903), *Bethany* (1904), and *The Life and Times of Andrew Jackson* which was published as a serial publication (1906) and as a book (1911).

was excellent preparation for his national speechmaking, encouraging the cogent arrangement of arguments to explicate or defend an idea. It forced productivity beyond thought—ideas had to be affixed to paper and survive outside the mind of the inventor. It involved the use of language, its refinement, and a respect for its power. It dictated adherence to the deadline. It offered prospective auditors an opportunity to preview his major premises before his arrival. Finally, it developed Watson into his own spokesman, free from the cadre of ghostwriters that subsequent politicians have found indispensable.[6]

At the time of his 1904 campaign, Watson had achieved notoriety as a successful lawyer, politician, journalist, historian, novelist, and lecturer. Although a spokesman for the downtrodden, he conservatively estimated the value of his estate at $121,000, or more than double his 1896 estimate when he ran for vice-president. He attempted to parlay some of this fame and fortune into more power as he stalked the countryside in search of votes. "Opening his campaign in Nebraska, he left no section unvisited, from Boston to California." In fact, Watson campaigned so hard that he suffered a physical breakdown "at the close" of a speech in Jackson, Mississippi, September 27. A physician advised him "to go home and spend a few weeks in absolute quiet." However, by October 5 he was back in New York City at a fund-raising dinner having "his fling at the Democratic Party and its standard bearer."[7]

But in 1904 Tom Watson was practically alone on the stump. In honor of the custom operative at the time, President Theodore Roosevelt did not campaign and Alton B. Parker, the Democratic nominee, remained at home for the most part, receiving political pilgrims who paid contrived visits. Early in the campaign, the GOP national committee chairman announced "that President Roosevelt would not make any political speeches this year" which was "in line with the course of President McKinley in the campaign of 1900." However, this decision did not preclude other famous GOP speakers from campaigning extensively on the president's behalf, such as former at-

6. Woodward, "The Political and Literary Career of Thomas E. Watson," 389, 379; Watson Papers.
7. Woodward, "The Political and Literary Career of Thomas E. Watson," 388, 403; New York *Times*, September 28, October 6, 1904.

torney general Philander C. Knox, Secretary of War William H. Taft, Senator Chauncey Depew, and the vice-presidential nominee, Senator Charles W. Fairbanks. A spokesman for the Democratic nominee declared that "Judge Parker has no faith in the utility of speechmaking for its own sake. . . . He believes a stumping tour by a Presidential candidate to be improper, and he will undertake no such tour." Later it was pointed out that "he will await the trend of events, and if they force an issue which he believes should be at once handled in a speech, then such a speech will be delivered." Even so, he entertained conflicting advice "to take the stump, take it quick, and hold it long," as opposed to those "against any appearance in the limelight at all." After announcing that he would not make any speeches away from his home, he ultimately consented to a speaking tour the final "whirlwind week" that included New York, New Jersey, and Connecticut and had no measurable effect on the result. Notable Democrats, such as former president Grover Cleveland, did not get involved in the campaign until the last two weeks, and throughout the campaign, reports from the Parker camp reflected an air of inaction and indecision.[8]

Initially, loyal Populists advised Watson to stay home, receive the notification committee, issue "a ringing letter of acceptance," deliver "one or two speeches," and avoid spending "any considerable sum of money." But other messages requesting Watson's appearance promised audiences, expenses, and ultimately votes to assure the imagined triumph. In addition, there were appeals to publish, in pamphlet form, those addresses already delivered as well as requests from editors and publishers for essays, personal profiles, or advance copies of speeches. One writer wanted to use copies of Watson's Cooper Union Address as a GOP campaign document, which must have made Watson wonder if the writer understood the speech. Thus, Watson was caught up in a campaign that came to be propelled by forces almost beyond his control.[9]

8. New York *Times*, August 13, 27, 23, September 3, October 7, November 1, October 22, November 4, 6, 1904.

9. J. M. Mallett to Thomas E. Watson, July 21, 1904, pp. 1–2; A. Benoit to Watson, July 28, 1904, p. 3; J. O. A. Bush to Watson, August 22, 1904; R. H. Reemelin to Watson, September 25, 1904; J. W. Shea to Watson, August 19, 1904; Harvey Studwell to Watson, August 21, 1904; Charles Maar to Watson, October 14, 1904; E. W. Baker to Wat-

II

Campaign issues often are revealed in the platforms of minor parties in national elections, whereas the major parties avoid these issues for fear of offending potential voters. The People's party platform of 1904 opposed "special privileges to the few," "force and militarism," "transportation monopolies," "trusts," "child labor," "sweat shops," "convict labor," "foreign pauper labor," and "alien ownership of land." It supported government ownership of the railroads, public utilities, telegraph, and telephone; government establishment of postal savings banks and parcel post; the "right of labor to organize"; the eight-hour day; initiative, referendum, recall; government regulation of interstate corporations; fairer federal taxation. In addition, Watson personally advocated a graduated income tax and the direct election of senators. The issues could be condensed into four categories: (1) economics, or the redistribution of wealth from the few to the many, (2) labor, or the strengthening of job quality and security, (3) enfranchisement, or the redistribution of electoral power from the select to the masses, and (4) federalism, or the expansion of central government power and services.[10]

Obviously these four categories overlapped and ensnarled other subissues that could erupt in importance according to time and locale. Likewise they invited venom, hate, even violence, from the majority. Advocates of such a platform in early twentieth-century America often were labeled Socialists, Communists, anarchists and were considered in concert with the likes of Eugene Debs and the Pullman strikers, even though Debs and the Socialists opposed Watson in both of his presidential campaigns. Watson's strategy of uniting the agrarians of South and West was a rebuke to the population bases of both major parties. Also, it was contrary to the nineteenth-century plea of his fellow Georgian, Henry Grady, for an industrialized "New South" developed in close concert with the urban East. The Populist platform advocated federalism—government power to oppose concentrated

son, August 21, 1904, pp. 1–2; Hamilton Holt to Watson, July 20, 1904; Albert Shaw to Watson, August 23, 1904; A. Brisbane to Watson, September 14, 1904; George M. Chapin to Watson, November 14, 1904, all in Watson Papers.

10. People's Party National Platform, adopted at Springfield, Illinois, July 4, 1904, in Watson Papers.

wealth and foreign competition; government use of taxation power; and government ownership of national transportation and utilities— whereas candidate Watson advocated "Jeffersonian democracy" which historically rejected federalism as odious despotism.

However, the opposition was not interested in debating such complicated issues as economics, labor, enfranchisement, or federalism. Democrats in particular wanted to use that old reliable appeal— fear—in order to keep the solid South in line. In Atlanta, Watson attacked the "hypocrisy of Democratic leaders" who claimed their party was the South's salvation from "Negro domination." His discourses in earlier years contended that dominant groups promoted animosity between blacks and poorer whites to destroy their combined power— "You are kept apart that you may be separately fleeced." His basic hope had been published in a famous treatise, "The Negro Question in the South": "Gratitude may fail; so may sympathy and friendship and generosity and patriotism; but in the long run, self interest *always* controls. Let it once appear plainly that it is to the interest of a colored man to vote with the white man, and he will do it. Let it plainly appear that it is to the interest of the white man that the vote of the Negro should supplement his own, and the question of having that ballot freely cast and fairly counted, becomes vital to the *white man*. He will see that it is done." He had expressed the same sentiment in his *People's Party Paper* in attempting to separate self-interest from social intermingling: "I can see no reason why I am any less a white man . . . simply because the black people are convinced that our Platform is a fair one, and vote for me upon it. . . . Social Equality is a question which every citizen settles for himself." Watson was a national leader in this appeal and continued to pursue it after his electoral failure of 1904. Although he "was hardly a friend of . . . integration . . . he was quite willing to encourage Negro political equality" and "was clearly more open-minded than his rivals." Even so, the seemingly debatable premise "that white Southern Populists were sympathetic, if only briefly, to the cause of Negro rights" continues to stimulate "one of the larger controversies in American historiography." [11]

11. Brief, Atlanta Speech, 1904, Watson Papers; as quoted in Norman Pollack (ed.), *The Populist Mind* (Indianapolis: Bobbs-Merrill, 1967), 360–61, 369, 375; C. Vann

Watson was decades ahead of his contemporaries in correctly identifying *economics* and not *race* as foremost on the southern agenda. But "self interest" did not "always" control. He had underestimated the intoxication of red-neck prejudice. Economics can be complicated, tedious, boring—especially for illiterate and semiliterate sharecroppers. Race, on the other hand, can trigger emotions and short-circuit reasoning. As he valiantly attempted to explain economics, the wonder is not that Watson failed but that he ever succeeded in obtaining a reasonable hearing. Much of the Populist platform and many of Watson's political speeches were neutralized by the threat of what Woodward calls "Negrophobia" and "race chauvinism." Ironically, Tom Watson succumbed to this threat in his latter years and thereby sacrificed much of his earlier noble efforts.[12]

III

Two speeches delivered during the campaign and one immediately following the election were chosen for study. The campaign addresses were delivered in major population areas of the East and border whereas the postcampaign presentation was made to a hometown audience in Georgia.

Watson gave the first selected speech at the Cooper Union in New York, August 18, 1904, early in the campaign as an attempt to establish some of the premises of his candidacy and the platform of his party. Delivered to a national audience within the shadows of the political camps of the major opponents, his Cooper Union effort represented a combination speech of acceptance and first major campaign address, although he later issued a formal letter of acceptance. He delivered the second selected speech in St. Louis, Missouri, Sep-

Woodward, *The Strange Career of Jim Crow* (New York: Oxford University Press, 1957), 43–45, 73; Thomson Address, 13; Carl N. Degler, *The Other South: Southern Dissenters in the Nineteenth Century* (New York: Harper & Row, 1974), 340, 349–55; Lawrence Goodwyn, *Democratic Promise: The Populist Moment in America* (New York: Oxford University Press, 1976), 297; Morton Sosna, *In Search of the Silent South* (New York: Columbia University Press, 1977), 10.

12. An excellent example of his appeal to a racially mixed audience during an earlier campaign is recorded in Pollack (ed.), *The Populist Mind*, 375–80; Woodward, *The Strange Career of Jim Crow*, 69; Theodore Saloutos, *Farmer Movements in the South 1865–1933* (Lincoln: University of Nebraska Press, 1960), 130–32.

tember 6, 1904, well into the campaign and after he had gained some experience speaking in other locales. Presumably, his arguments on the issues had been refined and he had settled into a predictable stance on the various questions of the day. The third selected speech was delivered at Thomson, Georgia, November 19, 1904, following the election that recorded his resounding defeat. In this speech, he could analyze any apparent campaign mistakes as well as register a mixture of warnings and hopes for the future.

The method of rhetorical criticism applied to Watson combines the theories of Kenneth Burke and Richard M. Weaver. Burke's essay, "On Human Behavior Considered 'Dramatistically,'" identifies three distinct stages in persuasion: "guilt," "victimage," and "redemption." Under "Ultimate Terms in Contemporary Rhetoric," Weaver employs the labels "god term," "devil term," and "charismatic term." This study applied the following Burkeian-Weaverian assumptions: (1) "Guilt" results when those qualities identified by "god terms" are absent. (2) "Victimage" is identified by "devil terms." (3) "Redemption" is promised by "charismatic terms." [13]

Cooper Union Address

At Cooper Union, Watson assumed that "principles" and "justice" operated as two god terms that were in serious short supply in 1904. He hammered away at the necessity for "ideals," "loyalty," "right," "character" that would surface as a "creed," or "articles of faith." These "principles" needed to be applied with a "judicial temperament" at the "bar of American public opinion" by the individual who had the "courage of his convictions," if necessary, "for which he would die" to assure "justice." Although seemingly verbose and idealistic by present-day standards, his capsulated point was (1) to vote Democrat reflected deficiency in "principles," (2) to vote Republican reflected deficiency in "justice." Either course would result in guilt.

---

13. Kenneth Burke, *Permanence & Change: An Anatomy of Purpose* (Los Altos, Cal.: Hermes Publications, 1954), 274–94; Richard L. Johannesen, Rennard Strickland, and Ralph T. Eubanks (eds.), *Language Is Sermonic: Richard M. Weaver on the Nature of Rhetoric* (Baton Rouge: Louisiana State University Press, 1970), 87–112. The author is indebted to Paul C. Gaske for theoretical ideas developed in his unpublished manuscript, "The Analysis of Demagogic Discourse: Huey Long's 'Every Man a King' Address," Western Speech Communication Association Convention, Phoenix, Arizona, November, 1977.

Presumably, if an endorsed god term, such as "justice" has evaporated or declined, some person or group deserves indictment for tolerating its demise. So, guilt emerges when god terms are nonexistent or incomplete. To avoid guilt, a voter should "be able to say, I belong to a party which will not strike its flag, which will not desert its creed, which stands to-day just where it stood on the day of its birth, which glories in its principles in the hour of defeat, which believes it has a message to mankind and a mission to perform, and which will never cease the struggle to restore our government to the Democratic ideal of the wise men, the good men, the great men who framed it." [14]

Guilt must be followed by a "ritual scapegoat." Absolute guilt must be "matched by a principle that is designed for the corresponding absolute cancellation of such guilt. And this cancellation is contrived by *victimage*." The victim is identified through Weaver's "devil term." Victimage, or the "ritual scapegoat" of "a sacrificial offering," [15] took two forms—the greedy and the unpatriotic. The greedy encompassed the conspiratorial wealthy; the unpatriotic were the political manipulators. The former were characterized by such devil terms as "Wall Street bankers," "Wall Street magnates," "the corporations," "the railroads," "moneyed aristocracy," "the trusts," "Sugar trust," "unscrupulous monopolists," "National Banks," "Rockefeller," and the Democratic nominee, Judge Alton Parker. The unpatriotic included the "partisan press" with its "subsidized organs of monopoly," "wily leaders," "bosses," and "professional politicians" who produced "class legislation," "protective tariff," "special favors," "legalized robbery," and "secret rebates" in their "unscrupulous hunt for office." With only rare exception, Watson's devil terms are general broadsides against familiar suppressors often condemned in previous Populist speeches of the nineteenth and twentieth centuries. As a son of the economically deprived South, Watson doubtlessly believed that victimage was a simple identity distinction between "them" and "us" that should be common knowledge to all. But he seemed to delight in devoting considerable attention to the recommended sacrifice even

14. Press release, speech typescript, Cooper Union, New York, August 18, 1904, in Watson Papers, hereinafter cited as Cooper Union Address; Johannesen, Strickland, and Eubanks (eds.), *Language Is Sermonic*, 88–89.

15. Burke, *Permanence & Change*, 286, 284; Johannesen, Strickland, and Eubanks (eds.), *Language Is Sermonic*, 99–100.

though the audience must have needed less information about victimage and more solutions addressed to deliverance. It was here that his language became "sermonic," to borrow Weaver's term, as he tied selfishness to unpatriotic behavior by indicting "lordly magnates," "corporation-kings," "moneyed aristocracy," for leading "corporations" to "corrupt the law-making power." Both financial power and political power became forces to be eliminated from the system.

Once the victims were sacrificed, from whence would come the redemption? For Watson, elimination of the devils contributed mightily toward the ultimate solution. He counted heavily on a single charismatic term, "Jeffersonian democracy," to carry the day for salvation. Early in the speech, he previewed the evils of Alexander Hamilton, that ultimate devil Tory "devoted as he was to the English model," and with "no confidence in the people, no love for the people; no sympathy with the people, but who believed that wealth should be taken into co-partnership with the government, given control of its laws, given command of its policies." In sharp contrast with this devil came the redemption of "Thomas Jefferson proclaiming the principles of democracy. With the idea of human brotherhood, with a perfect faith in the great body of the people, and with a constitutional love of right and justice which made class legislation abhorrent to him, he challenged the doctrines of Hamilton, and struggled to hold the government true to the principle of 'equal and exact justice to all men.'" [16]

It is not enough just to purge the victim from society. Many protest speakers through the ages have been deluded into believing that victimage equates remedy. Burke declares that redemption begins "in theories of *action*," which suggests audience pursuit of a prescribed public commitment. Watson offered several "theories of action" that were about as specific as political oratory ever becomes. Without equivocation, he stood for public ownership of the railroads, telegraphs, and utilities; a graduated income tax; a drastic revision of the tariff; and "Free Silver" or "any other equal amount of currency created by the government out of any material whatsoever." He opposed the system of national banks and taxes upon "the necessities of life." Although these recommendations seemingly satisfied Burke's call for

16. Cooper Union Address, 4, 5.

theories of action, they apparently were not, in Weaver's words, "rhetorical by common consent, or by 'charisma'" where "the charismatic term is given its load of impulsion without reference, and its function by convention."[17]

Prophetic in specifying many future legislative revisions that still are unfolding, Watson's call for "Jeffersonian democracy" did not trigger predictable affirmative response nor did it automatically short-circuit negative rebuttal. A charismatic term is assisted further when it is indelibly etched with the *ethos* of the speaker. Later twentieth-century campaigns built around such shibboleths as "New Deal," "New Frontier," and "Great Society" would immediately call to mind their human proponents. Watson finished fifth behind the Republican, Democrat, Socialist, and Prohibition candidates with less than 1 percent of the popular vote.[18] Given this final tally, much of the electorate apparently had problems defining "Jeffersonian democracy," understanding its value, or accepting Watson as its anointed guardian. Perhaps most charismatic terms are not fully understood, but speaker credibility offsets any information void. Thus, the widely popular and trusted speaker possibly could escape successfully with "Jeffersonian democracy" as a focal point for a forthcoming administration provided there was repetitive exposure and a large, loyal, well-financed party base.

The populace likely lacked sophistication on those monetary premises that formed the bedrock of Watson's arguments. His theories were more philosophical than personal and lacked "bread and butter" appeal. In addition, there could have been factors in his unsuccessful political past that mitigated against these terms being accepted "without reference." In 1892, during his first term in Congress, Watson caused a furor in the House by accusing members of drunken debating. The Democrats literally pushed him out of the party and gerrymandered his district by adding two more counties. Watson then ran as a People's party candidate, debating his Democratic opponent. Physical disturbances characterized the campaign

17. Burke, *Permanence & Change*, 274; Cooper Union Address, 21–28; Johannesen, Strickland, and Eubanks (eds.), *Language is Sermonic*, 105, 106.

18. Samuel Eliot Morison and Henry Steele Commager, *The Growth of the American Republic* (2 vols.; New York: Oxford University Press, 1960), II, 904.

and police were used to prevent violence. Watson lost but always claimed "vote fraud" as the cause. In 1894, Watson barely lost again to the same Democratic opponent and again claimed vote fraud. He thought about challenging the results, but Congress was now Republican and he did not want to owe his seat to the GOP. He lost again in 1895 after the Democrat resigned to force a new election. In 1896, Watson was nominated vice-president by the Populists in St. Louis on a ticket headed by William Jennings Bryan, who had been nominated earlier in Chicago by the Democrats. Bryan avoided him. Thus, Watson's theories were vague and his deportment was unpredictable, temperamental, evangelical, sacrificial. Even those philosophically inclined to agree with his premises could well have been repelled by his publicized conduct.[19]

There were multiple rhetorical and nonrhetorical forces simultaneously operative that often made any charismatic response difficult or impossible. In a closely reasoned letter from Frankton, Indiana, one of the faithful identified several "very perplexing problems" soon after the election: "the personality of Mr. Roosevelt"; "Mr. Bryan's eloquence" in support of Mr. Parker; the fragmentation of votes among Socialists, Populists, and Prohibitionists; "the chaotic condition of the People's Party"; and, probably most important, the "vast number of voters" who "saw not the slightest chance for your success." The "chaotic condition" of the party was characterized by such revelations as alleged fraudulent petitions that included "scandalous . . . frivolous . . . dead and fictitious names," and previously nominated candidates who bolted the Populist ticket late in the campaign to vote Democratic. Another writer noted that the statement "you have no chance" is "a favorite expression of a certain class of democrats, especially in the South." But perhaps even more unsettling, he wrote, were declarations from Socialists that "you talk such good socialist doctrine, and the Populist platform is so near to ours that I have no doubt we shall all come together in time, and that you will be our Socialist candidate for president in 1908" because "the *only logical opponent of capitalism is Socialism*." Also the letter from an "'Evolutionary' Socialist" declared, "I am for Eugene V. Debs for President. You

19. Brewton, *The Life of Thomas E. Watson*, 246–51, 263–73.

are my next choice." Obviously, the writer misunderstood Watson's appeal for public ownership of select enterprises such as railroads, telegraph, and utilities. Certainly Watson was capitalistic in his private affairs, and the records show steady growth in his estate. His law practice flourished, his farming paid good returns, his real estate holdings increased both in volume and value, he acquired stock in such capitalistic enterprises as a bank, and he managed all of his endeavors with frugal care.[20]

Finally, in Burke's words, "Every movement that would recruit its followers from among many discordant and divergent bands, must have some spot towards which all roads lead. Each man may get there in his own way, but it must be the one unifying center of reference for all." It could be "a centralizing hub of *ideas*" or "a mecca geographically located, towards which all eyes could turn at the appointed hours of prayer." Watson offered no "spot towards which all roads lead." Certainly his Thomson, Georgia, home hardly provided a geographical mecca that could rival Alton Parker's "Rosemount" at Esopus, New York, or Theodore Roosevelt's "Sagamore Hill" at Oyster Bay, New York, and the White House itself in Washington, D.C. The rustic, economically deprived, Rebel-dominated South was no match for the opulent, romantic, well-populated, international power bases of the major candidates. During the campaign there were violent racial incidents in Georgia that involved shootings, floggings, burnings, lynchings, attacks on the militia, and assaults on the jails that ultimately forced intercession by the governor. These violent acts often were major news stories that stimulated vigorous letters to the editor. Watson never subscribed to such violence, yet the outbreaks in his home state could have had only a negative impact on his candidacy. And no surrogate mecca, such as the naming of Thomas H. Tibbles from Bryan's home state of Nebraska as the Populist vice-presidential candidate, registered any recorded impact.[21]

20. Caleb A. Canady to Watson, November 21, 1904; H. J. Mullens to Watson, August 29, 1904, p. 3; E. F. Andrews to Watson, September 6, 1904; R. A. Dague to Watson, September 25, 1904, p. 1; all in Watson Papers, esp. Vol. 33; New York *Times*, October 24, 27, November 7, 1904.

21. Kenneth Burke, *The Philosophy of Literary Form: Studies in Symbolic Action* (Baton Rouge: Louisiana University Press, 1941), 192; New York *Times*, August 17 through September 26, 1904, *passim*.

St. Louis Address

Watson continued to assume that the absence of "principles" and "justice" as operational god terms was producing a state of guilt. He declared, "Let us write our principles upon our foreheads where they may be seen, and let us stand up for principle as against pretence. . . . I will work for the rights of the citizen and equal justice to all." He heavily emphasized the need for those political principles of "honor" and "honesty" as revealed in "plain words"; hence, the voter, in order to avoid guilt, "ought to demand a candidate who is brave enough and honest enough." Apparently, Watson saw differences between an "honest Bryan Democrat," a "Bryan Democrat," and a "Democrat." The god terms emphasized the need to demand a politician who "keeps his contracts." [22]

Victimage concentrated more on the political manipulators and less on the conspiratorial wealthy, although some of his subjects landed in both categories. At the outset, he realized that people did not attend such "a great Exposition . . . for the purpose of hearing a political sermon." Perhaps he should limit himself to nonpartisan comments, but "a non-partisan speech just wears me out," he said. Thus, after seeking and obtaining audience permission to "make a partisan speech," he took several swipes at the greedy few with references to "the rich," "national banks," "vast railroad corporations," "Wall Street," and "the Sugar Trust." But the full impact of devil terms was reserved for the unpatriotic, the political manipulator, the "pledge buster," who could never be trusted to keep "his contract." He did not agree with GOP politics although he could understand why a Republican selfishly supported the national ticket. His bafflement and venom were reserved for Democratic politicians who had mouthed humanitarian principles in the past, been elected to office, failed to fulfill promises, and engaged in devious acts for the sake of personal advantage. In this speech, far more than at Cooper Institute, Watson identified the specific objects of his disgust:

Grover Cleveland sent the United States army into the State of Illinois . . . in violation of the rights of the laborer to get justice for himself. . . . Vote for

22. Carbon typescript of speech, Louisiana Monument, World's Fair Grounds, St. Louis, Missouri, September 6, 1904, in Watson Papers.

Roosevelt, or vote for Parker, and no matter who is elected, Republican principles will succeed. . . . Grover Cleveland was elected President and we saw
the rottenest administration the American people every had. . . . Van Allen
wanted to go to the Italian mission; so he contributed $30,000 to the campaign
fund. Morgan, Belmont, and Rothschilds, wanted bonds. . . . Cleveland gave
them bonds in a midnight deal. . . . The same men that were around Grover
Cleveland then are around Judge Parker now. . . . Morgan is there, and according to Mr. Bryan, he is Belmont's partner. The one controls the L. & N.
and the other the Southern. One is driving Roosevelt and the other Parker.
. . . There is Olney, who sent the United States Troops into Illinois. There is
Gorman, the Senatorial agent of all the trusts. There is Belmont, the Rothschilds' agent; there is Lamont, and there is Carlisle, the Whiskey Trust
agent.

Watson was particularly hard on the Democratic presidential nominee, using the testimony of a Missouri favorite as his source: "Hon.
William J. Bryan, the man, who for eight years has been your leader
and prophet . . . [said] on April 23, 1904 . . . 'We now have evidence
enough to convict him [Parker] of total unfitness for the Democratic
nomination.' He said, 'Mr. Parker then stands by the New York platform, which crooked Dave Hill had put together.' Bryan said that nobody but an artful dodger could stand on the New York Democratic
platform. . . . Parker has been sitting on Hill's political knee and been
absorbing his political gospel from David B. Hill for the last twenty
years." Thus, the devils to be sacrificed are identified by name, the
circumstances leading to their victimage are itemized, the lack of
"principles" and "justice" inherent in their policies are revealed; the
constituency should shun them or forever bear the guilt of their elevation to power.[23]

Was there adequate provision for redemption? Did his address
offer a plausible road to salvation after the devils had been sacrificed?
The same charismatic term that predominated at Cooper Union—
Jeffersonian democracy—occupied center stage at St. Louis. Beyond
that expression, he mentioned the People's party, but without strong
reinforcement as he concentrated on Watsonian rather than Populist
ideals. The theories of action remained quite similar to those introduced in the acceptance speech: graduated income tax, government
ownership of railroads, revision of the tariff, eight-hour day, abolish-

23. *Ibid.*, 1–2, 7–9.

ment of child labor, direct election of such key officials as the judiciary, and initiative, referendum, and recall. In broad terms, he stood for "States' Rights" and "home rule." But how would these reforms be realized? His stirring peroration, though emotional and noble, possessed a ring of hopelessness and detachment: "We will not win this time, we may not next time, but in the name of the Jeffersonian Democracy, we will make this fight and we will appeal to the Democratic party to make it. I care nothing for the Presidency, as I cared nothing for the nomination. Let my name be blotted from the memory of man, but while I have life, I will work for the rights of the citizen and equal justice to all." [24]

As in the acceptance address previously analyzed, Watson's most serious rhetorical shortcomings were in the final category of redemption, salvation, charismatic terms, theories of action, and a "spot towards which all roads lead." He struck a contradictory and self-defeating rhetorical posture. Although specific remedies were advocated, he simultaneously assassinated any hope for his immediate election and, consequently, their implementation. Although he made an appeal to the Democrats to pursue his theories of action, he blasted their ineffectiveness in pursuing Jeffersonian principles in previous administrations. Rather than rally support based on hope, the St. Louis address catalogued gloom and predicted its continuance.

Thomson, Georgia, Address

The Thomson address, though twice the length of the one at Cooper Union and several times the length of the St. Louis discourse, established guilt in much the same way by assuming the absence of "principles" and "justice" as basic god terms. More so than at Cooper Union or St. Louis, the Georgia speech repetitively used the metaphors of combat and religion; the former through such phrases as "massing its forces," "a forward march," "fight to the death," "this battle," "fire upon our own flag of truce," "fight for the people," "take up your standard," "fight your battles." Intermixed were appeals to the spiritual: "sacred as ever," "altars of Duty," "redeem this Re-

24. *Ibid.*, 9–10.

public," "our sacred honor," "a new baptism," "a new consecration,"
"a blessed victory," "sack cloth and ashes." Politics probably invites
the mixing of militant and religious metaphors, but this characteristic
was more apparent in Watson's postelection address than in the earlier New York and Missouri campaign speeches. Perhaps he was attempting, albeit a little late for the 1904 election, a technique Eric
Hoffer calls "the art of 'religiofication'—the art of turning practical
purposes into holy causes." Thus, to support any other than the Populist cause was not only bad politics but a sacrilege.[25]

Smarting under a resounding defeat and facing a friendly audience at home, Watson's use of sectionalism came leaping forth with
considerable invective. Again, mixing purity with militancy, Watson
turned to the South for standards of "splendid manhood" and "pure
womanhood" where the "Old confederate soldier" was still revered.
The guilty were those who lacked religious commitment, the will to
fight, and qualities of heritage so common among southerners—at
least southerners of the Thomson, Georgia, variety. His earlier New
York speech avoided this regional identification that often characterized southern speakers of the century.

Victimage abounded throughout the address. Ritual scapegoats
remained the "soulless combinations of sordid wealth" in alliance
with "the corrupt politicians." Many of the same general broadsides
of Cooper Union, and some of the more specific devil terms of St.
Louis, were repeated. With the conspiratorial wealthy, Watson condemned individuals, corporations, and the state of New York—the
Rothschild family, August Belmont ("American agent of the Rothschilds"), Hamp McWhorter, J. P. Morgan, Standard Oil Company,
Atlantic Coast Line ("the railroad magnates of Wall street"), Southern
Railroad, Georgia Railroad ("collisions and smash ups"), Oceanic
Steamship Company ("the most sickening record on earth"), vast insurance companies ("they paid no federal tax whatever"), express
companies ("pay no federal taxes at all"), the telegraph companies
("pay no federal tax at all"), the telephone company ("pays no federal
tax at all"). With political manipulators, he was specific in condemning individuals, newspapers, and the East—Democrat Alton Parker

25. Thomson Address; Eric Hoffer, *The True Believer* (New York: Harper & Row, 1951), 15.

(who "said to [Theodore] Roosevelt 'You are right.'"), Pat McCarren ("paid lobbyist of the Standard Oil Trust"), Tom Taggart (Democratic national chairman, "the gambling hell man"), Boykin Wright (who "purchased the negro vote"), Brother Bryan ("having recently been close to Tom Taggart . . . went down on his knees to Wall street"), Judge Calloway (checked "to see who had not voted"), Augusta *Chronicle* ("using the fear of negro domination to hold your votes"), Atlanta *Journal* ("tell[s] you what the millionaires want"), Macon *Telegraph* (praises Tom Taggart for "his skill and diplomacy"), Savannah *News* ("which is for anything labelled 'Democracy'"), "Eastern Plutocracy," "the Eastern democrat," "Northern democracy," "Northern corrupt plutocratic money" ("voicing the sentiments of the corporations against the people"), and French Lick Springs, Indiana (as the retreat for Democratic politicians, "the biggest gambling hell in America"). These were all the victims, interwoven with devil terms, to be sacrificed before redemption could transpire. They were national except for the newspapers, which were all located in Watson's home state.

One demand for victimage was bogus in Watson's estimation— "the cry of Negro Domination" espoused by "your old time politician and editor" who wants to keep the southerner "under the rod of Eastern Plutocracy." Watson was a segregationist, yet he was more perceptive than most of his geographical generation in realizing that the plight of blacks and whites was a mutual dilemma: "And we said to those [black] people 'follow us and we will guarantee you'—what? Social equality? No. Political equality? No. We said, 'We will give you equality as a citizen, under the law that will protect your life, your limb, your property, your home and your fire-side, just as it protects ours. . . .' And the white man of the South who is not willing to go that far is not a man who believes in the Jeffersonian democracy."[26] Nevertheless, for years thereafter, southern politicians attacked the blacks with vigor on the stereotypical notion that they were the real enemy of the South.

Redemption still would flow from "Jeffersonian democracy." Salvation would become a reality when the South and "the great West

26. Thomson Address, 13.

which is also a grand agricultural section" unify on the "People's Party Platform" to "defy the Eastern democrat," to "defy the power of Wall street," and "break the chains that are binding us." He envisioned a South-West coalition not unlike the dreams of both nineteenth- and twentieth-century politicians during other campaigns. But "Jeffersonian democracy" and "People's Party Platform" did not provide charismatic terms for the future. In addition, his theories of action, so similar to those expressed at Cooper Union and St. Louis, had little apparent acceptance in the recent election.

Again prophetic, he repeated his advocacy of initiative, referendum, and recall legislation. As a postelection idea in 1904, however, the proposals had the ring of resentment. They were methods for removing the winners from office. Also, there were clever rebuttals to selections from William J. Bryan's book, *The First Battle.* The Nebraskan had been a friendly source to be quoted at St. Louis; now, reflecting upon Bryan's efforts on behalf of Parker, he was a source to be chided. According to Watson's running mate, T. H. Tibbles, Bryan had made a secret deal to go to Arizona and "get sick" rather than deliver any speeches on behalf of Parker. He was to "get well enough" only in time to present a total of five nonpolitical addresses in Indiana and Missouri as favors for old friends. By early September, Bryan was being scheduled for speechmaking during the entire month of October to capture voters "who in many cases might otherwise stand by the Populists." He proceeded to get considerable national press attention with his speeches on behalf of Parker in various areas of the country. Undoubtedly, Watson was giving vent to his resentment of Bryan's apparent hypocrisy in opposing those issues espoused in the Populist campaign. If he had been aware of the secret agreement alleged above, he had additional cause for anger.[27]

These taunts were too late for 1904 and too early for 1908. Perhaps Watson could foresee Bryan's return to the head of the Democratic ticket and desired to minimize the midwesterner's effectiveness or to strengthen his own negotiating position for a share of the ticket. Finally, Watson offered no philosophical or geographical mecca. The major rhetorical weaknesses at Cooper Union and St. Louis—the ab-

27. T. H. Tibbles to Watson, November 16, 1904, in Watson Papers; New York *Times,* September 1, September 17 through October 27, 1904, *passim.*

sence of redemption and the lack of charismatic terms—remained shortcomings in the Thomson address.

IV

There were two Tom Watsons. The era of the first was drawing to its close with his 1904 campaign for president. Forces of the opposition had stolen congressional elections from his grasp with fraud, intimidation, vote buying; he was threatened physically and was protected by friendly farmers during Populist meetings; he shared southern speaking platforms with black colleagues; at great personal risk, he harbored a young black campaign worker from mob violence. He was a voice for humane justice—at one level opposing the cruel convict lease system in his own state and at another level opposing an entrenched aristocracy that suppressed the economic lepers of his own age. Most of the Populist platform and many of his own proposals, undoubtedly shocking to contemporaries, subsequently were endorsed by the major parties and became law. Although he was not their sole advocate, his courage and foresight were unusual when compared with southern speakers of his generation.[28]

Although his oratory revealed considerable strength, its analysis yielded clues to future problems. Watson seemed to need "a hated enemy."[29] His speeches are loaded with tangible devils who must be purged in order to produce redemption. His god terms are vague, illusive concepts tied to individuals and theories of yesteryear. He could not compromise. "Jeffersonian democracy" was a doctrine of purity that demanded unconditional surrender from the opposition. His speeches were used as reactions to power—with enmity for any person or group who wielded influence. His theories of action were obscure. He did not focus on one single crisis, or on a limited number of manageable crises. He sprayed his shots; his arguments were di-

28. Pollack (ed.), *The Populist Mind*, 23–24, 380–85; Martin, *Georgia*, 139–40; E. Merton Coulter, *Georgia: A Short History* (Chapel Hill: University of North Carolina Press, 1960), 393–95; Lawrence Goodwyn, *The Populist Moment: A Short History of the Agrarian Revolt in America* (New York: Oxford University Press, 1978), 190; Kenneth Coleman (ed.), *A History of Georgia* (Athens: University of Georgia Press, 1977), 247.

29. See the analysis by Charles Arthur Delancey, "Tom Watson: Populist Spokesman in Georgia" (M.A. thesis, University of Georgia, 1974), 83–85.

luted. He was the "anti" candidate—the carping, third party doom-sayer. Operative political etiquette opposed luring his adversaries into serious debate. Consequently, much of his electioneering likely was perceived as idle ramblings by a malcontent trapped outside the system.

The second Tom Watson surfaced about 1906 and practically erased the positive achievements of the first. In popular writing to-day, "Georgia's fiery, red-haired Tom Watson" is remembered as the one "who raised the cross of the Ku Klux Klan"—"a demagogue in star-spangled cloth who would put power ahead of principle, ambition ahead of conviction." He supported a constitutional amendment that removed blacks from the Georgia franchise; he became violently outspoken against blacks, Catholics, and Jews; his writings probably provoked mob violence that led to the vigilante hanging of an imprisoned Jewish businessman. Although Watson died in 1922, some of this negative influence survived his death. Selected anti-Catholic Watson writings were published against Al Smith in 1928, and he became a folk hero for subsequent white supremacists.[30]

What caused the Watson reversal? Instead of supporting the only party that openly welcomed all races, blacks sold their votes for money, for cheap liquor, or out of fear. Poor whites cheered Populist oratory but would not break their habit of voting for the Democrats. The Catholic vote of Augusta had been solidly anti-Watson, possibly due to his Baptist faith or his agrarian roots. The East had long been an adversary with its northern Jewish organizations and moneyed class. So although his bitter indictment of entire population blocs is not condoned, it can be understood. The second Watson probably felt betrayed, used, abandoned. He did not desert previous supporters—they deserted him. He polled 114,753 votes, or .85 percent, in 1904,

30. Jack Anderson, "The Domestic Despots," Fort Collins *Coloradoan*, February 13, 1977; Coulter, *Georgia*, 398–400; Goodwyn, *The Populist Moment*, 325; Martin, *Georgia*, 145–50, 162–65, 169, 176; Pollack, *The Populist Mind*, 24; Hal Steed, *Georgia: Unfinished State* (Atlanta: Cherokee Publishing, 1971), 106, 239–41; Thomas E. Watson, *The Roman Catholic Church* (Thomson, Ga.: Tom Watson Book Co., 1928); Thomas E. Watson, *The Italian Pope's Campaign Against the Constitutional Rights of American Citizens* (Thomson, Ga.: Tom Watson Book Co., 1928); Thomas E. Watson, *How Rome Ruled the Philippines: A True Story of the Immorality of Catholic Friars* (Washington, D.C.: Fellowship Forum, 1928); William Anderson, *The Wild Man from Sugar Creek: The Political Career of Eugene Talmadge* (Baton Rouge: Louisiana State University Press, 1975), 9, 29–30, 39, 42–43, 48, 53.

and 28,131 votes, or .19 percent in 1908. The major party candidates aside, among third party competitors he ran a poor third in 1904 and a miserable fourth in 1908. The wonder is not that he altered his position so drastically, but that he persevered through repeated reversals and desertions.[31]

Tragically, Tom Watson is often characterized as only one of a long line of southern demagogues. Such a conclusion ignores the first half of his political life and discredits most of his Populist efforts.[32] Had Watson's political career ended in 1904, he would be remembered as the earlier spokesman for a group of people later individualized as "the forgotten man." He provided rhetorical groundwork for others who were destined to obtain those positions of power beyond his reach.

31. Martin, *Georgia*, 140–43, 148–49; Coulter, *Georgia*, 393–95, 398; Morison and Commager, *The Growth of the American Republic*, II, 904; Woodward, *The Strange Career of Jim Crow*, 73–74; Degler, *The Other South*, 342; Goodwyn, *Democratic Promise*, 296–97, 559.

32. Even Wilbur J. Cash falls into this trap in his classic text, *The Mind of the South* (New York: Vintage-Knopf, 1957), 245, 247–48.

Courtesy of South Caroliniana Library,
University of South Carolina

Associated Press Photo, courtesy of Wide World Photo

5 / M. L. MCCAULEY

Cole Blease and the Senatorial

Campaign of 1918

A Study in Ambivalent Apology

In an enthusiastically received address on April 2, 1917, Woodrow Wilson asked the Congress of the United States to declare war against Germany. Even as the president was challenging American legislators to "make the world . . . at last free," opponents from across the nation were demonstrating in the streets of Washington against American intervention in Europe.[1]

Among those American political leaders who would lead the opposition to Wilson and the American war effort was South Carolina's former governor, Coleman (Coley) L. Blease. No stranger to controversy, Coley—as he was known to his followers—had originally entered the South Carolina House of Representatives in 1890 as a supporter of "Pitchfork" Benjamin Tillman. With Tillman as his mentor, Blease employed, throughout his career, many of the rhetorical devices that have come to be associated with southern Populists of the era. He viciously lambasted political opponents, foreigners, and Wall Street, often conforming to no bounds of taste or courtesy. He pictured blacks as being immoral, shiftless, and in constant need of white superintendency. Moreover, despite little in the way of tangible programs, Blease championed the cause of poor, white South Carolinians.[2] In short, in his years on the stump, on the floor of the state

1. For a text of the speech, see *Congressional Record*, 65th Cong., 1st Sess., 102–105.
2. Two students of Blease recognize the hold he had on the millworkers and other poor whites of South Carolina. At the same time, these historians generally note that the South Carolinian's work on behalf of the state's lower classes led to little in the

house, in the governor's mansion, on the lecture platform, and in the United States Senate, Blease was known as a rabid racist, a vindictive and vitriolic campaigner, a defender of the farmer and the millworker, and as a man given to the most extreme use of hyperbole, over-simplification, and misrepresentation.

Consequently, it is not surprising that controversy ensued when Blease delivered a series of speeches in the summer of 1917 in which he strongly resisted not only the American entry into the war, but also the wartime policies of the Wilson administration. These addresses and the furor they created set the stage for the campaign of the follow-ing summer when Blease faced James F. Rice, N. B. Dial, and "Pitchfork Ben" Tillman in an election for the United States Senate.

Reaction by Governor Richard Manning and members of the reg-ular wing of the Democratic party to Blease's attacks was overwhelm-ingly negative. On the stump, in the halls of the state legislature, at a variety of deliberative meetings, in patriotic rallies across the state, and in many of the state's newspapers, these powerful Democrats de-nounced Blease and his Reform Democrats as disloyalists and traitors. Such allegations were constant and widespread. Deeply offended by the attacks, the former governor clearly believed his "*moral nature, motives* . . . [and] *reputation*" had been called into question.[3] So Blease assumed a rhetorical posture of self-defense. From the summer of 1917 until the Democratic primary at the end of August the following year, he attempted to extricate himself and his Reformers from the charges leveled against them.

In studying the rhetorical stances Blease assumed during the campaign, it becomes clear that he employed a variety of public argu-ments that B. L. Ware and Wil Linkugel suggest are commonly used in speeches of self-defense.[4] Each of these functioned as a mode of

---

way of concrete reforms. See Ronald Danton Burnside, "The Governorship of Coleman Livingston Blease of South Carolina, 1911–1915" (Ph.D. dissertation, Indiana Univer-sity, 1966), 235, 266; and Kenneth Wayne Mixon, "The Senatorial Career of Coleman Livingston Blease, 1925–1931" (M.A. thesis, University of South Carolina, 1970), 86, 92, 137–38, 140.

3. B. L. Ware and Wil A. Linkugel, "They Spoke in Defense of Themselves: On the Generic Criticism of Apologia," *Quarterly Journal of Speech*, LIX (1973), 274.

4. *Ibid.*, 275–82.

resolution for Blease as he attempted to counter the regular Democrats' disparagement of his patriotism. The manner in which these strategies worked and the outcome thereof are the focus of this essay.

The Rhetorical Situation

Wilson's call for mobilization against Germany's Hohenzollern monarchy on April 2 brought vigorous and vocal opposition from many Americans. "In South Carolina, this opposition was based on a mixture of political partisanship, ethnic considerations, and antimilitaristic sentiment."[5] During the summer of 1917, Blease, on the stump, and former Charleston mayor John P. Grace, through the pages of his paper, the Charleston *American*, gave voice to the political, religious, and ethnic values of many South Carolinians who could not support the war. With the aid of Congressman Fred Dominick, Blease's law partner and the only member of South Carolina's congressional delegation to vote against the declaration of war, plus a group of state politicians and a number of small-town papers, Blease and Grace appealed to (1) the nationalistic pride of the state's German population, (2) a partisan distaste for Wilson and Manning, (3) a strain of religiously based pacifism, and (4) the anglophobia of the state's voters.[6] One of the vehicles they used to further their views was the Reform Democratic party, a splinter group that Blease and his supporters had formed after his defeat for governor in 1916.[7] Throughout the summer and fall of that first year of war, "the antiwar people enjoyed their

5. Terry Lynn Helsley, "'Voices of Dissent:' The Antiwar Movement and the State Council of Defense in South Carolina, 1916–1918" (M.A. thesis, University of South Carolina, 1974), 1.

6. *Ibid.*, 53, 64, 68. The Abbeville *Scimitar*, Anderson *Farmers' Weekly Tribune*, Newberry *Herald and News*, and Gaffney *Ledger* editorially opposed the American entry into the war. Grace, a man of Irish ancestry, particularly found the Anglo-American alliance repugnant. Helsley surmises that Blease, who misjudged the strength of the prowar sentiment in South Carolina, saw the war as an issue on which to defeat the regular Democrats. Also see Robert Milton Burts, *Richard Irvine Manning and the Progressive Movement in South Carolina* (Columbia: University of South Carolina Press, 1974), 171, who concurs.

7. After his 1916 defeat Blease and his followers determined to follow Tillman's tactic of forming a party within a party. See Charleston (S.C.) *Evening Post*, October 26, 1916, and Columbia (S.C.) *State*, March 22, 1917, for accounts of the formation of the Reform Democrats of South Carolina.

greatest success and attacked the state and federal governments with abandon."[8]

Strangely enough, in Blease's campaign for the Senate in 1917 and 1918, the economic, racial, and social considerations that had dominated his rhetoric up to that time played only secondary roles. True to form, however, the campaign was characterized by exaggeration, misrepresentation, and personal attacks. In seven rather widely reported speeches in 1917, Coley charged that he would not have voted to enter the European conflict had he been a member of Congress; neither would he have voted for the conscription act. He poured out vituperation on his opponents, calling them liars and charging that many of them were war profiteers who capitalized on the military situation facing the nation. And it was not at all uncommon for him to label his political enemies cowards who sent the young men of South Carolina to do their fighting for them. From the time of his first address of the campaign when he spoke at a statewide meeting of Reform Democrats in Columbia on May 14, 1917, until his last stump speech of the summer to a group of Confederate veterans at Chapin, South Carolina, on August 30, 1917, he attacked Governor Manning for mismanagement of South Carolina's efforts at military preparedness. Repeatedly, he asserted that Reformers were denied roles in the decision-making councils of the state and relegated to serving on the front lines in Europe. After making such allegations, Blease frequently took a "hand primary" (a poll) of his audience to measure their support. Naturally, the partisan crowds that gathered to hear him gave their overwhelming endorsement.

Throughout the summer Blease continued his appearances across South Carolina, and the state's prowar forces began to mount a counteroffensive against Reform Democrats and their outspoken leader. Among those who responded was David R. Coker, chairman of the State Council of Defense. He took issue with remarks Blease made at a Lutheran-sponsored picnic at Pomaria on July 27 in the Dutch Fork region where most of the state's German population lived.[9] In addition, the Columbia *State* led the press in moving against the charges made by Blease. The editor, W. W. Ball, a long-time adversary of

8. Helsley, "'Voices of Dissent,'" 70.
9. Charleston (S.C.) *American*, August 1, 1917.

Blease, prophetically noted that the campaign of 1918 would center on the war.[10] For the next year, the criticisms voiced by Ball and Coker would not only continue but multiply.

Political opponents, editors, ministers—South Carolinians in all walks of life—questioned the patriotism of Blease and his party. These charges and countercharges created a rhetorical situation that drove Blease to assume a defensive rhetorical stance. Faced with the rising criticism of his loyalty to the nation and labeled a political opportunist, he could seemingly make only one viable, "fitting" response.[11] Were he to salvage his reputation, that of the Reform wing of the Democratic party, and their chances for victory in the Democratic primary in 1918, Blease had to "reconcile" these "derogatory charge[s] with a favorable view of his character."[12] To rebuild his image and that of his fellow Reformers, he turned to a distinct form of public address: the apology.

As a rhetorical type, apologetic discourse is a means by which an individual whose personal and ethical demeanor has been challenged moves to repair the damage in the eyes of the public. A speech of self-defense, the apology may be an attempt to justify behavior, to provide an explanation for misunderstood or misinterpreted motives, to turn the focus of attention away from the accused, or simply to deny the accusations that form the basis of the attack.[13] The seventy-five or so campaign addresses that Blease made in 1917 and 1918 clearly had the quality of apologia.

In each of the speeches, Coley had at his disposal four rhetorical strategies that are frequently used by apologists: *denial, bolstering, differentiation* and *transcendance*. Although the distinctions among these strategies may at times be somewhat arbitrary, the terms are useful in explaining the variety of ways in which a rhetor attempts to repair the damage done to his reputation. These techniques, which rhetorical theorists Ware and Linkugel adapt from psychologist Robert Abel-

10. Columbia (S.C.) *State*, July 31, 1917.
11. See Lloyd Bitzer, "The Rhetorical Situation," *Philosophy and Rhetoric*, I (1968), 1–14, for a discussion of the influence of particular historical circumstances on a rhetor's response to those conditions.
12. Jackson Harrell, B. L. Ware, and Wil A. Linkugel, "Failure of Apology in American Politics: Nixon on Watergate," *Speech Monographs*, XLII (1975), 261.
13. Ware and Linkugel, "They Spoke in Defense of Themselves," 273–75.

son's theory of the resolution of "belief dilemmas," were available to the former governor for his defense of the loyalty he and his fellow Reform Democrats felt for the nation.[14]

Rhetorical Strategies of Self-Defense

The most direct and easily imagined of the techniques was that of denial. As a means of negation, such arguments "do not constitute a known distortion of reality" in the minds of the speaker's audience. "Denial . . . strategies do not attempt to change the audience's meaning or affect for whatever is in question. Denial consists of the simple disavowal by the speaker of any participation in, relationship to, or positive sentiment toward whatever it is that repels the audience."[15]

Although some rhetors' disclaimers of guilt may be detailed and involved, in 1917 and 1918 Blease's were not. Instead, he seldom, if ever, used a simple statement of disavowal. Rather, he coupled his assertions that he was not disloyal with other rhetorical techniques. So although he denied the charges made against his patriotism, he never let the issue rest with simple statements that such allegations were untrue. In any one speech Blease took other lines of argument in defending himself and his party, and at times his remarks were inconsistent, even contradictory. Denial, as a rhetorical form for him, was simply a springboard to a more aggressive rhetoric.

One of the techniques he used in tandem with disavowal was that of bolstering. Blease tied his declarations that he and his party had been falsely charged to other statements that South Carolinians could in no way interpret as being treasonous. Bolstering, "the obverse of denial," allowed Blease clearly to align himself in the minds of the state's voters with patriotic sentiments that were widely held.[16] Even in what he termed his first statement on the war situation—an interview he gave on April 24, 1917—Coley asserted he was with his

14. *Ibid.*, 275–82. Herbert W. Simons, in "'Genere-alizing' About Rhetoric: A Scientific Approach," in Karlyn Kohrs Campbell and Kathleen Hall Jamieson (eds.), *Form and Genre: Shaping Rhetorical Action* (Falls Church: Speech Communication Association, n.d.), 37–38, observes that distinguishing one strategy from another may present difficulties.
15. Ware and Linkugel, "They Spoke in Defense of Themselves," 275–76.
16. *Ibid.*, 277.

"country right or wrong." [17] In virtually every speech he delivered for the next year and a half, in one way or another he used this supporting strategy as a means of defense.

A fine example of this strategy was the speech he gave in Danville, Virginia, to a crowd of four thousand at a meeting of the German-American fraternal order of Red Men on May 16, 1917. After the southern orator's tribute to Lee and a firm declaration that he would not have voted for war or the conscription bill, Blease demonstrated his loyalty when he boasted, "But we are in the war now. Now it is to do and die and we propose to stand as one man and fight to the finish. Germany is reported to have made the assertion that to burn the national capitol at Washington would . . . strike the greatest blow at democracy, but I am here to tell you fellow citizens that when this comes there will be no longer any American citizens living." [18]

Obviously, Blease wanted this audience to believe that he was proud of the nation's military strength. In fact, throughout both years of the campaign he tried to enhance his damaged reputation by identifying himself with the traditional southern admiration for the flag and military might. Thus, boasting became one means by which Blease bolstered his image. He particularly took delight in telling his audiences that the majority of South Carolinians who were in uniform were boys from Reform Democrat homes.

As the war wore on, as American casualties increased, and as his critics continued to denigrate his Americanism, Blease turned to even more emotional bolstering devices. During the final week of the campaign, he told an audience in the Piedmont:

Some of my dearest friends are in France fighting under the Stars and Stripes, the Lilies of France and the flags of other allies. Some of them have fought their last fight, and as a result of the supreme sacrifice which they made, they sleep in foreign soil—foreign, really, no longer because it has been joined to American by the ties of blood. Some of them were still in the trenches when last I heard from them. Some are officers, and some are privates—but, in whatever rank, they are the majority of the boys from this state who have answered the call of their country. [19]

17. Charleston (S.C.) *American*, April 25, 1917; Newberry (S.C.) *Herald and News*, May 1, 1917.
18. Danville (Va.) *Register*, May 17, 1917.
19. Charleston (S.C.) *American*, August 23, 1918.

Patriotic appeals were not limited to affirmations of admiration for South Carolinians who had sacrificed their lives or to boasting about the American military machine. Another dimension of Blease's overall strategy of support was his frequently repeated offer to raise a third military contingent of South Carolinians. Even as early as the first meeting of the Reform party after the United States had declared war against the Central Powers, Blease demonstrated his devotion to the nation when he told his fellow Reformers that he had offered to do just that.[20] Yet Manning had not responded. As a consequence of the rebuff, the former governor felt compelled to tell of his offer at every opportunity. He did so, for example, when he told the annual meeting of Company F, Fourth Regiment of South Carolina Confederate Veterans, on August 7, 1917, that he "offered to get up a brigade or regiment and save . . . [the] state the humiliation of fighting under foreign officers, but . . . [that the] red-headed cowardly governor refused to get up the third regiment."[21] Clearly, Blease's attempts at apology were never totally apologetic in nature.

Nevertheless, identifying himself with those values and beliefs that South Carolinians generally held demonstrated his desire to repair his damaged credibility. He even told those veterans that he had exhorted his party to obey the unpopular conscription laws. After all, he said, "It is not all of life to live nor all of death to die."[22] Other recurring themes that played roles in the former governor's strategy of bolstering were his personal accounts of having borrowed money to purchase liberty bonds and of allowing Camp Jackson, a new military training facility near Columbia, to use forty acres for a rifle range without costs.

Perhaps even more significant as a supportive ploy was the position Coley took toward Woodrow Wilson. Since the time presidential candidate Wilson had visited the home of William E. Gonzales, editor of the Columbia *State* and Blease's political enemy, the Reform leader only reluctantly had endorsed the president. Consequently, his efforts to benefit from his auditors' admiration for Wilson must have been an especially difficult stance for Blease to accept. Even so, as the

20. *Ibid.*, May 15, 1917.
21. *Ibid.*, August 10, 1917.
22. *Ibid.*

accusations mounted and he realized more fully how South Carolinians felt about the war, Blease included strong affirmations of support
for the nation's commander-in-chief. Although he had declared his
support of Wilson in earlier speeches, Blease introduced on July 12,
1918, a new argument to his strategy of establishing common ground.
He told the partisan crowd of four thousand at Wagener, "If it be necessary, in order to win this war, to break the precedent set by President Washington in reference to a third term, I shall tell President
Wilson that I will support him for a third term and make speeches for
him in any part of the American continent."[23] Almost every crowd to
which he spoke from that time forward heard Blease make a similar
statement. Recognizing the nation's devotion to the president, Blease
naturally hoped to capitalize on those sentiments and thus strengthen
his own faltering popularity.

His discussion of the Confederacy was the last recurring topic he
employed to identify himself with institutions, mores, and sentiments held dear by his auditors. At the time of this campaign, thousands of former Confederate soldiers were still alive. Indeed, the Civil
War and the aftermath of Reconstruction were still part of the living
memory of many South Carolinians. Regional educators, novelists,
newsmen, preachers, and politicians had kept the myths of the Lost
Cause, the Old South, chivalry, and the like fresh and vivid. At political rallies, on the lecture platform, in the pulpit, at veterans' reunions,
and on the floors of legislative assemblies, southern orators waxed
eloquent in the homage they paid these myths. So it is not surprising
that Blease, an astute politician, attached himself and his position on
the war to revered leaders of the Lost Cause.

On April 25, 1918, he celebrated these men in his address to a
standing-room-only crowd in Charleston's Artillery Hall. After having noted the opposition to the war of such loyal American political
leaders as the Democratic majority leader of the House, Congressman
Claude Kitchin of North Carolina, and the venerable Joe Canon,
Speaker of the House, Blease compared himself to two other men
who had opposed a war but eventually came to take the lead in that
effort: "When South Carolina and other Southern states seceded from

23. *Ibid.*, July 13, 1918.

the Union, Robert E. Lee, an officer in the Union army was opposed to secession; but when his native state signed the declaration of secession, Lee resigned from the Union army and took command of the Confederate forces. Where is the man who would dare charge Lee with disloyalty? One of the strongest opponents to [the] War of Secession who spoke . . . and wrote against it was chosen . . . to be the vice president of the Confederacy, Alexander H. Stephens. Were they disloyal? No."[24] The former governor used this favorable comparison between the two great Confederates and himself in a number of other speeches during that second and last summer of the campaign.

In fact, in one of his last speeches of the two-year battle Blease defended himself and the party aggressively. In still another address in Charleston's Artillery Hall on Wednesday evening, August 14, 1918, he resorted to most of his customary bolstering themes. Perhaps he felt the desperation of his situation. So, as a military band played the national anthem and before he began speaking, he grasped an American flag and waved it before a cheering crowd of twenty-one hundred.[25]

Surely, such an action was simply part of a larger rhetorical plan. Granted, he had not utilized much in the way of straightforward denials of the accusations that he and his party had been unfaithful to the American cause; but Blease recognized the need to bolster his flagging public image. His awareness of that fact lead him repeatedly to invoke a variety of arguments that would positively tie him in the minds of his campaign audiences to beliefs, values, and institutions that they held dear. Several persuasive devices formed the basis of his overall bolstering effort: his boasting about American military might and South Carolinians' in particular, his personal testimony about his financial support of the war, his affirmation of faith in the nation and its leadership, and his use of historical analogy to picture himself as a modern Lee or Stephens.

Neither his techniques of identification nor his disclaimers, as forms of persuasion, altered his audience's "meaning for the cognitive elements" involved in his discussion of the war issue.[26] But two other types of argument an apologist could employ were available to trans-

24. *Ibid.*, April 26, 1918; Yorkville (S.C.) *Enquirer*, April 30, 1918.
25. Charleston (S.C.) *American*, August 15, 1918.
26. Ware and Linkugel, "They Spoke in Defense of Themselves," 278.

form the perception of reality held by the state's voters. Blease hardly, if ever, used one of these—the strategy of differentiation, which would probably have been a detailed discussion of the distinction between his opposition to the war and that of such individuals as Eugene Debs or Emma Goldman. Rather, the South Carolinian turned to a posture of transcendance to complete his defense.

A transcendental approach allowed Blease to join his stand on the war with some larger context within which his audience did not view it. Such rhetorical tactics were transformative "in the sense that any such strategy affects the meaning which the audience attaches to the manipulated attribute," *i.e.*, his position in regard to the war. "The transcendental strategies," for Blease, "therefore, psychologically . . . [moved] the audience away from the particulars of the charge at hand in a direction toward some more abstract, general view of his character."[27] Such approaches symbolically lifted the issue to another level of significance. As a result, Blease's qualms about the war could no longer be seen as simply, straightforward opposition based on some pragmatic or political consideration.[28]

Two dominant themes formed the arguments of Coley's transcendental strategy. The first of these was theological or religious in nature; the second centered on his evaluation of the powerful Democratic regulars lead by Richard Manning. Upon close examination, the inconsistency of the former with the larger body of Blease's rhetoric becomes apparent.

A lack of logical consistency, nevertheless, did not hamper the Reform leader in his appeals to the religious beliefs and values of his listeners. His reservations about the war, he charged, grew out of his brotherly love. As early as in his speech to the Red Men in May, 1917, he ended his appeal in homiletic terms when he proclaimed, "There was never a quarrel which could not be settled upon reflection. There would be no sin if the doctrine of brotherly love was more generally accepted."[29] In his widely publicized speech at a Lutheran picnic in

27. *Ibid.*, 280.
28. John H. Patton, "A Government as Good as Its People: Jimmy Carter and the Restoration of Transcendence to Politics," *Quarterly Journal of Speech*, LXIII (1977), 249–57.
29. Danville (Va.) *Register*, May 17, 1917; Charleston (S.C.) *American*, May 19, 1917.

Pomaria later that summer, he also couched his opposition to American intervention in Europe in theological terms. In doing so, he shifted the issue of his opposition to the war to a higher scale: "It has been published of late in the anti-reform press that I and the party to which I belong are outcasts in the political world just now, but I want to say to you as far as I am personally concerned that I would rather be an outcast in the eyes of Woodrow Wilson and a follower of Jesus Christ, than to be a follower of Woodrow Wilson and an outcast from Jesus Christ." Why, asked Blease, did some ministers, "with one hand upon the Bible—a Bible which teaches them Christianity; a Bible which says to them, love the Lord, thy God, with all thy heart and thy neighbor as thyself . . . plea for this awful war, and for the destruction of human beings created in the image of their maker?" Answering his own question, Blease declared that the moneychangers were in the temple and that "characters like Judas Iscariot" were filling the pulpits of the state's churches.[30] Strangely enough, in that same speech, Blease the preacher had called for a speedy and successful conclusion to the war.

In his speech to Confederate veterans at the Carswell Institute, Blease continued to elevate his hesitations about American foreign policy to a higher level by turning to the Bible.

We have been for years and years sending missionaries and piles of our money to foreign lands to teach the gospel of Jesus Christ which He said is embraced in this command "Love the Lord thy God, with all thy soul, with all thy mind and with all thy body and thy neighbor as thyself." Now forsooth, because I am talking that same religion from the rostrum some fools holler that "Blease is against the government." Christ taught peace on earth. That's my doctrine, and "good will to men," that's me, and yet we are spending thousands of dollars to teach the heathens that religion and the command "Thou shalt not kill," and billions to make guns big enough and powder strong enough to kill our fellow men. I am for an honorable peace and for the doctrine of my Savior and saving our boys from death. "Onward Christian Soldiers, marching to kill your fellow men," would be a sacrilegious motto worthy only of the devil and his imps.[31]

Religious arguments, of course, were a staple for politicians in the South during this period; thus, preachers were not the only

30. Charleston (S.C.) *American*, July 29, 1917; Columbia (S.C.) *State*, July 23, 1918.
31. Charleston (S.C.) *American*, August 10, 1917.

speakers to quote the Bible. However, the former governor's use of Scripture to denounce proponents of American war policies must have been one of the reasons for the ultimate failure of his rhetorical defense. The percentage of pacifists has never been great among American churchmen and certainly not in South Carolina during the First World War. Consequently, these attacks on the clergy and churches probably negated much of the positive image he had endeavored to create with other aspects of his campaign discourse. He might have sensed this; in his later speeches, he simply placed his position on the war in the same tradition as that of Christian love and did not use religion, per se, as a whip with which to lash his opponents.

Besides planting his foreign policy remarks in the fertile bed of southern religion, Blease frequently used one other tactic to turn the voters' attention away from his stand on the war. He reversed the tables on his critics by challenging their patriotism and their devotion to the well being of the citizens of South Carolina and mounted his own defense by using vehement, and at times vicious, denunciations of Manning and Manning's candidate for the Senate, N. B. Dial. Fortunately for Blease, Tillman died on July 3, 1918. Prior to that time, the old Populist had either been too ill or too preoccupied in Washington to take an active part in the campaign. So Blease's primary targets became the governor, Dial, other regular Democratic leaders, and newsmen.

Repeatedly Blease accused Manning of discriminating against Reform Democrats in the composition of conscription boards and other state and local wartime agencies. In his speech at Filbert on August 2, 1917, he said Manning's formation of the South Carolina militia was the "most outrageous method of organizing a militia" as had "ever been known in the history of the world." As a result, "Manning used every power he could," said Blease, "to send the reform boys of . . . [South Carolina] into the trenches under the command of political opponents, caring nothing for the lives of these boys." After declaring Manning to be "the worst governor this state has ever had," Coley told the crowd, "Scott and Moses [two corrupt Reconstruction governors] dealt with theft of your money, but Manning is trying to steal the bodies and souls of the Reform boys of South Carolina." Finally, he proclaimed that if Manning said Blease was not a loyal

American, then Manning was a "contemptible liar."[32] He was to make this final charge for the remainder of the campaign.

At Pickens on August 25, that first summer, Blease accused his adversaries of doing anything to win the upcoming election. Using typical Populist arguments, he warned that "millions of Wall street money, coming from such corporations as the steel trust, the powder manufacturers, the ship builders, and such like, will be sent into every state to debauch the voters and save war candidates." He further asserted, "The world has never seen such a political campaign of debauchery as will be waged in the election of next year to save those who favor war and death in behalf of money and credit, even though it take the honor of the voter." Cautioning his auditors about efforts to purchase support, Blease thanked God some could not be influenced by "postmasterships, R.F.D. carrier positions, little appointments around the capitol . . . United States marshalships, district attorney-ships, or any other position that can be handed out from Washington or Columbia."[33]

Denunciations of political corruption and opportunism were commonplace in Coley's stump speeches. On occasion, he even called his antagonists cowards who hid behind a bottle or age to avoid the draft. But his most vicious and cruel remarks came in a campaign address at Branwood the evening of July 18, 1918. Speaking to a crowd that numbered somewhere between twenty-five hundred and five thousand, Blease sarcastically remarked, "The governor brags that he has five sons who are in the [military] service. It is so. Yet all of them are strutting about in pretty uniforms and holding commissions and are in no more danger of meeting the bullets than this electric light under which I stand." Although the Branwood audience apparently approved of these comments, the more objective voter surely did not. Six of the governor's seven sons volunteered for the service; the seventh was too young. And that same fall, Manning's son, William Sinkler, was killed in action in the Argonne Forest.[34]

32. *Ibid.*, August 3, 1917. The Columbia (S.C.) *State*, August 3, 1917, was more modest in its estimate of the crowd. It reported only four thousand gathered for the meeting. Congressman Tom Heflin of Alabama had been scheduled to speak at Filbert, but business in Washington detained him.
33. Charleston (S.C.) *American*, August 26, 1917.
34. Yorkville (S.C.) *Enquirer*, July 23, 1918; Burts, *Richard Irvine Manning*, 179.

Standards of good taste and fair play obviously did not limit the Reform campaigner. A few days after the Branwood address, Blease spoke to about five hundred people in the mill village of Olympia in Columbia. He again used personal attacks as a means of shifting his listeners' attention away from himself and turning it toward the hostile press. In denouncing Charlton R. Wright, editor of the Columbia *Record*, Blease claimed that Wright had not only been expelled from a Columbia club for cheating at cards, but that Wright's employer, Edward Robertson, had inherited money from a father who had "laid the foundation of his fortune while a United States Senator by [the] grace of a negro and scalawag legislature in reconstruction days." Besides the racial slur, a rarity in this particular campaign, and in addition to his appeals to southern antipathies concerning Reconstruction, Blease concluded his allegations against Wright by declaring the editor to be "a common, everyday, card thief." [35] The accused Reformer showed equal vehemence in denouncing W. W. Ball, the editor of the Columbia *State*, who had played a key role in seeing that Blease's speeches on the war were made an issue. [36] Blease asserted that Ball, who had married the daughter of the German consul in Charleston, drove an automobile purchased with German money. Moreover, observed Coley, Ball's own children had German blood "in their veins." [37] Such was the case, he added, with the children of the editor of the Charleston *Evening Post*, who had also married one of the consul's daughters. Finally, Blease charged that the Charleston *News and Courier* was owned by persons of German ancestry. The sum of his remarks was that these newsmen had called his patriotism into question when their own credibility was open to criticism.

Such allegations allowed the former governor to refocus the attention of his listeners in another direction, away from himself. With his political enemies tainted with the possibility of German sympathies and political corruption and opportunism, Blease's own stand on the war, he no doubt hoped, was not as subject to criticism. However, the violent style in which Coley attacked the prowar forces back-

35. Charleston (S.C.) *American*, July 28, 1918.
36. John D. Stark, *Damned Upcountryman, William Watts Ball: A Study of American Conservatism* (Durham, N.C.: Duke University Press, 1968), 74–79. Ball shrewdly used Blease's speeches—particularly those of 1917—against the former governor.
37. Charleston (S.C.) *American*, July 28, 1918.

fired with most South Carolinians. Again, the excess that characterized his transcendental strategy probably worked against him rather
than as an effective means of self-defense.

Summary and Conclusions

A number of historians, such as Terry Helsley in his study of the antiwar movement in South Carolina and Robert Burts in his biography
of Manning, lay the blame for the Reform defeat on Blease, who, they
argue, misread the political climate of the period. He—supposedly attempting to capitalize on such factors as a partisan dislike of Wilson
and Manning, the doctrine of states' rights, the ethnic pride of South
Carolina's German population, a strain of religious pacifism, a sense
of isolationism, and a hatred of moneyed interests—chose the wrong
side of a controversial issue. Without a doubt, the position Blease and
his followers assumed in regard to American war policies was the one
overriding concern of the 1918 campaign. To suggest that Blease
simply made a political mistake by expressing doubts about American
military intervention in Europe, however, is an inadequate analysis of
the election and its outcome.

First, this contention rests on the assumption that Blease, without qualm or compunction of conscience, voiced his opposition to the
war purely on the basis of political expediency. This charge is made
without sufficient evidence. Judging the motives of any political figure is difficult at best. A variety of considerations, with varying de-
grees of importance, may ultimately determine a given course of action. To attribute the positive values of patriotism and altruism to
Manning and Dial and the negative qualities of political opportunism
and selfishness to Blease and his party is somewhat naïve. Both
groups were politicians seeking either to win or to retain office and at
the same time to adapt to the beliefs and values of their constituents.
No doubt Manning and his supporters (and Blease and his) ration-
alized in their own minds their private behavior and public utter-
ances. In short, Cole Blease probably was as altruistically motivated
in regard to his stand on the war as were Manning and Dial.

The acrimony that existed between Manning and Blease helps explain the bitterness of the campaign of 1918. The election of 1916 and

earlier rivalries had left their marks. Personal differences were only compounded by differences of cultural and social backgrounds. Manning, the scion of an old, aristocratic family, and Blease, the son of an upcountry tavern keeper, represented two divergent strains in southern politics. Naturally, Blease, the experienced stump speaker, resorted to rhetorical extremes, particularly in his *ad hominem* attacks. Nevertheless, with few exceptions, at least, he did refrain from the use of the racial issue, a tactic that characterized both his earlier and his later speechmaking. While espousing the pacifism and love of Christ, at the same time he verbally assaulted—at times in the most unfair, false, and outrageous manner—his opponents. Not only was his practice incompatible with his preachments on Christian love, but his addresses were often internally inconsistent. Frequently, this Reformist criticized his adversaries for fighting a war despite the Christian admonition to be makers of peace. But in the same address, he himself declared that the war should be concluded speedily and with American success. As often as not, he even boasted of American military prowess. By doing so, he was guilty of the same inconsistency of which he accused his opponents.

Blease manifested the fervent nationalism of the day. In the approximately seventy-five speeches made during the period of this study, Blease consistently supported the American government. Granted, he opposed the declaration of war and many of the wartime policies of Manning and Wilson, and he did cry discrimination in regard to such matters as membership on conscription boards and other agencies. His motives were probably political. On the other hand, Reform Democrats had reason to expect to play a larger part in the national emergency. Whether Manning's fears about disloyalty among them were justified or not, Blease's campaign rhetoric was not "treasonous." Accusations that it was appear unfounded. Had his addresses genuinely reflected treachery, steps would have been taken to curtail his freedom of speech. Other South Carolinians, such as John P. Grace, certainly found themselves at odds with national authorities. In fact, had Blease's political adversaries not attacked his early speeches, the subject probably would have died in the early summer of 1917. But the Newberry native obviously felt the need to defend his early remarks and those of fellow Reformers against the criticism of editors, politicians, and other leaders. The effect was snowballing. One speech led to another. Blease seemed perpetually caught up in a rhetorical situation that demanded a response.

Consequently, his speaking throughout 1917 and until the primary in late August, 1918, could properly be termed apologetic discourse. Because "apologetic discourse involves a favorable view of his character,"[38] the Reform leader basically employed two rhetorical techniques in self-defense. First, Blease strove positively to identify himself with the beliefs, values, and institutions of most South Carolinians. He attempted to enhance his credibility by boasting about the American war machine and specifically South Carolinians' contributions to it, by giving personal testimony about his monetary assistance to the American effort, by affirming his faith in the nation and its president, and finally, by picturing himself in the same mold as Robert E. Lee and Alexander H. Stephens.

As a second technique, Coley redirected the interests of the Palmetto state's voters by asserting that his reservations about American involvement in a European dispute grew out of his conviction that Christians should be makers of peace and not war. However, his comments about those who did not adhere to the Christian standard of brotherly love were anything but those of a peacemaker. The former governor castigated his political antagonists as another ploy to transfer attention from himself. This tactic, coupled with the religiously based denunciations, failed adequately to restore faith in his own credibility. Therefore, one could safely say that Blease's transcendental strategy negated any positive good that may have resulted from his attempts at bolstering. In sum, the more he spoke, the more he needed to speak to make amends for what he had previously said.

His efforts to extricate himself would perhaps have been more successful had he not continued the personal assaults on Manning and Dial. A more fitting rhetorical campaign, and perhaps a more appealing one to the state's electorate, would have been to have sought an early closure on the matter of his patriotism by a thoroughgoing apology. In this way his opponents would have been denied an issue that clearly proved detrimental to the Reform ticket's chances for elec-

38. Harrell, Ware, and Linkugel, "Failure of Apology in American Politics," 261.

tion. After having disposed of the charge of disloyalty, he then could perhaps have amplified his discussion of matters that received only peripheral attention in the election, *e.g.*, the price of agricultural products, road construction, and postwar adjustment. Unfortunately, Blease was too much the southern Populist stump speaker, caught up in his own rhetorical excessiveness. As a consequence, his apologetic efforts were ambivalent and inadequate. However, his career was not ruined with the election of 1918. The voters of South Carolina sent him to the Senate, in place of Dial, in 1924.

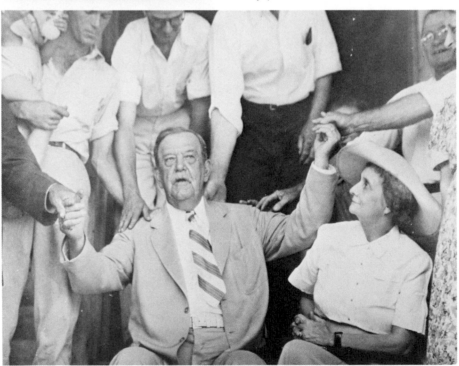

"Cotton Ed" Smith

The South Carolina Farmer in the United States Senate

Ellison Durant Smith was born and reared in the country near Lynchburg, South Carolina. Having a good life on the family farm became the heart of his existence, though it was not farming itself that he enjoyed. For, according to his nephew, the Rhodes scholar John Rice, as a farmer his "Uncle Ellie" was a "model of irresponsibility," whose management of the farm was "restless and restive." Smith's life in the country, Rice believed, "revolved around two centers, game birds and cotton. . . . [O]ut of one preoccupation came a minute knowledge of edible birds, out of the other a political career."[1] This career began with two uneventful terms in the Columbia statehouse in the 1890s, but Smith's political star truly rose almost a decade later with his election at the age of forty-four to the United States Senate. There the self-proclaimed advocate of the South Carolina farmer remained for the next thirty-six years. After his first and only loss in a senatorial race, a sick and broken old man returned to his country home to die before his elected successor was sworn into office.

Throughout his Senate career the name of "Cotton Ed" Smith was linked to five issues: agriculture, tariff, immigration, states' rights, and racism. His communication—verbal and nonverbal—on these five issues during his campaigns and while in the Senate was basically emotional rather than logical; he was essentially a showman

1. John Andrew Rice, *I Came Out of the Eighteenth Century* (New York: Harper and Brothers, 1942), 14.

who delighted in the use of anecdotes and plain folks appeal, who used emotionally loaded words and personal invectives in his attacks against all opponents, and who thrived within the raucous, carnival-like atmosphere of South Carolina political campaigns of the period. He lacked the analytical and organizational skills to achieve legislative leadership in the Senate.

I

Campaigning in South Carolina was, in "Cotton Ed's" own words, a "monkey circus." The state required that all candidates for any state-wide office schedule joint appearances in each county seat. Journalist Harry Ashmore, a native South Carolinian, remembered these political rallies as "a sort of touring stock company, with the principals, their handlers, and the press traveling together through the hot summer months."[2] In his very first Senate campaign Smith used this circus-like atmosphere to dramatize his link with Carolina cotton farmers. His usual plan was to ride from the railroad station to the speakers' platform atop a cotton-bale throne in a parade of cotton wagons, sometimes accompanied by a band. The candidate and his supporters wore cotton bolls for boutonnieres, and the Lynchburg farmer—sporting a cotton suit—spoke of this fluffy, white staple as "my sweetheart, my old sweetheart."

In dramatizing himself as a cotton grower, Smith was emphasizing his already established identity as a spokesman for South Carolina farmers. Eleven years before he first announced for the Senate he had begun working with farm organizations. He was active in establishing the Farmers' Protective Association in South Carolina in 1901, was one of the "men of prominence" who assembled in Shreveport, Louisiana, in 1904 for the National Cotton Convention, and was an attendant at the January, 1905, Southern Interstate Cotton Convention in New Orleans.[3]

Out of this last convention came the Southern Cotton Association with E. D. Smith as a member of the executive committee. In that

2. Harry S. Ashmore, *An Epitaph for Dixie* (New York: W. W. Norton, 1957), 99.
3. Shreveport (La.) *Journal*, December 12, 1904; New Orleans *Daily Picayune*, January 23, 1905.

capacity he worked in South Carolina as well as in other southern states to win members and support for the organization. The Southern Cotton Association proposed to carry out its ideas through an extensive system of committees: one to bring about a permanent reduction in cotton acreage, one for organizing farmers in each state (however, state and local committees were to be headed by a farmer, a banker, and a merchant), another for financing and holding present crops, and still others for warehousing and financing future crops, for gathering statistics and reports on all matters related to cotton, for establishing direct trade between farmers and textile manufacturers, and for improved transportation and more favorable freight rates.[4] All of these were goals that continued to be a part of Smith's thinking on the subject of cotton.

Not only had this South Carolinian's cotton premises been clearly established before he ran for the Senate, but his speaking style had also received some notoriety. For example, reports of the Shreveport convention suggested that his delivery was dramatic, his speech organization rambling, and his language emotional. Of one of his speeches at this gathering the New Orleans *Picayune* observed: "Prof. E. D. Smith, of South Carolina, rose and made a fiery Confederate address, composed of almost equal parts of the boll weevil, the bear evil, and the Civil War. 'New England beat us once with the bullets,' he said. 'They have just beaten us again with the ballots; now, for God's sake, let's try and beat them with the bolls!'"[5]

Such rhetoric apparently pleased the delegates, for the next day, "by the unanimous voice of the gathering," "Carolina Smith" was again summoned to speak. Describing Smith's platform antics on the second day of the Shreveport convention, the *Picayune* observed that he "harked back to the Civil War," "danced about in the aisle in excitement," and "shook his fist in the face" of an opposition delegate, accusing him of "trying to destroy the entire crop of the South."[6]

A month later at the 1905 Southern Interstate Cotton Convention in New Orleans, the delegates apparently remembered Smith for these colorful performances. The *Picayune* account of this convention

4. New Orleans *Daily Picayune*, January 25, 1905.
5. *Ibid.*, December 13, 1904.
6. *Ibid.*, December 14, 1904.

noted that when "Carolina Smith" took his place at the rostrum he "was greeted with laughing cheers" and "the Convention settled down for a good time":

Smith was introduced as "The Gatling Gun of South Carolina." The Convention laughed, but Mr. Smith swung suddenly round on them with an uplifted hand. "Gentlemen, if I am a Gatling Gun," he cried, "I am loaded for bear!" They cheered.

"Gentlemen," he continued, "it is not bull or bear but our fool selves that we have to blame for this condition of affairs. The fact of the matter is we haven't got the sense to take care of ourselves. Organization is God's law. It is the force of life, it resists disintegration. Let us come out of the woods! . . ."

"Speculation is a monstrous proposition. Let us combine and cut him out. Let field, mill, and factory get together and clasp hands; let us agree upon a price and sell direct to each other, and let the cotton exchanges go to the devil, where they belong!"

Such discourse, however, did not please all of the delegates, for when Smith finished his address a "motion was made to limit all speeches to two minutes." This motion was then amended "to cut them out all together, the plea being advanced that the Convention had convened to transact business and not to listen to hot air."[7]

With his image as a cotton spokesman established, in each of his Senate campaigns Smith asked the people to vote for him simply because he was a farmer. In fact, in these elections he did not always defend his previous votes on agricultural issues; it was enough that he was a farmer. Martha Bouknight has demonstrated how the senator employed the strategy of identification in all of his campaigns and concludes that in the 1908 campaign, for example, "So evangelical was Smith's crusade for cotton and so compelling his explanation of the rise in cotton prices, that almost every farmer in South Carolina saw in Ellison DuRant[8] a personal friend and benefactor." In 1932 Smith proclaimed, "Do you know, I'm the only farmer in the United States Senate. Most of them are pesky lawyers." And in 1938 he shrewdly attempted to disassociate himself from the decline in the price of cotton: "I'm the only farmer in the United States Senate and a

7. *Ibid.*, January 27, 1905.
8. This is not a pun on the senator's name but a spelling apparently used in his early years. Bouknight employs it consistently; S. K. Smith and Daniel Hollis prefer Durant.

cotton farmer at that. If I'm responsible for the low price of cotton, I'm a bigger man than I thought I was. Where is our administration?" In the words of historian Ernest Lander, "If the price of cotton went up just before election day, Senator Smith took credit for its rise. If cotton prices dropped, he blamed Wall Street speculators."[9]

Once he was elected, however, despite his allegiance to states' rights Smith supported many federal programs for agriculture. He endorsed federal assistance to establish grading standards for cotton, to improve seed, to control the boll weevil and the army worm, to train extension agents and put them in the field, and to regulate transportation rates. He favored the Muscle Shoals and Tennessee Valley Authority projects because he saw them helping farmers through the production of cheap power and of nitrates for fertilizer. He wanted federal regulation of the cotton exchanges, he voted for farm banks and loan funds, and he assisted in the enactment of the agricultural reform measures in Wilson's New Freedom program.[10]

However, Smith's support for these agricultural causes should not be considered evidence of great influence in federal agrarian policy. Even though he was viewed as cotton's spokesman in the Senate and though he eventually chaired the Committee on Agriculture and Forestry, Smith was not an effective advocate for farmers. Because he had few leadership skills, he personally did little to solve the farmers' problems. One historian, for example, summed up Smith's position in the 1920 farm crisis: "The senator clung to no doctrinaire positions of states rights or laissez faire economics. His response to the depression of 1920 was that of a demagogue politician motivated by practical politics."[11]

"Cotton Ed's" opportunity to be influential in the design of farm policy should have increased in 1932 when the election of Franklin Delano Roosevelt returned a Democratic administration to Washington, but that is not what happened. The senator had supported

9. Martha Nelle Bouknight, "The Senatorial Campaigns of Ellison DuRant ('Cotton Ed') Smith of South Carolina" (M.A. thesis, Florida State University, 1961), 34, 117, 130; Ernest McPherson Lander, Jr., *A History of South Carolina, 1865–1960* (Chapel Hill: University of North Carolina Press, 1960), 77–78.

10. Dewey Grantham, Jr., "Southern Congressional Leaders and the New Freedom, 1913–1917," *Journal of Southern History*, XIII (1947), 454–56.

11. Selden K. Smith, "Cotton Ed Smith's Response to Economic Adversity," *Proceedings of the South Carolina Historical Association*, 1971, 23.

the Roosevelt-Garner ticket and was doubtless looking forward to becoming an important part of the New Deal. Seniority had given "Cotton Ed" the chairmanship of the Agriculture and Forestry Committee, but it could not make him a presidential advisor. Roosevelt sought advice and assistance from other southern senators, especially majority leader Joseph T. Robinson from Arkansas, Pat Harrison of Mississippi, and South Carolina's junior senator James F. Byrnes. For advice on cotton the president and Secretary of Agriculture Henry Wallace turned to Senator John H. Bankhead of Alabama. Chairman Smith's probable frustration in the early Roosevelt years was portrayed in these words: "If Senator Smith expected a return to the halcyon days of the New Freedom he was grievously disappointed. . . . He reluctantly supported the AAA, but he felt that it was too complicated and required too much regimentation. The old agrarian wanted subsidies for the farmer but he opposed mandatory acreage controls. Although he became chairman of the senate agricultural committee, he had little influence in shaping the New Deal's farm program." [12]

In the 1940s Roosevelt remained president, Smith still chaired the Senate Committee on Agriculture and Forestry, and the South Carolinian continued to exert little positive influence in the establishment of national farm policy. In 1943 he was referred to as the "titular head, but not really leader, of the farm bloc" and as "the epitome of that twist of history which has left Democratic President Roosevelt with senior key congressmen out of tune with his policies." [13]

Thus, except for a relatively brief period of the Wilsonian era, during the South Carolina farmer's thirty-six years in the Senate he had little direct effect on the nation's farm policy. He presided over but did not lead the Senate Committee on Agriculture and Forestry. His lack of success was due to his inability to formulate detailed solutions for farm problems, Roosevelt's reliance on other senators and on Secretary of Agriculture Wallace for the promulgation of his programs, and Smith's own paucity of organizational and leadership talents. Still, in his campaigns he continued to claim that being a farmer

12. Daniel W. Hollis, "'Cotton Ed Smith'—Showman or Statesman?" *South Carolina Historical Magazine,* LXXI (October, 1970), 248.

13 Wesley McCune, *The Farm Bloc* (Garden City, N.Y.: Doubleday, Doran and Co., 1943), 36–37.

uniquely qualified him to represent his state in the Senate. He assumed credit for any agricultural good and blamed Wall Street and his ninety-five colleagues for farm depressions.

II

Tariffs for revenue only was a principle on which the South Carolinian was always consistent. Indeed, each of his campaign platforms included that plank. Because his opponents usually took an almost identical stand, however, this position never became much of an issue in South Carolina. Palmetto state politicians had studied their Calhoun.[14]

Smith looked at the tariff primarily in terms of its effect on cotton growers. Therefore, his major argument was that if farmers had to sell their cotton and grain abroad on an open market, they should not have to pay a tariff on necessary imports such as fertilizer, bagging, and ties. He also reasoned that Americans should not have to pay high prices for bread, shoes, or other necessities simply because domestic manufacturers of these items wanted to get rich from the protective tariff.

In the spring of 1909 discussion of the Payne-Aldrich tariff was a major item on the Senate agenda, and it was during this debate that the freshman senator from South Carolina gave his maiden speech. In this address he argued that it was "absolutely idle to talk about the protective tariff being a benefit to the cotton and grain growers of America," reasoning that tariffs on fertilizer and on jute for bagging and ties were an unjustifiable expense that the farmer had to pay. Furthermore, cotton growers could not pass this expense on when they sold their cotton because they could not determine the market price of their product. He also claimed that tariffs on textiles did not benefit laborers in the cotton mills but only the owners who reaped large dividends by keeping wages low while selling their textiles at an artificially high price, a price made possible by the protective tariff. Smith concluded this address by declaring, "It is vastly more important to the American people that they shall have bread at a reasonable

14. Selden Kennedy Smith, *Ellison Durant Smith: A Southern Progressive, 1909–1929* (Ann Arbor, Mich.: University Microfilms, 1970), 53. The South Carolina stance on protective tariff dated back to the tariff controversy of the 1820s.

price . . . than that a miserable system of high protection shall be guaranteed in spite of their hunger." [15]

A second tariff debate—in this instance precipitated by consideration of reciprocity agreements with Canada—was again an occasion for a major senatorial speech by "Cotton Ed." On March 2, 1911, the South Carolinian spoke in opposition to a proposed tariff board authorized to study the need for tariff revision. Smith felt that approval of this board would mean the Senate had abrogated its constitutional responsibilities. But the speech—which consumes more than three full pages of the *Congressional Record*—was not confined to a discussion of the board. Soon the whole tariff issue was its subject. The speaker argued that it made sense for the South and the West as producers of raw materials sold on the free market to oppose protectionism. He charged that manufacturers who wanted protection were not unselfishly seeking it for the benefit of their workers, since these same manufacturers also favored unrestricted immigration which would, he said, "fling wide the doors to the scum and offscouring of Europe and bring this element into our country in direct competition with our native-born American labor." He told his colleagues, "The matter with the American Senate is this . . . most of us are too far removed from the bleeding, suffering hearts of those that produce that out of which we roll in wealth."

In concluding this speech, Smith alluded to the Crucifixion of Jesus and told a long hypothetical story about a man and his wife who "drudge" all year on a farm that produces bountifully, only to receive for their crop low prices, "disappointment and pain." "In studying these conditions, seeing this tragedy on the oppressed," he said, "I pledged myself then—as I pledge the Senate now—that I shall strive to see to it that those who produce the wealth of this country shall enjoy the proceeds of the wealth they produce." [16]

Four months later Senator Smith again spoke at length in the Canadian reciprocity agreements debate. This time he concentrated on trying to establish the "justice" of his tariff position. "We are not here for the purpose of saying whether it [the agreement] will impoverish the North East States or enrich the South or impoverish the South or

15. *Congressional Record*, 61st Cong., 1st Sess., 2586–90.
16. *Ibid.*, 3rd Sess., 3853–57.

enrich the North East States. . . . We are here to argue what is right, what is just under the law." Protectionism at the expense of the South, he reasoned, was not "just," and any struggle against such practice was a "battle of righteousness." Smith's rambling discourse on this occasion included paragraphs on the founding of the American colonies and the Revolutionary War along with attacks on oil, tobacco, sugar, and steel trusts, which he called "a scandal and stench."[17]

The Underwood-Simmons Tariff Act debate in 1913 provided an opportunity for Smith to vent his feelings about the New York Cotton Exchange. An amendment to the tariff proposed a tax of one-tenth cent per pound on undelivered futures contracts in cotton with the hope that this would curb wild speculation on the exchange. Although "Cotton Ed" agreed with the goal, he thought the means would only depress the market price of cotton, and this he apparently felt would hurt the farmer more than speculation would. "For the last 60 years," he said, "we have not got anything like a fair price for cotton. I believe that the cotton growers of the South today would be independent and have good homes and educated children if it had not been for that miserable inequity [the Cotton Exchange] in New York."

In this same debate the South Carolina farmer employed a technique that probably had little influence on the Senate but that doubtless pleased his constituents. He sent copies of the proposals being debated to the home folks with a request for their opinions, and he then read into the *Record* a number of their replies. Two months earlier, when the debate had centered around the tariff on cotton bagging and ties, he had used the same technique without inserting the verbatim replies.[18] Although he may have sought the advice of his constituents earlier, these are the only times in his first term that he read their letters and wires to the Senate. Perhaps his action was influenced by the fact that he soon would be running for reelection.

In summary, on the tariff issue in the Senate, the South Carolinian's position was more consistent than it was on agriculture. On both topics, however, his speeches were rambling and emotional.

17. *Ibid.*, 62nd Cong., 1st Sess., 3121–25.
18. *Ibid.*, 63rd Cong., 1st Sess., 2515–16, 4019, 4021.

III

Just as Smith's stand on tariffs was an outgrowth of his perspective as a cotton farmer, so was his position on immigration. He believed that relaxed immigration restrictions were being used to import alien labor to expand cotton acreage in the Southwest, and he favored a reduction in cotton acreage. An increase in such acreage, made possible through lax immigration regulations, would, he felt, keep the South in servility.[19]

But "Cotton Ed" argued against immigration on yet another ground, charging that an increased flow of immigrants onto American soil would harm the nation's political, social, and economic systems. These newcomers, he said, were "poverty stricken," "politically incompetent," and not "worthy of receiving the wage that an intelligent American citizen doing like work should receive." It was "a crime against the boys and girls in this country" "to allow foreigners to come in and preempt our lands," acreage that these children might otherwise someday own. He asked who favored this cheap labor and answered that it was the "already overrich, overgreedy and overselfish" corporations.[20]

All of these arguments were in strict accord with voter attitudes in South Carolina. In fact, in the state's 1908 senatorial campaign, each of the candidates voiced a need for tighter controls on immigration. According to historian S. K. Smith, "The 'new' immigration had not touched the Palmetto State, but the fear persisted that American institutions were in danger of corruption."[21]

When Smith entered the Senate his first committee assignment was one that pleased him, the Immigration Committee. He became chairman of the committee in 1913, and in this capacity he coauthored the Immigration Act of 1917; however, S. K. Smith has argued that the Palmetto state senator deserved little credit for this accomplishment. "Although Smith coauthored the act," reasoned this critic, "there is no indication that the senator had any original ideas on the

19. Bouknight, "Senatorial Campaigns," 36.
20. *Congressional Record*, 62nd Cong., 2d Sess., 5018.
21. S. K. Smith, *A Southern Progressive*, 121.

subject. . . . As floor leader for the legislation, the senator displayed no special legislative skill or finesse."[22]

Thus, Senate debates on immigration demonstrate "Cotton Ed's" penchant for using emotional language and for making villains of unidentified corporations and special interests. As usual his speeches lacked both original ideas and clear organization.

IV

The farmer from South Carolina let his agricultural views determine his vote on tariff and immigration issues, and on these questions his basic positions coincided with the sentiment of his South Carolina constituents. Although there may have been an occasional local disagreement with him on the nature of national agricultural policy, any such disagreement would have been far less likely relative to his states' rights and white supremacy stands. For "Cotton Ed," states' rights and white supremacy were synonyms, and during his lifetime few white South Carolinians in or out of politics would have disagreed with him. "States' rights" was a shibboleth long popular in South Carolina. Therefore, for a politician who grew up during the Reconstruction period to pledge his allegiance to it was not surprising.

In an address to the annual reunion of the Confederate veterans of South Carolina, delivered in July, 1935, the senator, as he rambled along from Runnymede to FDR, made the following arguments regarding states' rights: the treaty of peace between Great Britain and the colonies was between his Britannic majesty and the thirteen colonies; the Constitution established a dual system of government; the Bill of Rights was added to protect the rights of individuals and of the several states; the war between the states did not modify in any respect the Bill of Rights, or the dual form of government; President Roosevelt endorsed the principle of delegation of powers; social and economic powers must remain in the hands of the states; the Wagner-Costigan antilynching bill was a usurpation of power. The speaker fought against it and would continue to fight to protect the constitutional rights of the state.[23]

22. *Ibid.,* 132.
23. "State Rights, an Address delivered on July 31, 1935, by United States Senator

Smith, however, rarely raised the issue of states' rights when questions of race were not involved. In fact, he supported many measures that had the effect of extending the powers of the central government and even the powers of international compacts. For example, in addition to his advocacy of federal programs for agriculture and for Muscle Shoals and the Tennessee Valley Authority, he also supported federal aid to roads and the federal reserve system. After World War I, he endorsed the League of Nations, World Court membership, and United States loans to Austria and Germany to enable them to buy agricultural products here. Furthermore, he voted for the National Recovery Act, Works Progress Administration, Rural Electrification Administration, and social security. But states' rights became an issue for him in Senate debates on abolition of the poll tax, antilynching proposals, wage-hour and fair employment practices legislation, and certain measures for aid to education. Each of these had a link to race and thus was viewed by Smith as federal intervention.

Political scientist V. O. Key described this connection in answering the question, "Southern Solidarity: How Much and on What Issues?" Through an analysis of roll call votes in the Senate, 1933–1945, he concluded:

By a process of elimination we have identified those few issues on which the South stands solidly against both Republicans and non-southern Democrats and those issues reflect a common determination to oppose external intervention in matters of race relations. The common element in the critical votes is objection to Federal intervention. The southern Senators voted against Federal investigators who would look into lynching, against Federal inspectors who would inquire whether Negroes were discriminated against in the expenditure of educational funds, and against Federal officials who would seek to prevent discrimination against Negroes in employment.[24]

During Senator Smith's day, South Carolina white audiences expected their politicians to be advocates of white supremacy. As W. J. Cash pointed out in his *The Mind of the South*, the Democratic party throughout the South was "the institutionalized incarnation of the

Ellison D. Smith of South Carolina, before the annual reunion of Confederate Veterans of South Carolina, in Drayton Hall, University of South Carolina, Columbia, S.C.," typescript in South Caroliniana Library, University of South Carolina.

24. V. O. Key, Jr., *Southern Politics in State and Nation* (New York: Alfred A. Knopf, 1949), 352.

will to White Supremacy." Indeed, as political scientist Allan Louis Larson, writing in 1964, put it, "There has never been a campaign in the Deep South where a major candidate has taken a stand against segregation."[25]

Having established the premise—that understanding any phase of the southern political process revolved around the position of blacks—Key investigated the southern states individually. In the chapter on South Carolina he declared: "South Carolina's preoccupation with the Negro stifles political conflict. Over offices there is conflict aplenty, but the race question muffles conflict over issues latent in the economy of South Carolina. Mill worker and plantation owner alike want to keep the Negro in his place. In part, issues are deliberately repressed, for, at least in the long run, concern with genuine issues would bring an end to the concensus by which the Negro is kept out of politics. . . . In part, the race issue provides in itself a tool for the diversion of attention from the issues."[26]

Prior to 1932 it was not candidate Smith but his opponents who tried to exploit the race issue in senatorial campaigns. Coleman Blease, "Cotton Ed's" major foe in 1914, portrayed the senator as a "dire threat to the maintenance of 'white supremacy,'" and the campaign of 1920 saw the widespread circulation of an anti-Smith pamphlet, which charged that Smith favored "Negro Social Equality" in the District of Columbia. Furthermore, Edgar A. Brown, the senator's opponent in the 1926 second primary, attacked Smith's support of the World Court on the grounds that the court had black judges, an allegation that backfired when Brown was unable to substantiate it. Still, the court issue gave Brown the support of the Ku Klux Klan, which burned a cross near Smith's home.[27]

In developing his white supremacy plank in the campaign of 1932, "Cotton Ed" said he had voted against women's suffrage be-

25. Wilbur J. Cash, *The Mind of the South* (New York: Vintage-Knopf, 1941), 132; Allan Louis Larson, *Southern Demagogues: A Study in Charismatic Leadership* (Ann Arbor, Mich.: University Microfilms, 1964), 168.

26. Key, *Southern Politics in State and Nation*, 5, 131.

27. Hollis, "Showman or Statesman?," 235–36, 246; Bouknight, "Senatorial Campaigns," 47–48; H. L. Scaife, *The Record of Senator Ellison D. Smith*, an eleven-page published letter to Senator Smith in the South Caroliniana Library, University of South Carolina. Bouknight, "Senatorial Campaigns," 74–79, quotes the Scaife document extensively.

cause it gave black women the right to vote. This was the campaign in which he allegedly described the rape of a white woman by a black man in language "so raw that it has never been printed" and which is "still referred to in the hills of South Carolina as The Speech." Authors Allen Michie and Frank Ryhlick, who offer no source for this story, seem to have been the first to mention it in print. Their account was cited by both Bouknight and Hollis. The latter, however, questioned the authenticity of the account, stating that one of his senior students, after searching South Carolina newspaper accounts of the 1932 campaign, could find only limited references to race, and "interviews and other sources" revealed no indication of "The Speech."[28]

"The Phillidefy Story" was "Cotton Ed's" 1938 campaign contribution to the race issue. He had twice walked out of the 1936 Democratic National Convention, assembled in Philadelphia—once when a black minister gave the invocation, and again when a black congressman was presented as a speaker. The New York *Times* reported that in the South Carolina primary Senator Smith

spent considerable time rehearsing the next speech to make it high-toned and learned. But here, according to his own story, is what happened: "Oh, I was going to make it highbrow if there ever was a highbrow speech. I got away up there in the clouds and began it. I started off on the Plains of Runnymede, got down through the Battle of King's Mountain and was headed for the Civil War via the cussed protective tariff, with a lot about the immortal John C. Calhoun.

"I felt somebody down in front was watching me. Of a sudden I looked down and there on the front seat was an old farmer with a torn black hat on his head and tobacco juice running down both sides of his mouth. I hesitated a moment and looked at him. When I did he growled:

"'Aw, hell, Ed, tell us about Phillidefy.' After that I came on down and never did get back up on that high plane. I know what the people of South Carolina are interested in. White supremacy, that time-honored tradition, can no more be blotted out of the hearts of South Carolinians than can the scars which Sherman's artillery left on the State House at Columbia. And, please God, I'm tellin' about it."

But in the same article of the *Times* is a remark made by Smith's opponent Olin Johnston on the stump at Greenwood: "Why, Ed Smith

28. Allen A. Michie and Frank Ryhlick, *Dixie Demagogues* (New York: Vanguard Press, 1939), 275; Bouknight, "Senatorial Campaigns," 115; Hollis, "Showman or Statesman?," 247.

voted for a bill that would permit a big buck Nigger to sit by your wife or sister on a railroad train." Thus, both senatorial contenders pandered to what they perceived as the racial prejudice of their audiences.[29]

Harry Ashmore, who heard Ed's account of "The Phillidefy Story" in the 1938 campaign, provided one interpretation of the occasion: "[T]here was a sort of innocence about it. The white men who gathered under the chinaberry trees to whoop and holler as Ed built his climaxes didn't really object to being prayed over by a Senegambian, and didn't believe Ed did either. And, most remarkable of all, nobody enjoyed the performance more than the Negroes who stood, white teeth gleaming in the dark, at the rear of the crowd. 'Hot damn,' they would chortle, 'Old Ed's pourin' it on tonight.'" Hollis, on the other hand, presented a different view, commenting that although he heard the story at three rallies, no blacks were present.[30]

Believing that "The Phillidefy Story" appealed to South Carolina whites, "Cotton Ed" revived the account for his 1944 race, but then it was not enough. The eighty-year-old farmer lost in the first primary to Olin Johnston.

So on the stump there was "The Phillidefy Story," and in the Senate there was "Cotton Ed's" defense of lynching. "The virtue of a woman is a thing which should not be displayed in court," he declared during a 1935 debate over an antilynching measure. "Nothing is more dear than the purity and sanctity of our womanhood and, so help us God, no one shall violate it without paying the just penalty which should be inflicted upon the beast who invades that sanctity." Later he added that he blamed not "the colored race" for these acts of bestiality but "carpetbaggers, scalawags and camp followers" who had led the blacks astray.[31]

"Cotton Ed's" nephew believed his uncle was guilty of hypocrisy in making many of these emotional appeals to race. Rice stated: "He mouthed 'white supremacy,' when he knew that white-trash was ruining the state. Tears came to his eyes as his voice throbbed of Southern womanhood and the sanctity of marriage, when he knew

29. New York *Times*, June 25, 26, 1936, August 23, 1938.
30. Ashmore, *Epitaph*, 102; Hollis, "Showman or Statesman?," 251.
31. *Congressional Record*, 74th Cong., 1st Sess., 5749, 6616.

all the time that the state was cursed with the sacrament of bigamy. He flattered and cajoled those whom he despised." [32]

V

Why was Ellison Smith so successful in his senatorial campaigns? His position on the issues—agriculture, tariff, immigration, states' rights and white supremacy—did not differ materially from those of his major opponents. All of them catered to the perceived prejudices of the South Carolina electorate. And although Smith employed all of the emotional techniques of the demagogue, his opponents performed similar acts for the South Carolina monkey circus. Nevertheless, "Cotton Ed" seems to have been more adept at namecalling than his opponents. Consider, for example, the following account of Smith's 1938 campaign: "From the beginning Ed referred to his leading opponent, former Governor Olin Johnston, as 'Brother Oleander' and to the secondary contender, State Senator Edgar Brown, as 'Satchel Edgar.' One inspired evening he arose after Brown, who had promised more and bigger WPA projects, to toss off of his capacious cuff this devastating line: 'Satchel Edgar says if you send him to Washington he will bring home the bacon. I have only one question: To whose home?'" Thereafter "Bacon Brown" was synonymous with "Satchel Edgar." [33]

This Lynchburg farmer's facility at stump speaking was not his only campaign asset. Sheer good luck, according to Hollis, was also an important element in the senator's repeated successes:

"Cotton Ed's" entry into the political arena came at a propitious time— part of the good political fortune that was to continue until 1944. . . . [In 1908] circumstances made it impossible for the strong man of Palmetto politics [Tillman] to intervene.

Once again [in 1914] Smith had benefitted from political good fortune. . . . [H]is contests with the iron man of Palmetto politics [Blease] came at a time when the political tides were running against him.

Smith's good luck had continued. . . . [He] was safely reelected before the terrible agricultural collapse of 1920–1921 took place.

On the eve of the [1938] election, Brown . . . withdrew from the race.

32. Rice, *Eighteenth Century*, 14.
33. Ashmore, *Epitaph*, 99–100.

Once again Smith's uncanny political luck continued. Had the supporters of the two New Deal candidates combined forces, "Cotton Ed" would have been in serious difficulty, but . . . after the two men exchanged insulting telegrams, much of Brown's support went to Smith.[34]

Showmanship and luck, however, were not enough to make him a leader in the Senate, where the seniority system gave him his only leadership roles. Perhaps his major handicap was his inability to organize effectively. His tendency to include irrelevancies reveals itself in all of his speeches—on the floor of the Senate, before the South Carolina electorate, or to a fraternal group. In discussing issues, Smith relied heavily on emotional appeals, which made his reasoning hard to follow. Furthermore, he labeled but did not analyze problems. He seemed unable to work wholeheartedly at anything or to comprehend principles of organization. His nephew Rice commented on his "uncentered nature": "He never had the courage completely to accept or reject anything. He was half pious and half profane, half good and half bad, half everything, half slave and half free. And yet, in spite of his uncentered nature . . . I loved him very much."[35] Fortunately for the senator, he did not need to organize his campaign speaking schedule, which was established by the state of South Carolina. In these campaigns, one sign of his lack of concern with organization was that he apparently never even tried to build a state political machine. The conclusion seems inescapable: Smith's lack of organizational ability was a major shortcoming, explaining in part his weakness as a Senate leader.

Among the serious students of "Cotton Ed's" career, praise for him is only lukewarm. Bouknight stated her intention thus: "It is hoped that this thesis will neither criticize nor praise but instead will rediscover a political antediluvian whom South Carolina once cherished and revered and on whom she bestowed a United States senatorial toga for thirty-six years." And she suggests that the eulogy in the Columbia *Record* correctly concluded that "Cotton Ed's tragedy was one of time." "He represented another epoch," declared the *Record*, "another way of life." S. K. Smith said of the Senator, "His own longevity and personal conduct have obscured his earlier years of

34. Hollis, "Showman or Statesman?," 239, 243–44, 254.
35. Rice, *Eighteenth Century*, 16.

constructive service to his state and nation." However, in an earlier chapter that writer stated: "'Cotton Ed's' role of partial leadership during the legislative struggles of almost two decades was the result of political happenstance rather than personal endeavor. . . . Although Smith was tenacious, he was neither fertile nor original in political imagination. . . . The South Carolinian lacked the mental discipline so necessary for sustained leadership; his support was vital, but the ideas came from others." Hollis concluded that "Ellison D. Smith was a senator of ordinary ability who remained in office too long." [36]

What, then, can be concluded about "Carolina Smith," the Gatling gun speaker whose name became "Cotton Ed"? His position on agriculture, tariff, immigration, states' rights, and white supremacy was essentially the same as that of his South Carolina political opponents. His Senate speeches were generally consistent with his campaign platform, but his discourse rambled from topic to topic whether he was in the Senate or on the stump. Indeed, his lack of all kinds of organizational skills may explain in part his ineffective leadership. His speech style was always dramatic and emotional, employing humor, anecdotes, plain-folks appeal, and namecalling. The same allusions appear repeatedly—the plains of Runnymede, the Civil War, and the Crucifixion of Jesus. In presenting issues he did not rely on logical analysis, but included emotional appeals to justice, virtue, and "Americanism," together with attacks on special interests, lawyers, the rich, and the black. Ellison Durant Smith, this South Carolina farmer who spent thirty-six years in the United States Senate, bears the marks of a demagogue.

36. Bouknight, "Senatorial Campaigns," iii, 195–96; S. K. Smith, *A Southern Progressive*, 283, 243–44; Hollis, "Showman or Statesman?," 256.

*Courtesy of Theodore G. Bilbo Collection,
University of Southern Mississippi*

Associated Press Photo, courtesy of Wide World Photo

Theodore G. Bilbo

Evangelist of Racial Purity

It is essential to the perpetuation of our Anglo-Saxon civilization that white supremacy in America be maintained. We have only to look about us and to read what time has recorded about race relations to realize that there are only two permanent solutions to the race problem—separation or amalgamation. If the first—a physical separation of the races—is not chosen, then the results will inevitably be the latter—amalgamation, a mixing of the blood and the destruction of both races.[1]

These words of Mississippi's Theodore "The Man" Bilbo reflect what ultimately became the central theme of his political career and the apparent *raison d'etre* of the last years of his life. During the period in which he acquired a nationwide reputation as the country's foremost racist demagogue, Bilbo's "dream" was the actual government-financed "repatriation" of all American blacks to Liberia. He twice introduced a bill in the Senate to provide free transportation and resettlement which he hoped would make migration to Africa so attractive that large numbers of blacks would leave the United States. But even his southern senatorial colleagues, themselves diehard segregationists, refused to take the Mississippian's "back-to-Africa" ideas seriously. He therefore contented himself with participation in southern filibusters which successfully killed federal civil rights legislation and preserved racial segregation in the South—at least for the time being.

1. *Congressional Record*, 75th Cong., 3rd Sess., 881; Address to the Mississippi Legislature, March 22, 1944, *ibid.*, 78th Cong., 2nd Sess., A1798.

Like George Wallace in his symbolic last stand in the "schoolhouse door" at the University of Alabama a generation later, Bilbo and other prominent southerners in Congress at the time, such as Georgia's Richard Russell, Tom Conally of Texas, and Allen J. Ellender of Louisiana, assumed a defensive "fight-to-the-last-ditch" bunker mentality. Theirs was a holding action against the inevitable triumph of the civil rights movement. All—including Bilbo—must have suspected that their cause was doomed in the end. Of this group, only Bilbo was willing to speak on the subject of race with apparent abandon and with what many colleagues regarded as recklessness. In his last years he became an embarrassment to the South and to his home state because of the notoriety given his racist comments by the nation's press. But the resentment of Mississippi's voters toward the ever-increasing crescendo of attacks on Bilbo by "outsiders" and by the "northern press" outweighed their embarrassment. They returned him to the Senate in 1947 to begin his third term—a term he never served. A group of senators led by Robert A. Taft of Ohio prevented his taking the oath of office and being seated, and two days later, on January 5, 1947, "The Man" left Washington for the last time to enter a hospital in New Orleans for cancer surgery. The cancer continued to spread and, following several operations, Theodore Gilmore Bilbo died on August 21, 1947, at the age of sixty-eight.[2]

How had this diminutive country lawyer from Juniper Grove, Mississippi, become one of America's most notorious demagogues? This essay will seek to answer that question, first through an examination of Bilbo's early life, his years in state politics, and his involvement during his senatorial career with three major "civil rights" debates over the Wagner-Van Nuys antilynching bill, abolition of the poll tax, and the Fair Employment Practices Commission. Second, Bilbo's two principal rhetorical themes, their supporting sources, and the senator's relations with his Mississippi constituents and with the urban and northern press will be explored. A concluding section will

2. Bilbo was nicknamed "The Man" because he habitually referred to himself in the third person. The best biography of him is A. Wigfall Green, *The Man Bilbo* (Baton Rouge: Louisiana State University Press, 1963). The best source for his last days is Richard C. Ethridge, "The Fall of the Man: The United States Senate's Probe of Theodore G. Bilbo in December 1946, and Its Aftermath," *Journal of Mississippi History*, XXXVIII (August, 1976), 241–62.

offer an assessment of Bilbo as an orator based on his use of available rhetorical choices.

I

Life began for Theodore Bilbo in 1877 as the youngest of the eight children of James Oliver and Beddy Wallace Bilbo. Bilbo's father was a small landowner and part-time sawmill operator. The future senator's earliest education preceded the establishment of schools in his county, and he was thus probably educated by his parents and by itinerant ministers through his thirteenth year. At age fourteen he entered the third grade at Poplarville School. Because of poor transportation between his home in Juniper Grove and the school six miles away, young Bilbo became a boarding student. He showed an early interest in public speaking by participating successfully in the school's debate program and by becoming active in church affairs. In 1896 he was "authorized" or licensed by the Baptist church to preach, which he continued to do occasionally in Juniper Grove, even in his later years.

Within a period of four years young Bilbo completed nine grades in the Poplarville School, an accomplishment of which he frequently boasted in later years. During the years 1897–1900 he attended Peabody College in Nashville, Tennessee, returning to Mississippi in 1900 to teach Latin and mathematics at several schools in the southern part of the state.

Then in 1903 Bilbo decided to enter politics. He campaigned for the post of clerk of Pearl River County, but lost the election by 56 votes to W. W. Mitchell, the Baptist minister who had performed Bilbo's second marriage ceremony and with whom he had boarded during part of his four years in Poplarville School.[3] Following this defeat, Bilbo returned to teaching until 1905, when he entered the Vanderbilt School of Law. Although he failed to receive a law degree, he was admitted to the Tennessee bar in 1906 and to the Mississippi bar the following year. Then, in 1907 at the age of thirty the young country lawyer again decided to pursue a career in politics.[4]

3. Bilbo's first marriage in 1898 had ended with his wife's death in 1900. Green, *The Man Bilbo*, 16.
4. An excellent source of information on Bilbo's political career in state politics is

Bilbo's career in the state politics of Mississippi spanned the twenty-seven-year period from 1907–1934. He was senator in the state legislature from 1907–1911; lieutenant governor, 1912–1916; and governor, 1916–1920 and 1928–1932, the first person ever to be elected a second time to that office.

The key to Bilbo's success in state politics was his ability to exploit sensational political events. For example, he achieved instant state-wide notoriety in a bribe-taking scandal that shook the state legislature in 1910. A member of the Mississippi senate at the time, Bilbo testified before a grand jury that he had accepted a bribe to change his vote in the legislature's election to fill a vacancy in the United States Senate. Bilbo claimed, however, that he had accepted the bribe in order to expose the corruption of the Bourbon politicians who were attempting to "buy" the seat in the Senate. This confession caused the state senate to bring a bill of impeachment against Bilbo, which failed by only one vote. That body then passed a resolution condemning Bilbo's acceptance of the bribe, declaring him "unfit to sit with honest, upright men in a legislative assembly," and asking him to resign. Bilbo defiantly ignored this request.[5]

This event set Bilbo off on a statewide stump-speaking campaign during which he made 125 speeches. He was thus enabled to create a popular conception of himself as protector of the "little people" against the Bourbon "interests" that had traditionally ruled the state. He easily won the race for lieutenant governor in 1911 and began to build statewide support for a gubernatorial campaign in 1915. He was again fortuitously provided with a sensational political event when, on December 1, 1914, both he and state senator G. A. Hobbs were indicted on a bribery charge in connection with a proposed bill to create a new county in the Delta. Both men were subsequently acquitted, and Bilbo used the publicity of the incident to initiate his campaign.

By now Bilbo's popularity in Mississippi was so great that he was easily elected governor with a clear majority in the first primary, out-

Larry T. Balsamo, "The Political Career of Theodore G. Bilbo: 1877–1932" (Ph.D. dissertation, University of Missouri, 1967). Also see Thurston Ermon Doler, "Theodore G. Bilbo's Rhetoric of Racial Relations" (Ph.D. dissertation, University of Oregon, 1968).
5. Green, *The Man Bilbo*, 34.

polling the combined votes of his four opponents. During his term as governor, 1916–1920, Bilbo, with the help of a cooperative state legislature, was able to carry out his campaign promises of popular reform. His administration built a charity hospital and the state's first tuberculosis sanitarium; stopped the practice of public hangings; restored the state capitol building; increased the pensions of Confederate soldiers; established lime-crushing plants in the state; began a successful program requiring the dipping of all cattle in the state to eradicate Texas fever; created a state tax commission which, by the end of the term, had received five million dollars for construction and two million dollars in building materials from the federal government; and increased appropriations for education.[6]

In 1920, at the end of his term as governor, Bilbo returned to his farm and the private practice of law. In 1923 he moved to Jackson and established his own weekly newspaper, the *Mississippi Free Lance*, which he sent to every registered voter in the state who would accept it.

He was elected to a second term as governor in 1927 on a platform of sweeping reforms, but this time the state legislature refused to enact any of his campaign proposals. Moreover, during his second gubernatorial term Bilbo was responsible for what became known as "the rape of education in Mississippi." Secret records were kept at all state institutions of higher learning on those faculty members who had opposed Bilbo. Students burned the governor in effigy when he dismissed forty-five faculty members in a purge that cost the University of Mississippi and the four state colleges their accreditation.

Bilbo left office in 1932 with Mississippi deeply in debt, its educational establishment in disgrace, and with a second-term record barren of the popular reforms that had characterized his first administration. Fred Sullens, editor and proprietor of the Jackson *Daily News* and an avowed enemy of Bilbo, gleefully conducted a mock epitaph contest to celebrate "The Man's" political death. The winning entry:

Here lies the body with Bilbo's name
Of shame he had no terrors.

6. Doler, "Bilbo's Rhetoric of Racial Relations," 65–66; Green, *The Man Bilbo*, 57–66.

He was born a "ham" and died the same;
No hits; no runs; many errors.

The "epitaph" seemed prophetic of the next two years. Alone,
and unable to attract clients for a law practice in Jackson, Bilbo appealed for help to Mississippi's United States Senator Pat Harrison,
who used his influence to obtain a six thousand dollar per year position for the former governor. The job consisted of clipping and past-
ing news references for the Agricultural Adjustment Administration,
a position Bilbo referred to as "Pastemaster General." But during this
period of eclipse that seemed at the time to be political oblivion, "The
Man" vowed to return to Mississippi in 1934 to conduct a campaign
for a seat in the United States Senate.[7]

He kept his vow and entered the 1934 senatorial race against the
lackluster and ineffectual second-term incumbent, Hubert D. Stephens. During the campaign, Bilbo "whipped through Mississippi
like a tornado, speaking six or eight times a day, running up nearly a
thousand speeches, covering thirty thousand miles, and gaining ten
pounds." He portrayed his opponent as an enemy of the people and
friend of the wealthy. He presented himself as "one of the people"
who knew their problems, sorrows, privations, hopes, and ambi-
tions. He declared himself "Mississippi's foremost and greatest humanitarian," who would work for an orderly redistribution of the
nation's wealth.[8] His campaign appearances had all the theatrical ex-
hibitionism of an evangelistic, tent revival meeting:

Hands clasped as if to restrain emotion, he steps before his audience.
Sonorously, with mock solemnity, he announces that it is not too late for
those who have sinned to return to the church; the doors are open to those
voters who have strayed. In a moment he has the crowd at ease, laughing at
his biblical paraphrases, impressed by his verbatim quotations, pleasantly
shocked by his minor profanities.
As his listeners are carried along by his emotional outpourings he increases his tempo. His voice takes on a quiver, his hands a theatrical palsy as
he raises them slowly over his head. Then extravagant invective begins. He
tries to link his opponents with the power and oil interests, he booms out a
crackling broadside at Wall Street, and then swiftly, solicitously, he speaks of

7. Green, *The Man Bilbo*, 67–87.
8. *Ibid.*, 91; Doler, "Bilbo's Rhetoric of Racial Relations," 88.

the veterans, the farmers, the masses and all the other victims of corporate interests.

Coatless men leap into the aisles and shout approval. Others join in the uproar. "Hit it, Bilbo!" "Ahmen!" "Hallelujah!" they shout. For two hours they are borne along, laughing, shouting applauding. He leaves them in a happy glow. They know that Bilbo will take care of them in Washington.[9]

Bilbo's 1934 Senate campaign revealed his evangelical style to a much greater degree than would his more formal pronouncements later printed in the *Congressional Record*. The full measure of his down-home, King Jamesian choice of words may be seen in the following passage from one of his more inspired moments of rhetorical abandon during this first campaign for election to the Senate:

Friends, fellow citizens, brothers and sisters—hallelujah. My opponent— yea, this opponent of mine who has the dastardly, dewlapped, brazen, sneering, insulting and sinful effrontery to ask you for your votes without telling you the people of Mississippi what he is a-going to do with them if he gets them—this opponent of mine says he don't need a platform. . . . He asks, my dear brethren and sisters, that you vote for him because he is standing by the President. . . . I shall be the servant and Senator of all the people. . . . The appeal and petition of the humblest citizen, yea, whether he comes from the black prairie lands of the east or the alluvial lands of the fertile delta; . . . yea, he will be heard by my heart and my feet shall be swift . . . your Senator whose thoughts will not wander from the humble, God-fearing cabins of Vinegar Bend . . . your champion who will not lay his head upon his pillow at night before he has asked his Maker for more strength to do more for you on the morrow. . . . Brethren and sisters, I pledge.[10]

Bilbo's opponent, although lacking a clear majority, narrowly won the first primary in the 1934 senatorial race. But in the second primary, the colorless incumbent was probably defeated because of Bilbo's superior and ubiquitous crowd-pleasing showmanship.

On his arrival in the capital, the newly elected senator boasted that in Washington he would "out huey Huey Long and raise more hell than Roosevelt." Most observers, however, agreed that Bilbo's first year in the Senate was "less conspicuous than an unlisted phone number."[11]

9. New York *Times*, September 20, 1934.
10. V. O. Key, Jr., *Southern Politics in State and Nation* (New York: Alfred A. Knopf, 1949), 242–43.
11. Doler, "Bilbo's Rhetoric of Racial Relations," 90.

During his two terms in the Senate Bilbo introduced and sponsored legislation that was primarily local or regional in scope, such as flood control measures for the Mississippi River, construction of a bridge over the Pearl River, appropriations for extermination of the bollworm, and aid for the tenant farmer.[12] In matters of national significance, "The Man's" most important contribution was his introduction and sponsorship of legislation that established four regional research laboratories in Philadelphia, Peoria, New Orleans, and San Francisco to discover uses for the products of these areas of the country. In recognition of his role in this project, Bilbo was invited to give the dedicatory address at the laboratory in New Orleans.[13] The later development of penicillin at the Peoria laboratory provided the Mississippian with one of his proudest moments.

Throughout his career in the Senate, Bilbo was generally a Democratic party loyalist and faithful supporter of Roosevelt and his New Deal policies. In the late 1930s, however, division began to develop among congressional Democrats over the race issue. Party leaders realized that they must win and retain the increasingly important black vote in the northern states or risk losing Democratic control of the Congress and presidency. This realization led to the introduction in Congress of "civil rights" legislation designed to improve the lot of the black man and to protect his welfare. Southern Democrats, all doggedly determined to preserve segregation as the basic "Way of Life" in their states, were forced into a defensive posture against their northern colleagues.

An early instance of this conflict developed in 1938 during the extended debates and ultimate southern filibuster on the Act to Guarantee Equal Protection of the Laws—commonly known as the Wagner-Van Nuys antilynching bill. This bill proposed to protect accused persons from injury or death at the hands of a mob, not by punishing the participants in the mob, but by penalizing law enforcement officers in the event of a lynching and by compensating the victim or his family. Further, the bill indirectly focused on southern blacks as victims by eliminating from its purview the lynching victims of "labor

12. Green, *The Man Bilbo*, 94.
13. A reprint of Bilbo's address is found in the *Congressional Record*, 76th Cong., 3rd Sess., A122.

disputes" and "gangsters or racketeers." Southerners in the Senate interpreted the bill as an attack on the South and immediately raised the issue of the bill's constitutionality. The federal government, they argued, had no business meddling in the affairs of the states. All states already had antilynching laws on their books, and they were, the southerners argued, fully capable of enforcing their own laws without federal interference. Ultimately the antilynching bill was defeated because of the Senate's rejection of cloture to end the southern filibuster in which Bilbo played a substantial role.[14]

A second controversy developed among Senate Democrats over the series of bills introduced between 1942 and 1944 designed to repeal the payment of a poll tax as a prerequisite for voting in most southern states. Debates on these bills focused on their constitutionality, the relevant provisions of the Constitution being:

Article I. Section 2. phrase b: The Electors in each State shall have the Qualifications requisite for the Electors of the most numerous Branch of the State Legislature.
Section 4. The Times, Places, and Manner of holding Elections for Senators and Representatives, shall be prescribed in each State by the Legislature thereof; but the Congress may at any time by Law make or alter such Regulations, except as the Places of choosing Senators.
Article IV. Section 4. The United States shall guarantee to every State in this Union a Republican form of Government.[15]

Those who supported the legislation to abolish the poll tax argued that although the poll tax met the letter of the law, its ultimate effect was the disfranchisement of most blacks and many poor whites —thus depriving these groups of a "Republican Form of Government" as prescribed by the Constitution. Southern and strict-constructionist opponents of the legislation replied that the management of elections was constitutionally delegated to the states and that both the poll tax and the literacy qualifications of some states had been repeatedly upheld by the Supreme Court. During these debates, Bilbo expressed his opposition to the poll tax in his own state but opposed

14. *Ibid.*, 75th Cong., 3rd Sess., 872–96, contains a lengthy Bilbo speech on the subject.
15. Quoting these constitutional provisions as the cornerstone of his arguments, Bilbo inserted a lengthy discussion of Supreme Court decisions favoring his position into the *Congressional Record*, 78th Cong., 2nd Sess., 4416–25.

the legislation as federal interference with state affairs. He recommended repeal of the poll tax by Mississippi itself—probably because its elimination would permit a greater number of his poor white constituents to vote. Blacks could still be denied voting rights in Mississippi on the basis of literacy qualifications, which were always strictly applied for black applicants, whereas whites were given simple constitutional passages to interpret. Bilbo was forced to argue this point strenuously in his 1946 campaign for reelection when opponents cited his earlier advocacy of poll tax repeal in his home state as an effort to make it possible for blacks to vote. The Senate finally dropped the poll tax issue, however, following another lengthy southern filibuster and an unsuccessful attempt to vote cloture.[16]

The third major controversy that divided Democrats during Bilbo's tenure in the Senate was the debate over the establishment of a permanent Fair Employment Practices Commission (FEPC). By executive order under special wartime powers, FDR had in 1941 created the first such organization and had strengthened it in 1943 by a second executive order. Roosevelt had acted in response to blacks who charged that they were not being employed in wartime industries in proportion to their percentage of the nation's population. The purpose of the FEPC was to receive complaints of job discrimination based on race, creed, color, or national origin and to adjudicate such complaints. The FEPC set up regional offices throughout the United States, but it abruptly ceased operations at the end of the war with the termination of budget and wartime executive powers. Probably in pursuit of black votes, many members of Congress favored the creation of a permanent FEPC, and various bills with this intent were introduced in the Congress between 1943 and 1945. These bills provoked another confrontation among Democrats. Southern Democrats argued that such legislation would disrupt established patterns of race relations in the South, that it would violate states' rights by imposing federal authority in areas not indicated in the Constitution, and that it would violate the individual's freedom to manage his affairs as he wished without federal government supervision.

The central issue was again constitutionality. FEPC proponents

16. *Ibid.*, 4470.

argued that such legislation would be constitutional because the Supreme Court had always upheld the principle of no discrimination on the basis of race, color, creed, religion, or ancestry. Opponents raised their usual cry to maintain the separation of state and federal powers: the dual system of government that had been created by the Constitution and permitted state and local jurisdictions to manage all affairs not explicitly delegated to the federal government. Like the antilynching and anti-poll tax bills, the proposed FEPC legislation was ultimately killed by southern filibuster and the unwillingness of enough senators to invoke cloture.

II

What was Bilbo's oratorical role in these three major controversies of his time? His rhetoric reveals the recurrence of two predominant themes representing his basic objectives. His first objective was preservation of states' rights against encroachments of the federal government. He saw states' rights, in turn, as the major means for attainment of his second objective—maintenance of white racial purity in the United States.

In pursuit of the first of these objectives, Bilbo often observed that if the Congress were to permit the federal government to interfere with such affairs of the states as punishment for lynching, poll tax, or employment, this would be the "entering wedge" by which the federal government would ultimately control *all* matters formerly reserved to the states—including race relations.[17] The southerners were supported in their efforts during Bilbo's two Senate terms by such influential northern Republican strict constructionists as William E. Borah and Robert A. Taft.

Moreover, Bilbo himself was a knowledgeable student of the federal Constitution and its interpretations. In his speech of January 21, 1938, opposing the antilynching bill, he ably quoted at some length a contemporary constitutional law scholar of Cornell University, David O. Walter, who had published a history of the many previous attempts at federal antilynching legislation. Such attempts had begun

17. See, for example, Bilbo's address to the Mississippi Legislature, March 22, 1944, *ibid.*, A1797.

in 1891 in an effort to protect aliens living in the United States. Other similar bills designed specifically for the protection of blacks from lynching had begun as early as 1892. All had died in the Senate, victims of the constitutional argument that they were an invasion of powers reserved to the states and, in some cases, because of southern filibusters. Bilbo also quoted Supreme Court Justice Hugo Black's opposition to the Wagner-Costigan antilynching bill of 1935 when Black had been a U.S. senator.[18]

In his attacks on the anti-poll tax legislation before the Senate in the years 1942–1944, Bilbo again demonstrated his familiarity with the intricacies of the federal Constitution. In an address before the Mississippi Legislature on March 22, 1944, "The Man" presented one of his most cogent attacks on the constitutionality of the proposal. He directly quoted section 2, article 1 and the Seventeenth Amendment of the federal Constitution and argued that "nothing is more clearly shown by the debates in the Constitutional Convention than the intention of the founding fathers that each State should have the power to fix the qualifications of the electors within its borders. The power to fix such qualifications was one which the States zealously guarded." He noted further that "nowhere in the Constitution is Congress given the power to strike down or add to the qualifications for electors as set up by the sovereign States nor is the Congress given the power to define the qualifications or prerequisites for electors. The decisions of the United States Supreme Court are unanimous in holding that the poll tax laws are constitutional and nondiscriminatory." On May 12, 1944, Bilbo, on the floor of the Senate, inserted into the *Congressional Record* as part of his remarks of the day a lengthy and carefully prepared statement that reiterated relevant sections of the federal constitution, elaborated on the intentions of the founding fathers by quoting several of them directly, and reviewed a number of crucial Supreme Court decisions that had upheld the constitutionality of the poll tax.[19]

In the FEPC controversy, neither side could cite specific passages of the Constitution to support their arguments. Bilbo joined his southern colleagues in what had by now become their customary, even ritualistic states' rights arguments based on the Constitution's

18. *Ibid.*, 75th Cong., 3rd Sess., 877–81.
19. *Ibid.*, 78th Cong., 2nd Sess., A1797, 4416–25.

traditional separation of powers, but he focused most heavily on the racial purity theme, sometimes mixing both themes: "We are fighting for principles, for our constituencies, for the sovereignty of our States, and the integrity of the blood of the Caucasian race." [20]

Thus, in his development of the states' rights arguments based upon a strict interpretation of the federal Constitution, an interpretation the U.S. Supreme Court largely continued to uphold during Bilbo's Senate tenure, the Mississippian showed himself to be a highly competent and knowledgeable spokesman for the preservation of "our dual system of constitutional government," as he frequently phrased it.

But the preservation of constitutional government was, of course, not Bilbo's most urgent cause. With the fanaticism not of a cynic but of a "true believer," "The Man" single-mindedly pursued until the end of his days the second of the two objectives discussed here—his avowed life's goal of preserving what he saw as the purity of the Caucasian race in the United States.

Bilbo's views on race were reducible to two fundamental propositions, the first of which was his belief in the superiority of the Caucasian race and its accomplishments.

The white race, or Caucasian, has three well-marked divisions—Nordic, Alpine, and Mediterranean. These three races of Europe constitute what is properly called the Caucasian or European race. The three, led by the Nordic, especially in modern times, have contributed to civilization all its higher achievements. The Nordics might be termed the aristocrats of the human race. The Teuton, which is a branch of the Nordic race, has for 2,000 years played the chief role in history and in civilization, and it is for the preservation of this race, its ideals, its culture, its institutions, its civilization, I am making this plea today. [21]

As a corollary of his belief in Caucasian superiority, Bilbo's second fundamental proposition was that racial amalgamation would destroy the civilization that the white man had built. He often included in his oratory lengthy historical examples of the downfall of white civilizations which he attributed to racial mixing. He epitomized this view in one summary statement in a speech against the antilynching

20. *Ibid.*, 79th Cong., 2nd Sess., 1050.
21. *Ibid.*, 75th Cong., 3rd Sess., 885.

bill in 1938: "The amalgamation of the white with the colored races has destroyed the civilization of the Caucasian race not only in Egypt and India but in Abyssinia, Nigeria, Uganda, Mashonaland, Babylonia, Phoenicia, Persia, Cambodia, Ceylon, Java, New Zealand, Polynesia, northern China, Korea, Portugal, Spain, Italy, Greece, the Balkans, Mexico, Yucatan, Peru, and Haiti; and today the same curse of amalgamation between the white and colored races is threatening the destruction of the civilizations in practically all of the Latin Americas and many of the colonial white possessions in Africa."

Later in the same address he illustrated the intensity of his belief in this subject with the exclamation that "one drop of Negro blood placed in the veins of the purest Caucasian destroys the inventive genius of his mind and strikes palsied his creative faculty." [22] He believed that the breakdown of racial segregation in the United States, and particularly in the South, would result in a tragic "mongrelization" which would destroy both races and cause a similar decline in the culture of this country. The extent of his fanaticism was such that he ultimately wrote that he would prefer to see the white race destroyed by the atomic bomb rather than slowly exterminated by amalgamation with blacks. [23]

Based on the twin postulates that the superior white race had provided the world with its highest accomplishments and that history had shown a decline in all Caucasian civilizations which had tolerated racial amalgamation, Bilbo set out on a crusade during his last years to effect a solution that would preserve Caucasian purity in the United States. There were three possible ways of accomplishing this salvation, he argued: "First, draw the color line between the white man and the black man while we live together, denying to the colored man social and political equality, and under no conditions permitting intermarriage or miscegenation or amalgamation of the two races at any time or in any place. . . . The second thing is segregation of the Negro race in some chosen territory within the United States or on

22. *Ibid.*, 889, 894.
23. Theodore G. Bilbo, *Take Your Choice: Separation or Mongrelization* (Poplarville, Miss.: Dream House Publishing, 1947), ii. This book provides the best and most concise compendium of Bilbo's views on racial matters.

some islands of the sea, where none but the black man shall live; and, third, repatriation or the deportation of the entire Negro race to its native heath in Africa." [24]

For the rest of his life, Bilbo pursued the third of these possibilities with the single-minded doggedness of a dedicated zealot. He twice introduced a bill in the Senate to provide for resettlement of American blacks in West Africa. The necessary lands for implementation of his "Greater Liberia Act" would come from the African colonial holdings of England and France, which could, he reasoned, be credited for their unpaid World War I debts to the United States. The United States would finance remaining land purchases as well as transportation and settlement expenses. The territory would at first be managed by a corporation in which the United States would own 51 percent of the stock; but ultimately the new homelands could either be annexed by Liberia or could become independent. Realizing that massive deportation of American citizens was out of the question, "The Man" hoped to make his repatriation plan attractive enough that blacks would want to migrate to the new territory. Bilbo claimed to have millions of signatures of American blacks who supported his views and wanted to migrate back to Africa. [25] He never relinquished this far-fetched and costly scheme, even during and after World War II, when such financial commitments on the part of the U.S. government were even more inconceivable than when he had first proposed the idea.

Although Bilbo continued to advocate black repatriation until his death, by 1944 he apparently realized that lack of support among his colleagues in the Congress would force him to settle for the first of his recommended solutions to the problem—drawing the color line. In his widely circulated address before the Mississippi Legislature on March 22, 1944, he admonished: "The time has come when we must draw the color line so tight that no man, whether he be sinner, saint, steward, elder, deacon, pastor, priest, or bishop, shall be permitted in

24. *Congressional Record*, 75th Cong., 3rd Sess., 882.
25. *Ibid.*, 76th Cong., 1st Sess., 4671–77. Bilbo claimed to have one million such names on file in 1938 and three and one-half million by 1944. See *ibid.*, 75th Cong., 3rd Sess., 883, and 78th Cong., 2nd Sess., A1798.

the name of the church or the Bible to expound theories of God's teachings that would certainly lead to sin, miscegenation, intermarriage, or social equality in any form between the Negro and the white man."

Bilbo was aiming his remark specifically at northern ministers who were agitating for racial integration on the basis of the biblical brotherhood of man. "The Man" clearly intended the drawing of the color line to go beyond the province of the ministry, however. He elaborated: "We people of the south must draw the color line tighter and tighter, and any white man or woman who dares to cross that color line should be promptly and forever ostracized. No compromise on this great question should be tolerated, no matter who the guilty parties are, whether in the church, in public office, or in the private walks of life."

The Mississippian then demonstrated the extent to which he was willing to go in drawing the color line by citing the example of a speech teacher at Delta State Teachers College in Cleveland, Mississippi, who, he claimed, had made a "vicious attack on southern ideals and customs" by telling her students that the ability of blacks was equal to that of whites and that, if blacks were given the same opportunities, their accomplishments would be equal. He further accused her of saying that marriage to a "high class Negro" would be preferable to marriage to "a man of poor white trash." The enraged senator concluded the illustration with the exclamation: "God help us if we do not prohibit such teachings in every white school as well as every Negro school in Mississippi."[26]

Bilbo's admonition to draw the color line reached its peak, however, during his reelection campaign for the Democratic primary in 1946. He attracted nationwide notoriety through comments such as those chronicled by one on-the-scene observer: "'Lots of good religious folk say that Christians should treat the nigger as a brother.' The voice becomes menacing. 'I don't mind having the nigger for my brother in Christ, but I'm damned if I want him for a son-in-law. . . . I'm the best friend the nigger's got in the state of Mississippi.' He grins. 'I'm trying to do something for 'em. I want to send 'em back to

26. *Ibid.*, 78th Cong., 2nd Sess., A1801.

Africa where they belong. . . . You know and I know what's the best way to keep the nigger from voting. You do it the night before election.'" [27]

Any attempt to portray the development of the racial purity theme in Bilbo's rhetoric would be incomplete without an examination of the materials he used to develop and elaborate upon his ideas. Supporting sources for Bilbo's beliefs on Caucasian racial superiority and the perils of racial amalgamation were generally lacking in credibility and, for the most part, had been published twenty to forty years before Bilbo began to use them as a part of his repatriation ideas. Only two of his frequently quoted sources on race as an important historical determinant possessed any academic or scholarly qualifications at all, and their works were considerably dated by the late 1930s. [28]

"The Man" was more fortunate, however, in seeking credible sources in support of his repatriation scheme. Thomas Jefferson had said that "nothing is more certainly written in the book of fate than that these people are to be free; nor is it less certain that the two races, equally free, cannot live in the same government." Alexis de Tocqueville had written: "There are two alternatives for the future: The Negroes and the whites must either wholly part or wholly mingle." But Bilbo's favorite, and probably most credible source in support of physical separation of the races was none other than the Great Emancipator himself. Bilbo must have relished quoting Abraham Lincoln's statement that "there is a physical difference between the white and the black races, which I believe will forever forbid the two races living together on terms of social and political equality." Lincoln had personally favored recolonization of American blacks in Africa and had even proposed a constitutional amendment to provide for such resettlement in his second annual message to Congress submitted in December, 1862. Bilbo was also fond of quoting Lincoln's well-known statement from the Lincoln-Douglas debates that blacks were inherently inferior to whites and that he was not in favor of blacks becoming

27. Hodding Carter, "'The Man' from Mississippi—Bilbo," New York *Times,* June 30, 1946.
28. Doler, "Bilbo's Rhetoric of Racial Relations," 141–43.

jurors, of their holding political office, or of their intermarrying with whites.[29]

Not to be overlooked in this examination of Bilbo's sources is the person who may have served as his role model and inspiration for his racial ideas: his earliest mentor, Mississippian James K. Vardaman. In his four-hour Senate speech that accompanied his first introduction of the Greater Liberia Act, Bilbo quoted Vardaman extensively, noting that "no man of his time devoted more thought and more study to this great problem."[30] Vardaman had also favored recolonization of American blacks in Africa and had used the words of both Jefferson and Lincoln in support of such a proposal. Bilbo's early political association with and admiration for Vardaman could have been a decisive factor in "The Man's" more detailed development of the ideas and proposals of his predecessor.

Venerated as some of Bilbo's sources were, they all had lived in a different world from that of America approaching the mid-twentieth century. For the country as a whole, Bilbo's ideas, like the sources that supported them, were hopelessly out of date and would soon become relics of interest only to historians and others who habitate the musty corridors of libraries.

But Mississippi and the other states that had comprised the Old Confederacy were not like the country as a whole. Bilbo knew his constituents; his oratory was intended for them. Who were they? What were they like? And why did they support and continue to re-elect as their senior U.S. senator a man who, with obvious relish, aroused the animosity of most non-southern Americans, the Washington Establishment, and particularly the northern press?

Both Bilbo and his constituents were the white, rural, agrarian segregationists of economically depressed Mississippi. His people were insular, resentful, even fearful of "outsiders," and above all dedicated to the maintenance of the racial status quo that kept blacks disfranchised and "in their place." Bilbo's constituency was, moreover, below average in literacy and education because of Mississippi's inferior educational facilities; and they were largely "born again"

29. *Congressional Record*, 75th Cong., 3rd Sess., 886, 78th Cong., 2nd Sess., A1798.
30. *Ibid.*, 75th Cong., 3rd Sess., 7360.

Protestant fundamentalists, accustomed to the rousing revivalistic preaching style of itinerant southern evangelists. It is hardly surprising, therefore, that Bilbo's manner of speechmaking closely adhered to the evangelistic model with which both he and his constituents were so familiar.

During his career in Mississippi state politics, Bilbo had cultivated the enmity of the state's wealthy Bourbon elite to the delight of his own "redneck" supporters. His impact on the national stage was at first far less noticeable, probably because he was a loyal supporter of FDR and the Democratic administration in power. The controversy over the race issue which arose in the late 1930s, however, again provided Bilbo with a target for his evangelistic wrath: in this case, such meddling "outsiders" as northern members of Congress and members of the urban and especially northern press, who would destroy Mississippi's white supremacist "way of life."

In the Senate debates over the antilynching bill, repeal of the poll tax, and the FEPC, Bilbo, in the eyes of his constituents, could once again play the role of their "savior," valiantly struggling against the "devilish" northern senators who would erode the rights of the states to govern many of their own internal affairs—principally elections and racial segregation.

Another powerful group of enemies Bilbo encouraged was the urban and particularly the northern press. In his own state both Jackson dailies, the *Daily News* and the *Clarion-Ledger*, consistently opposed him throughout his political career. In response to Bilbo's efforts to repeal the poll tax in Mississippi, for example, the *Daily News* argued editorially that Bilbo was not in the class with those great Mississippians who had included the tax as part of the state's constitution in 1890. The newspaper further accused him of attempting to build a political machine upon the "riff-raff and the ignoramuses" who would be enfranchised by abolition of the tax.[31]

One of the most significant speeches of "The Man's" entire career was his address to the Mississippi Legislature on March 22, 1944. The *Clarion-Ledger*, however, chose to "bury" its report of Bilbo's impor-

31. Jackson *Daily News*, February 12, 1940.

tant address on the eighth page of next morning's issue. The story was restricted to a cursory sampling of excerpts from the speech, and the *Clarion-Ledger* editorially ignored this hometown speech of the state's senior U.S. senator.[32]

During Bilbo's 1946 reelection campaign in the state's Democratic primary, the *Daily News* commented editorially that Bilbo's "thinly veiled incitations to mass terrorism" went too far and expressed the hope that he would be prosecuted by the Justice Department.[33]

One of Mississippi's major daily newspapers, however, the Meridian *Star*, proved consistently supportive of Bilbo in its editorial comment. During one of his many filibusters, the *Star* editorially expressed its gratitude: "To protect our right to rule ourselves, Bilbo stands ready to stage a one-man filibuster for eighteen months, if need must be. . . . We agree with Mr. Bilbo that righteous ends justify any—every legal means. . . . Our Mississippi senior senator appears a Godsend in time of vital threat. . . . We need more Bilbo-minded senators in Washington!" Far from ignoring Bilbo's 1944 speech to the state legislature, the *Star* both reported the event prominently on its first page and praised the address editorially: "Our former barnstorming Mississippi governor becomes a sedate and respected U.S. senator. Mr. Bilbo has far outgrown average congressional measurements. . . . Bilbo no more stands forth as the stormy petrel of Mississippi factional politics. Senator Bilbo has attained national dignity and thinking in a war-scarred, tired world."[34]

Bilbo's racist rhetoric in the 1946 primary, particularly his alleged attempt to incite intimidation of black voters the "night before" election day, later resulted in an investigation by a special Senate committee to determine whether he should be seated in the Eightieth Congress. This investigation moved the usually restrained New York *Times* to observe editorially that "the real issue is what has come to be know as 'Bilboism,' a combination of racial hatred, Ku Klux Klannery, intimidation at the polls and a narrow parochialism to which all national interests are subordinate."[35]

32. Jackson *Clarion-Ledger*, March 23, 1944.
33. Jackson *Daily News*, July 1, 1946.
34. Meridian *Star*, July 14, 1943, March 22, 1944.
35. New York *Times*, November 18, 1946.

One important regional daily newspaper, previously in agreement with most of Bilbo's public positions, was no longer able to endorse his candidacy in the 1946 election:

The Senator is not a credit to his state or his section. Thousands who voted for him would have preferred to cast their ballots for a candidate of finer character and better qualification. Mississippi does not lack men of full senatorial stature. But the major issues in her senatorial campaign were shaped by outside extremists and propagandists of demagogue stripe whose stupid tactics made Bilbo's election all but inevitable from the campaign start. The Senator shrewdly capitalized and exploited their stupidity.[36]

Most important national publications such as *Time, Newsweek, U.S. News & World Report, The New Republic,* and *Christian Century* were critical of and often condescending toward Bilbo during and after his 1946 campaign. Syndicated columnists and radio commentators such as Walter Winchell also kept up the public attack against Bilbo. Reminiscent of his earliest successes in campaigns that permitted him to play the persecuted martyr, the Mississippian simply became louder and more vociferous in his racist rhetoric. This, in turn, escalated the press attacks, thus giving Bilbo ever larger groups of enemy "outsiders" bent on destroying him and his people's most cherished beliefs and values.[37] The press attacks were, of course, self-defeating. They simply added to the perceived polarization that already existed between the Mississippi electorate and the urban North and further elevated Bilbo's standing as principal spokesman for his side.

III

What judgments must ultimately be made of Bilbo the orator? His command of fervent, evangelistic oratorical tactics was unsurpassed in his own time. He intuitively performed with perfection the public role that learned scholars of political science have since characterized as a leader "coping with an opposition that can be identified and personified."[38] But Bilbo labored rhetorically to preserve the antiquated

36. New Orleans *Times-Picayune,* July 3, 1946.
37. See Doler, "Bilbo's Rhetoric of Racial Relations," 224–57, for an extensive review of press and individual responses to Bilbo's rhetoric in the 1946 campaign.
38. Murray Edelman, *The Symbolic Uses of Politics* (Urbana: University of Illinois Press, 1964).

social mores of a backward-looking and recalcitrant constituency.

In the end, the critic of oratory may raise the question of rhetorical choices. Bilbo could have prepared his followers for the social changes he knew would come, by taking the rhetorical role of spokesman for racial moderation. Instead, he consciously chose to exacerbate racial animosities. He deliberately contributed to a hardening of racial attitudes which were ultimately manifested in bloodshed rather than orderly change when a new social order was finally forced upon Mississippi. It is for this premeditated demagogic choice—his calculated decision to become a zealous missionary, an evangelist of racial purity—that Bilbo must be condemned.

Today, with the benefit of three decades of historical hindsight, "The Man" should not be viewed merely as an anachronistic rhetorical curiosity of another era. Rather, the political career of Theodore Gilmore Bilbo should serve as a tragic reminder of the social consequences that have frequently followed a talented orator's unfortunate rhetorical choices.

Huey P. Long's 1927–1928 Gubernatorial Primary Campaign

A Case Study in the Rhetoric of Agitation

In August, 1927, in a speech in Alexandria, Louisiana, Huey Pierce Long formally inaugurated his candidacy for the Democratic nomination as governor of Louisiana.[1] In January, 1928, he won the nomination and became governor in the general election. Within a year he had established the base for one of the most powerful political organizations ever witnessed in America. At the time of his assassination in 1934, he had initiated a strategy he hoped would make him president of the United States within the space of two national elections. The present rhetorical study considers the 1927–1928 gubernatorial campaign because it typifies characteristics of Long's speaking that later earned him the title of "demagogue."

Probably no southern "demagogue" has received more attention than Long. Historians and public address scholars alike have produced numerous studies of the Louisianian's life and speaking.[2] Differing from these earlier studies, the present essay analyzes the cam-

1. The writer wishes to acknowledge the assistance of the staff of the Department of Archives and Manuscripts, Louisiana State University, Baton Rouge, in the research for this essay.
2. The definitive biography is T. Harry Williams, *Huey Long* (New York: Alfred A. Knopf, 1969). Speech studies include Ernest G. Bormann, "An Analysis of the March 7, 1935, Radio Address of Senator Huey P. Long" (M.A. thesis, University of Iowa, 1951); Ernest G. Bormann, "A Rhetorical Analysis of the National Radio Broadcasts of Senator Huey P. Long" (Ph.D. dissertation, University of Iowa, 1953); Karl Edward Faser, "A Rhetorical Analysis of the Use of Invective by Huey Long" (M.A. thesis, University of Oklahoma, 1965); Frederick Haberman, "Persuasion in the Power of Huey Long" (M.A. thesis, University of Wisconsin, 1935); Olan Buford Lowery, "An Analysis and Evalua-

paign as an example of the rhetoric of agitation, drawing upon the methodology suggested by John Waite Bowers and Donovan Ochs in *The Rhetoric of Agitation and Control*. Long functioned as an agitator in that he stood outside the political establishment in 1927, he advocated significant social change, and he encountered resistance from the establishment to his proposed reforms. Applying Bowers' and Ochs's methodology, this essay will consider briefly the necessary historical background of the campaign, delineate the ideologies of Long and his opponents, and then examine the rhetorical strategies that led to his victory in the January, 1928, gubernatorial primary.

Historical Background

In heavily Democratic Louisiana of 1927, to win the Democratic nomination was tantamount to winning the office. Therefore, the key race for the governorship was the Democratic primary. Since campaigns customarily began well in advance of the January election, Long entered the primary on July 17, 1927.

His opponents were incumbent Governor Oramel H. Simpson and Congressman Riley J. Wilson of Ruston, Louisiana. Simpson had been a candidate since succeeding Governor Henry Fugua, who had died in office in 1926. However, Simpson lacked the support of the powerful political leadership, because members did not feel he could be elected.[3] Instead the political establishment switched to Riley J. Wilson as their candidate. Thrust to the forefront by events connected with the disastrous Mississippi River flood in 1927, Wilson had assisted in the passage by Congress of a flood control bill. The resultant publicity cast the congressman in the role of expert on a subject of vital interest to the people of Louisiana and provided the political bosses with an issue they could exploit to win the election. On July 11, in a carefully staged convention in Alexandria, Wilson was nominated.[4]

---

tion of Huey Long's 'Share Our Wealth' Speech, May 15, 1935" (M.A. thesis, University of Iowa, 1951); Molly Minehan, "A Theoretical-Rhetorical Study in the Nature of Demagoguery: Huey Pierce Long, a Case Study" (M.A. thesis, San Francisco State College, 1962).

3. Williams, *Huey Long*, 244–45.
4. *Ibid.*, 247–48, 275–78.

The ensuing campaign lasted from August, 1927, until the primary election on January 17, 1928. When the votes were tabulated, Long was clearly the leader, though he lacked the necessary majority to win the nomination. Desperation attempts failed to put together a coalition of Wilson and Simpson backers in support of Wilson, and Long became the nominee without a second primary.

The Conflicting Ideologies

Long and his opponents stood clearly identified as representatives of opposing ideologies.[5] Simpson and Wilson represented the conservatives in Louisiana, who had controlled the state since Reconstruction.

V. O. Key observes that "while no measuring rod is handy for the precise calibration of the tightness of oligarchies, a plausible argument can be made that the combination of ruling powers of Louisiana had maintained a tighter grip on the state since Reconstruction than had like groups in other states." That combination included a powerful, old-fashioned New Orleans political machine, which effectively manipulated voting and which had strong ties to business and financial interests. Other elements included the New Orleans commercial interests, the powerful sugar cane growers, the cotton planters, the lumber interests, the petroleum industry, and the utilities. Collectively these factions exercised total control over the state.[6]

The common man's resentment against the political establishment was intensified by the absence in Louisiana of strong popular leaders similar to those of other southern states. Jeff Davis of Arkansas, Cole Blease of South Carolina, and Tom Watson of Georgia stirred the imaginations of the poor from the hills and piney woods, and the hope they offered, even if unfulfilled, gave their followers a means of venting their frustrations and angers. No such commanding figure had appeared in Louisiana to challenge conservatives and become a hero of those who had received little attention from state government.[7]

5. In the present context, "ideologies" are not intended to suggest organized systems of belief. As applied to Long and his opponents, "ideology" refers to the basic premises that underlay the politics of these men.

6. V. O. Key, Jr., *Southern Politics in State and Nation* (New York: Alfred A. Knopf, 1949), 159.

7. *Ibid.*, 159–60.

178 / HAROLD MIXON

As their campaign speeches show, Long's two opponents personified the conservative ideology. For the most part Long, Simpson, and
Wilson discussed the same issues: roads, education, agriculture, labor and capital, free bridges, penal institutions, charitable institutions, and the state agencies. But the three candidates differed dramatically in the positions taken on these issues. Simpson and Wilson,
basically in agreement, affirmed the status quo. Perhaps spurred by
Long's criticisms, both made gestures in the direction of reforms.
For example, both men advocated the construction of free bridges
throughout the state, and particularly on the major approaches to
New Orleans. And each man spoke vaguely of the need for econo-
mies in state agencies and guarantees that those offices could not be
used for political purposes. But in all of their pronouncements they
offered no significant criticism of the status quo. Indeed, they were
careful to praise the accomplishments of Louisiana in the past and to
offer platforms designed to extend the praiseworthy achievements of
former administrations.

A few examples will illustrate their positions. The two conservatives praised the level of education in 1927, insisting that a good education was available to all the children. His two opponents agreed
that Long's proposal to provide free textbooks to all children was ad-
mirable in principle, but should only be implemented without raising
additional taxes. Wilson emphatically opposed increasing taxes to pay
for textbooks if parents were already able to buy them for their children. Discussing the issue of charitable institutions, Simpson and
Wilson agreed that all should be done to provide for the state's mentally and physically handicapped citizens within the existing financial
capabilities of Louisiana, but again both opposed any increase
in taxes to provide additional services. And on the issue of hard-
surfaced roads, though not conceding any major inadequacies in
Louisiana's road system the conservatives pledged to develop and to
improve major highways and to convert to hard-surfaced roads over a
period of years, preferably with federal aid.[8] The one apparent breach
in conservative philosophies of the two men was their support of free
bridges, a proposal that opposed the machine interests. However, the

8. New Orleans *Times-Picayune*, August 12, 1927.

political establishment probably viewed that support as a move to get votes rather than any liberal political tendency.[9]

In summary, most of Simpson's statements and actions suggest that he strongly adhered to a conservative philosophy. According to T. Harry Williams, Simpson's "long service as secretary of the senate had left him with what might be called a 'caretaker' psychology; he instinctively operated to please all the elements in a power structure, giving highest priority to the most powerful." His supporters openly characterized him as the representative of the "conservative element," and the opponent of "radicalism and demagogues." Riley J. Wilson extended the same establishment philosophy.

In contrast to Simpson and Wilson, Long envisioned far-ranging participation of the state government in improving the lot of the average man. A native of Winn Parish in north central Louisiana, Long brought to the 1927 campaign a reputation as the champion of the little man against the corporate interests represented by the ruling oligarchy of the state. Early in his career he began an attack on the unequal distribution of wealth, a position that later became his "share-the-wealth" program. In a letter published in the New Orleans *Item*, March 1, 1918, he asserted that 2 percent of the people possessed 65 to 70 percent of the nation's wealth, and that the inequality was increasing.

A second issue for Long was the inequality in educational opportunity, which he termed one of the greatest causes for "industrial unrest." Pinpointing a connection between the lack of education and economic inequality, he contended: "This is the condition, north, east, south and west; with wealth concentrating, classes becoming defined, there is not the opportunity for Christian uplift and education and cannot be until there is more economic reform. This is the problem that the good people of this country must consider."[10]

A third expression of Long's concern was his attack on the corporate interests, particularly the major oil producers represented by Standard Oil. By controlling pipelines, he argued, the major oil producers threatened the existence of the independent producers by denying them a market. In 1918, at twenty-five years of age, Long began

9. Williams, *Huey Long*, 245, 264.
10. New Orleans *Item*, March 1, 1918.

a fight against the Standard Oil Company that spanned most of his career. Injecting the oil issue into the 1920 gubernatorial campaign, he expressed disappointment in the law the successful candidate (whom he had supported) had passed.[11] Thus, Long proposed a state government that would promote human rights rather than exploiting the people, as he asserted the ruling oligarchy had done.

Rhetorical Strategies

Long relied heavily on public speaking to carry his crusade to the people. Even today, with good roads and efficient means of transportation, his itinerary would be impressive. In 1927, with poor roads and relatively primitive means of transportation, he conducted a tour that was nothing short of incredible. According to his estimate, at the end of his campaign he had spoken five hundred to six hundred times, a figure verified by a friendly newspaper. A careful survey of the Shreveport *Times* from August, 1927, to the primary in January, 1928, confirms the extent of his stumping. The *Times* carried many complete or partial texts of the Long addresses, as well as mention of numerous others. Crisscrossing the state in a pattern that carried him into every parish, Long often spoke in five to seven different towns in one day. He began in smaller towns in a parish and concluded with an address in one of the largest towns. According to the Shreveport *Times*, Long drew huge crowds for most of his meetings, his listeners often overflowing the meeting place. In some cases he used amplification to carry his speech to other rooms in the building and to the lawn outside.

In his speeches, Long employed two basic strategies, "polarization" and "solidification." As defined by Bowers and Ochs, polarization "assumes that any individual who has not committed himself in one way or another to the agitation is supportive of the establishment." It includes those methods by which the agitator seeks to move individuals from commitment to the establishment to support of the agitator. In Long's case, polarization consists of techniques by which he attempted to secure audience commitment to the progressive cause rather than that of the conservatives. Used by Long to a lesser

11. Key, *Southern Politics in State and Nation,* 158.

degree than polarization, solidification includes "the rhetorical processes by which an agitating group produces or reinforces the cohesiveness of its members, thereby increasing their responsiveness to group wishes." [12]

Polarization

In attempting polarization, Long employed the techniques of flag issues and flag individuals—that is, the issues and individuals especially vulnerable to the agitator's charges. [13] In his campaign, he used the flag issues to contrast the progressive and conservative programs. Flag individuals he offered as focal points for his attacks on the conservative ideology.

FLAG ISSUES Partially in common with his two opponents, Long organized his platform around ten issues. He introduced most of these in his opening speech in Alexandria, and he substantially modified some as the campaign progressed. The issue that received most of his attention was the political use of state agencies. Long contended that state money supported the status quo in that agency payrolls promoted political patronage. Employees were paid for work not done, in order to subsidize their political activities in support of the incumbents. Long also attacked the awarding of contracts for materials on the basis of political expediency, contending that such contracts went most frequently to companies that supported the reelection of the incumbent governor. Criticizing a number of state agencies, he made his two special targets the highway commission and the conservation agency.

A second issue was education, about which Long made four specific proposals. First he argued that every child should receive an adequate education, something he asserted was not being done in 1927. Second, he supported vocational training, especially for the indigent and mentally or physically handicapped. Such training, Long implied, had been delayed by "the influence of ring politicians" and was in general so inadequate that it was ineffective. Third, Long also proposed making higher education available to all deserving students,

12. John Waite Bowers and Donovan Ochs, *The Rhetoric of Agitation and Control* (Reading, Mass.: Addison-Wesley Publishing, 1971), 26.
    13. *Ibid.*, 27.

regardless of their parents' financial means. And finally, by far his most popular educational proposal, he suggested a plan to provide free school books for all children.

Long's third issue was the care of the mentally and physically handicapped. He argued that mentally defective persons in need of treatment were being held in jails because state mental institutions had no place for them. He accused state administrators of knowing about the needs of the blind, deaf, orphaned, deformed, and crippled, but refusing help because of alleged insufficient funds.

Turning his attention to roads as his fourth issue Long claimed that the conservatives were responsible for the poor system of highways in Louisiana. In 1927, Louisiana had relatively few hard-surfaced roads, and most "improved" roads were of the gravel variety. Long insisted that these roads were insufficient and expensive to maintain, sometimes wearing away in less than a year's time. Therefore he proposed paving highways, beginning with the more important ones and gradually extending the program to virtually every other public road in the state.

In a fifth issue, Long pledged a fair deal for labor. Indicting the political establishment, he asserted that in 1927 Louisiana offered no relief for disabled workingmen. In fact, he insisted, the existing administration had deliberately aggravated the plight of these unfortunates by making state assistance so impractical or insufficient as to be virtually worthless. Long promised legislation to solve the problem, without hurting agriculture, commerce, or industry.

In the sixth issue, Long focused on trade and port activities, charging that the state officials were responsible for the steady decline in activity at the port of New Orleans. He proposed that Louisiana seek federal aid to make New Orleans competitive with neighboring ports and also to increase the extent of navigable inland waterways.

A seventh issue Long emphasized was the state's farm problems. Here he noted that in spite of excellent agricultural conditions, Louisiana farmers were not doing well financially. Adopting elements from the Populist program, he argued that the state should provide a system of warehouses and storage facilities and assist with the marketing of produce.

Long's eighth issue argued for the need to conserve Louisiana's

HUEY LONG / 183

natural gas. Throughout the campaign Long opposed the waste of natural gas in the manufacture of carbon black and advocated that it should be "reasonably and steadily reduced." Instead of producing carbon black, he suggested that gas should be made available to induce industries to locate in Louisiana and to supply natural gas to every city and town in the state. In particular, he mentioned the need to get natural gas to New Orleans for residential and commercial purposes.

Long's ninth issue was flood control. Inasmuch as Louisiana had recently experienced a damaging flood, and because his opponent Riley Wilson based much of his campaign on flood control, Long needed to address the issue. He pointed out that the levee system clearly had failed to provide adequate protection, but suggested that the problem was national in scope, and that the federal government appeared to be moving to correct it. He pledged that as governor he would coordinate efforts to seek effective federal flood control, specifically promising that he would propose enactment into law of the Chicago flood conference's recommendations. He further promised to enlist the ablest men available to work at the state level to bring about whatever action was possible to prevent further flood problems.

In a tenth issue Long advocated free bridges throughout Louisiana. In particular he promised free bridges at Chef Menteur and the Rigolets in New Orleans.

Finally, interwoven into his treatment of many of these ten issues was the subject of ring politics. He accused the political machine based in New Orleans, but operating statewide, of being responsible for many of Louisiana's problems.

Not all of these issues were of equal importance in Long's speeches. His opponents clearly preempted some in that they also supported nominally at least free bridges, conservation of natural gas, and road improvements. About the only difference between Long and opponents Simpson and Wilson on these three issues was that he may have been more specific in his proposals. Long hoped to remove flood control as an issue, because it was Wilson's strongest claim for support in the election. And he was less interested in such issues as the proposal to correct problems associated with New Orleans's Lake Pontchartrain, since they were limited geographically in their appeal. As a skillful politician, Long could sense either that he clearly carried an issue or that it was not popularly received, in which case he permitted it to recede into the background. For whatever reasons, he seemed to concentrate upon those issues that permitted him to call attention to the culpability of his opponents.

Rhetorically Long employed his flag issues with great effectiveness, first of all because of excellent adaptation to his audiences. He was noted for his ability to adapt his appeals with equal ease to audiences in Louisiana's Protestant north as well as those of the Catholic south, a facility well illustrated in an anecdote with which T. Harry Williams began his biography of Long. According to Williams,

The first time that Huey P. Long campaigned in rural, Latin Catholic south Louisiana, the local boss who had him in charge said at the beginning of the tour: "Huey, you ought to remember one thing in your speeches today. You're from north Louisiana, but now you're in south Louisiana. And we got a lot of Catholic voters down here." "I know," Huey answered. And throughout the day in every small town Huey would begin by saying, "When I was a boy, I would get up at six o'clock in the morning on Sunday, and I would hitch our old horse up to the buggy and I would take my Catholic grandparents to mass. I would bring them home, and at ten o'clock I would hitch the old horse up again, and I would take my Baptist grandparents to church." The effect of the anecdote on the audience was obvious, and on the way back to Baton Rouge that night the local leader said admiringly: "Why, Huey, you've been holding out on us. I didn't know you had any Catholic grandparents." "Don't be a damn fool," replied Huey. "We didn't even have a horse." [14]

In adapting to specific audiences, Long was careful to choose issues particularly salient to the group of people whom he faced. When he spoke in Alexandria and Shreveport, he discussed the necessity for increasing navigable inland waterways, with obvious reference to the Red River which could bring commercial shipping into these cities. Speaking in Baton Rouge, he emphasized his support of the state university located there. And in New Orleans, he stressed the need for free bridges connecting that city with major traffic arteries within the state and along the Gulf Coast.

In addition, Long's flag issues gained rhetorical effectiveness from his skillful selection of specific examples. At the beginning of his stumping he developed the issues in fairly general terms, but as the

14. Williams, *Huey Long*, 1.

canvass progressed he cited specific examples of the problems. His attacks on the state highway commission illustrate his technique. In the early weeks of his campaign, Long made general accusations, indicting the incumbent's use of the highway commission for political purposes. In Lake Charles he continued this line, suggesting that commission payrolls were overloaded with useless jobs created for purely political reasons to help keep the "ring" in office. However, in later weeks he substituted for these general accusations more specific examples. Not only did he become more specific, naming the individuals involved and quoting the amounts of money expended, but he frequently chose his examples to fit his particular listeners, providing them local incidents with which they were likely familiar.

In a speech in New Orleans Long demonstrated this technique when he described how in a neighboring parish the state highway commission paid far more for gravel than was necessary in a road-paving deal with the Washington Parish police jury. Narrating the episode in detail, he showed how the public bid process had been circumvented, and one company was paid a premium price for the gravel. According to Long, in 1926 the Washington Parish police jury entered an agreement with the highway commission for the police jury to prepare certain roads for paving, after which the highway commission would gravel them. The subsequent developments were somewhat complex. The highway commission requested bids in January, 1927, for both construction and gravelling of the roads. However, when the highway commission changed, J. M. Fourney, the new highway engineer, discovered the contract and reminded the police jury that Washington Parish was to prepare the roads, and highway commission responsibility was limited to gravelling. Withdrawing the bids, Fourney asked Washington Parish to provide the money to grade and drain the roadbed. According to Long, it then became known that the former commission members had privately connived for the state to pay the entire cost of the construction. In return, the speaker claimed, the Washington Parish police jury would assist J. Y. Sanders in his bid for the United States Senate.

Engineer Fourney insisted on the initial written agreement and demanded in February, 1927, that Washington Parish deliver to the highway commission the $79,000 that represented the parish's share of the project. Commission records were silent on the matter until a new engineer, a Mr. Bowden, took office, when bids were requested in July, 1927.

According to Long, all bids were rejected, and a decision was made to build the road on the "force account," a procedure that formally classified the project as a maintenance item and required no bids. Under that arrangement, the contract to supply the gravel went to the Bogue Chitto Gravel Company, which previously had been high bidder. Long revealed that the company was headed by "an ardent supporter" of Governor Simpson, and the no-bid price was even higher the the same man's original bid. As a result the taxpayers paid substantially higher prices than any quoted in the bids, or $14,724 above what the cost should have been. Long also related that the Washington Parish police jury never paid its share, with the highway fund paying the full amount of the project.[15]

This extended description has been given to illustrate Long's excellent rhetorical application of these examples. Outwardly he gave them the form of a straightforward narrative in which he recited the facts about the incident, but he added touches that increased their impact. The narrative contains numerous specific details; the listeners were given dates, names, places, and statistics which enhanced Long's credibility. At crucial points, he inserted questions that must have echoed those of his listeners and that reinforced the conclusion they had already formed: "Why was the Bogue Chitto Gravel Company favored over other contractors? Was it to get support for Simpson in Washington parish? Have any of the profits of the Bogue Chitto Gravel Company . . . found their way into the Simpson campaign fund? If so, how much?" There was no need for Long to supply the answers.

Long also used his supporting material to arouse the emotions of his listeners, especially their anger, and to attack the character of his opponents. Describing the lack of educational opportunities, Long posed a hypothetical example in which he demonstrated that the average farmer in Louisiana would have to pay more than he made annually to support a child for one year in college, concluding that

15. Shreveport (La.) *Times*, November 16, 1927.

only the wealthy could afford a college education for their children. Bringing a box of school books to the platform with him, he told his audiences that each book cost two dollars, whereas in neighboring Texas education officials confirmed that Texas supplied free textbooks for children at a cost to the state of only ninety cents per book. Since Louisiana changed textbooks so frequently, Long noted, the books could not be passed on from child to child, and a family had to buy new ones each year for each child. This was an unreasonable expense, Long declared, and he further increased his audience's anger by inferring that the procedure existed primarily so that certain individuals could profit from it. And when Long related an example such as the one involving construction of a road in Washington Parish, he carefully chose his language so as to arouse the anger toward officials who appeared not only dishonest, but reprehensible for misusing and wasting the financial resources that properly belonged to the people of the state. Thus in Long's hands the supporting materials became more than logical proof of his claims; they also acquired strong emotional and ethical overtones which further intensified the negative feelings toward political bosses and corrupt incumbents.

Long's rhetorical use of these flag issues suggests four conclusions. First, they contained something to appeal to virtually every group of voters important to Long's political aspirations. He addressed himself to the problems of the working man, the farmer, the city dweller, and the rural population. Second, the issues contained appeals directed to specific geographical areas. Third, Long adapted his appeals well to specific listeners, with local references pertinent to particular audiences. It is obvious, as others have noted, that he utilized blocks of material from which he selected units for individual audiences. However, he individualized those blocks by references to local persons and places and changed the development of these blocks as the campaign progressed, as is evidenced particularly in the case of the attacks on waste in state agencies. Fourth, the issues were intended to polarize his audiences, who were offered an "either-or" choice. There was no way, according to Long, to get rid of these problems as long as the political status quo remained; the only way effectively to solve the problems was a fresh approach, which was not bound by the past commitments. In effect, Long said, his audience could vote for either of his opponents to continue the status quo, or they could choose a new approach to the problems by voting for him. Thus in the choice and use of the flag issues, Long showed himself a skillful rhetorician, with a keen perception of what material would be most effective for a specific audience.

FLAG INDIVIDUALS Long concentrated upon four individuals to further his attempt at polarization. Early in his canvass he insisted that he would not attack the character of his opponents, a promise that quickly fell by the wayside. Frequently Long engaged in personal criticism of his opponents and, going even further, often used these flag individuals to personify the bad aspects of ring politics.

Throughout the campaign Long attacked incumbent Governor O. H. Simpson, whom he identified with the "system" against which he professed to run. In some instances he challenged Simpson indirectly, as when he talked about the politicalization of the state agencies the governor controlled. But on other occasions he was more direct, referring to Simpson by name and making specific accusations against him.

The most notable such assault occurred during a debate between Long and Simpson at Colfax, Louisiana, on November 11, 1927. The encounter is particularly interesting because it illustrates Long's ability to control the ground of an argument so as to make his case appear in a favorable light. For weeks Long had sought a direct public confrontation with Simpson, but he had been unable to arrange one. Then, on November 11, he appeared unexpectedly at a rally where Simpson was to speak, and in the ensuing exchange between the candidates he used Simpson's past activities and remarks to discredit him. First Long chose an issue that offered strong emotional potential, Simpson's failure to provide a pension for old soldiers. Simpson attempted to defend his administration's position on the pension by claiming that banks would not advance funds because the act authorizing the pension was illegal and a special act would have to be passed. Long countered that there had been a special session of the Louisiana legislature but that Simpson had included no pension act in that call. Emphasizing that the necessary pension legislation could have been included, Long demanded that Simpson tell the audience "Why you didn't do it?" Simpson made no reply. Attempting to take the initiative, the incumbent governor turned to Long's school book proposal and remarked that he would like to provide clothes, free automobiles, and everything else for school children; he would approve a tax on racing to provide for school needs, he asserted. Long pursued this reference to racing, as it offered a chance to damage Simpson's character before the rural audience. Agreeing that racing should be taxed, he immediately shifted the grounds of the argument. "Let's see who it is that is so close to the races," Long began and then insisted that he had never been to horse races, had never bet on them, and had never asked racing interests for a single favor. Pressing his point, he asked Simpson, "How about you?" Simpson replied that he had been to one race in two years, to which Long responded, "That's one more than I have been." Continuing, Long asked if Simpson had written the New Orleans race track requesting numerous passes to be used by the governor and his friends. When Simpson admitted he had, Long used the admission to advantage: "There you have it, my people. He is the man who has seen to it that his friends and himself were made the free patrons of the racetrack and provided ways for them to go there."

The debate then turned to Long's criticism of the highway commission. The governor asserted, "The propaganda they are circulating against this commission is false." Long replied by stating that "a few months ago" the highway commission had had 1,039 employees. But on September 30, after the campaign had begun, the payroll numbered 2,776 men, an increase of 1,737. When Long challenged Simpson to deny it, the governor was silent. Relating the situation more closely to his immediate audience, Long claimed that recently forty men had been employed cutting weeds on a thirty-mile section of road—cutting weeds in October that frost would kill in November. Again Long challenged Simpson to deny it, and again the governor remained silent.

When Simpson did not respond to Long's repeated challenges for a denial, Long added that if Simpson or his supporters did deny the charges, Long would supply names. He then named one individual to demonstrate that he had such information.[16]

16. *Ibid.*, November 12, 1927.

The exchange undoubtedly produced the image of the governor desired by Long. The accusations, unanswered by Simpson, presented him as the recipient of special privilege and a man quite willing to use the powers of his office to secure his own reelection. It reinforced Long's contention that Simpson represented a system that was more concerned with self-perpetuation than with meeting the needs of the people.

In other speeches Long mounted a direct attack on the incumbent, as exemplified in an address at Lawrence Square in New Orleans when he offered an uncomplimentary picture of Simpson's role in the Sabine River bridge affair. A bridge had been built across the Sabine River connecting Louisiana and Texas; however, after its completion the bridge was unusable because Louisiana had not finished the approach to the bridge from the Louisiana side. As Long related the story, Simpson had received delegations of Texas and Louisiana citizens who petitioned him to complete the approach, but the governor was unreceptive until public indignation became very high.

Indeed, indignation ran so high, Long asserted, that when Simpson's headquarters announced a speaking tour through Calcasieu Parish, Simpson advisors from that area notified the governor that he could not afford to face the people in the region because of their strong resentment of the manner in which the highway commission had managed the project. He thus changed the speaking tour to a hand-shaking tour. According to Long, when Simpson arrived in Vinton, he suddenly professed that he neither understood nor appreciated the problem, in spite of personal interviews with delegation after delegation which had brought the problem to his attention.

Turning to sarcasm, Long then described how Simpson had performed "a marvelous acrobatic feat," suddenly becoming the hero who pushed the project to completion, utilizing all the workers and equipment from adjacent areas. Obviously, Long asserted, Simpson expected the public to view him as the hero in the episode, but Long predicted that the people would not be deceived and would remember that a few days before Simpson had visited the site, his highway commission chairman had stated the impossibility of completing the project on time without a waste of state funds.[17]

17. *Ibid.*, November 20, 1927.

Again, Long made Simpson a focal point in order to polarize voter attitudes. He suggested that Simpson acted only out of expediency and concern to retain political control of the state, behavior that would continue another four years if Simpson were reelected governor.

In a New Orleans speech, Long continued his attack on the incumbent governor insisting that not only had Simpson personally participated in the politicalization of the state highway commission, but he had done so even at a time when he professed to be leaving politics aside to give full attention to the flood crisis. His "high-sounding interviews and statements" saying that he was devoting his full attention to the flood problems and would not resume political matters or his campaign until relief was available to the flood-damaged areas were insincere, Long insisted. For the record from Simpson's own office refuted his claims and stamped "him as a politician who all along was trying to fool the people into believing that he only had their own interests at heart." To substantiate this charge, Long cited specific individuals who had secured positions for their relatives on the state payroll as a reward for past or promised political support for Simpson.[18]

Thus Long mounted a full-scale attack on the governor's character. Mixing sarcasm with examples and statistics, Long sought to portray Simpson as a man whose principal concern was to retain the governorship regardless of the cost to the people. In so doing, Long achieved two rhetorical objectives. First, he raised doubts about the character and credibility of his opponent. Secondly, he implied that Simpson's behavior was typical of the political oligarchy that had controlled Louisiana for so long. He implied that a vote for Simpson would be a vote to continue the practices of that oligarchy; a vote for Long would be a vote against these practices and for a government of the people.

Long also chose as a main target Major Frank T. Payne, head of the highway commission under the Simpson administration. In his speeches he described Payne as a man directly responsible for using the highway commission to advance Simpson's political objectives.

18. *Ibid.*, November 24, 1927.

In denouncing Payne, Long introduced a new strategy. In a speech in New Orleans he promised that in each of his twelve speeches in that city he would present a sensational new charge. He kept his promise, producing letters written to Payne asking for jobs for various individuals. In all of the instances, Long followed the same pattern. He pointed out to his audiences that no specific duties were mentioned, but in each case the individual was recommended for employment on the basis that he would secure votes for Simpson. For example, in one letter the writer urged Payne to assign a highway employee in plain clothes to north Louisiana because the employee had many relatives in the area and could greatly aid the Simpson cause.[19] Insisting that these were typical examples of exploitation of state funds for political purposes under Payne's administration, Long asserted that the need for the services of such men was never a consideration. Instead, Long alleged that such individuals were always scrutinized for four qualifications: the employment must actively enlist the person in the ranks of O. H. Simpson, the employment must enlist the man's family in Simpson's cause, he must be from a large family with many relatives, and he must show capacity as a campaign worker.

Long added emotional impact to the incidents by causally linking them to the state's inadequate provision for the mentally and physically afflicted, the orphaned children, and education. In Long's analysis, money that should have gone to these worthwhile causes was spent instead by the highway commission to support Simpson's campaign. Long also made one of his few references to the Lost Cause, noting that because of the political use of funds "the old Confederate veterans may be denied their pension while the thin gray line is steadily perishing." Undoubtedly the speaker hoped to arouse his listerners' anger by suggesting that insufficient funding to solve these vital programs resulted from the administration's misuse of the public's money. Long concluded that all of these conditions would continue until the controlling political machine was removed from power.

In a speech in New Orleans' Eighteenth Ward, Long changed his

19. *Ibid.*, November 15, 1927.

strategy slightly, this time attacking Payne's use of his office to award contracts for political purposes. Specifically, Long hinted that highway commission records showed Payne had awarded most of the state's gravel contracts to two companies headed by political friends. According to Long, this practice had resulted in excessive costs. From April to October, 1927, gravel purchases from these two firms had cost the state $8,846 above the lowest bids. In addition, freight savings of $5,300.40 could have been realized if the other companies had received the contracts, or a total savings to the state of $14,146.40. In another instance, Long claimed that Payne's favoritism had inflated the cost by $6,900 over the prices of lower competitors.

In the same speech, Long attacked Payne's credibility, citing the commissioner's denial that he had given any company a monopoly. According to the speaker, one of the companies he cited had received 75 percent of the sand clay gravel contracts from May 1 to October 1, whereas during the same period the other company supplied 60 percent of the washed gravel. Long further insisted that the contracts were awarded while the lower rates were on file in Payne's office, and that Payne had used "the cloak of the maintenance department" to circumvent the law requiring bids on all projects costing over $2,000. Long suggested that "Payne's methods are nothing short of an illegal juggling of funds to give orders and contracts to a favored few individuals and concerns."

Such favoritism, Long contended, was politically motivated, the two men whose companies had received the gravel contracts being active supporters of Simpson. Long wondered out loud if a part of their excess profits made its way into the Simpson campaign fund and suggested that the voters render a verdict on January 17.[20]

In his Lawrence Square speech on November 19, Long used the Sabine River bridge affair to further portray Payne in an uncomplimentary light. According to Long, Payne also had been personally visited by "delegation after delegation" urging rapid completion of the project, and "at times seemed to be irritated by these special pleas and not infrequently made this irritation quite evident to his visitors."

20. *Ibid.*, November 19, 1917.

Long suggested that the project would not be finished until Payne wanted it completed, and that Payne, as an obstructionist, was acting as the administration's representative in the matter.[21]

Professing to have many other such cases documented from the highway commission files, Long concluded that under Payne the commission was "politicalized from top to bottom in the interest of O. H. Simpson," and that no man from New Orleans could hope for a position in the agency unless endorsed by the New Orleans ring or Simpson ward leaders.

In this manner Long used Payne to personify the highway commission practices that he had indicted as being political in nature. The speaker characterized Payne as a representative of the philosophy of the ruling oligarchy and suggested to his listeners that a vote for Long would be a vote against the kind of practices followed by Payne.

Long singled out L. E. Thomas as a third major "flag individual" in his campaign speeches, and Thomas played a role somewhat different from the first two flag individuals. Payne was an appointee of Simpson and supported administration policy. Thomas, however, supported Riley Wilson, Long's other opponent, and by denouncing Thomas, Long could also attack Wilson. Long's diatribes also were prompted by a bitter political rivalry between Long and Thomas, and by Thomas' role in the Alexandria convention that had nominated Wilson.

In his attack on Thomas, Long's basic strategy was to impugn Thomas' character. Long's first major denunciation of this rival came in a Shreveport speech on September 17, when he rebuked Thomas for his role in the Alexandria convention. Employing sarcasm, Long referred to Thomas as "the Honorable L. E. Thomas, mayor of the city of Shreveport, who, by the rules of seniority, had become a leader of all the brigade of chronic pie-eaters and perpetual trough-feeders in the state and whom I have helped to defeat in three of his recent campaigns." Then referring specifically to Thomas' role in the Alexandria convention, Long declared that the mayor had "announced a deliverance of the people of Caddo parish into the camp of one of my political adversaries." Later in the same speech, Long ridiculed Thomas by

21. *Ibid.*, November 23, 1927.

asserting that Thomas had tried unsuccessfully in 1924 to deliver Caddo Parish voters to Thomas' candidates. A few months later, the speaker asserted, Thomas unsuccessfully opposed Long's reelection to the public service commission. In the same election, Long claimed credit for assisting in the defeat of Thomas in his bid for a seat in the United States Senate. Long carried his "home box" in each of those contests, whereas Thomas lost his "home box" and the city hall "box" by a two to one majority.[22]

In another Shreveport speech, on November 24, Long devoted a large part of his speech to answering charges made against him by Thomas at a Simpson rally one week earlier. In the response, Long challenged Thomas' credibility and insisted that the mayor had lied and switched positions so often that it was difficult to determine what he believed.

Thomas had been on the public payroll for thirty-three years and was reluctant to leave it, began Long, and he derisively compared Thomas' tenure to weaning a calf. When the calf reached eighteen to thirty months of age it had the decency to wean itself, but of Thomas —"that 33-year-old babe, that pie-eating and pap-sucking L. E. Thomas"—Long declared, "you can't even wean him or get him out of the pay trough."

Long then reviewed Thomas' campaigns for public office. In 1919, the speaker pointed out, Thomas ran third among three candidates for the railroad commission. In 1920, he ran fifth among five candidates for state senator, and in another race with three candidates he again ran third. Only in one race, Long noted, did Thomas run second, and that was when he opposed Edwin S. Broussard for the office of United States senator and there were only two candidates in the race. However, even in that instance he lost by the largest majority ever recorded in the state. Long then turned to his central theme that Thomas was for Thomas only, and that he had no regard for the truth or for honor.

Only after this attack on Thomas' character and accomplishments did Long deal with the specific charges Thomas had made against him. First, Long denied Thomas' claim that in 1923 the Southwestern

22. *Ibid.*, September 18, 1927.

Gas and Electric Company had made a ten thousand dollar campaign contribution to Long, calling it "a deliberate falsehood" supported only by an affidavit made by Gus Williams of New Orleans. Long insisted that Williams was not to be trusted, noting that earlier in the campaign Williams had stated that every public service corporation in Louisiana opposed Long. Now, however, he was claiming that a public service corporation was supporting Long. Obviously Williams was wrong in one of the allegations, since he contradicted himself, and therefore, the speaker asserted, nothing Williams said could be believed.

Secondly, Long took up Thomas' charge that the whiskey and gambling interests were behind his campaign. To the degree that gambling was a problem in either New Orleans or Shreveport, responded Long, it was the fault of governing authorities, because gambling could not exist without their sanction. Although actually this claim was irrelevant, the assertion made it possible for Long to further smear Thomas, who was mayor of Shreveport. If the audience accepted Long's position it followed that Thomas had protected the gambling interests in his city. Furthermore, Long applied the same argument to the governor, noting that Simpson himself was engaged in the manufacture of punchboards, a form of gambling device, an activity Long had forced Simpson to admit earlier.

Returning to Thomas' actual charge, Long contended that the accusation of support from the whiskey interests stemmed from the allegation that John P. Sullivan of New Orleans was supporting Long. Long responded, "What's wrong with him [Sullivan]?" Suggesting that Thomas was inconsistent, Long then reminded his audience that when R. G. Pleasant ran for governor of Louisiana in 1916, with Thomas as his manager, that group accepted money from the distillers for whom Sullivan served as an attorney. In 1920, Long continued, Pleasant, Thomas, Sanders, Sullivan, and Long all joined in support of John M. Parker, and Thomas raised no objections then. In 1924, when Thomas ran for United States senator, he received Sullivan's aid and even paid $7,500 to Ben Moran, Sullivan's leader in the Eleventh Ward, for campaign expenses. Long concluded that the only difference was that Thomas had gone to Sullivan to seek support, whereas Sullivan had come to Long to offer it.

The speaker then turned to the racial issue, which he rarely used. He related how, in the campaign for the United States Senate, Thomas formed an alliance with Walter J. Cohen, a black Republican. As an outgrowth of that alliance, Long suggested, "Thomas' negro political affiliations were such that no honorable or respectable person could accept his support from that day." In a further reference to the racial issue, he claimed that Thomas had sided with the black Republicans "against those who were trying to save the white democracy of this state."

Next Long took up Thomas' references to Long's war record—or lack of it. Thomas had renewed the frequently repeated charges that Long had evaded service in the military in World War I. In answer Long responded in the most general terms, referring to documents that he had "lately produced" from government officials showing Thomas to be "a malicious and wilful perverter of the truth." Long gave no further explanation of the nature of these "documents." However, he continued, the certificates had brought only a temporary halt to Thomas' allegations, and Thomas had resumed "the same old falsehoods that he put out several years ago."

Long then turned to several episodes in Thomas' career which Long said cast doubt on the mayor's integrity. In 1916, according to Long, Thomas and R. G. Pleasant conducted a sham fight against prohibition while accepting the financial backing of the liquor interests. Long accused Thomas during that campaign of creating the "falsehood" that a Thomas C. Barrett, a prohibitionist, had faked appendicitis to evade the contest. However, when incontrovertible evidence had refuted the story, Long insisted, even Thomas privately admitted the charge to be untrue; nonetheless, when occasion permitted Thomas had continued to tell the story in isolated sections of the state.

In another episode, Long recalled that when Sanders was governor, Thomas had tried to become Speaker of the Louisiana House of Representatives, only to be beaten by another candidate. In retaliation Thomas denounced Sanders. But when state funds became available for deposit in banks, Thomas made an effort to acquire a large sum for himself and wrote a letter pledging support to Sanders and his administration, even though he was at this time publicly denouncing Sanders. Thomas would do anything for money, Long concluded.

In a third episode, Long charged that, after having received the support of the liquor interests for many years, Thomas and Pleasant double-crossed those interests by seeking to prevent liquor sales in the area around Camp Beauregard. Later they double-crossed the prohibitionists, said Long, though he provided no clarification of this last assertion.

Long accused Thomas and Pleasant of betraying "everybody in the state" with the board of state affair; with Thomas as chairman, that board increased the taxes, according to Long, by 110 percent. Then, Long asserted, Thomas, who had been made bank examiner, closed several banks because they were "not supporting the scheme that he [Thomas] had been projecting." Long claimed that other banks were permitted to remain insolvent for years. Amplifying the charge of tax increases, Long contended that Thomas and Pleasant had misled the people by telling them that though the basis of assessment would be raised from fifty cents to one hundred cents on the dollar, the millage rate would be cut in half with the result of no net tax increase. Long claimed that after the assessment Thomas and Pleasant actually raised the millage, resulting in a tax increase of "about 110 percent."

Thomas had charged that Long received $10,000 from the gas and electric utilities, a charge Long denied. As Long described the situation, Thomas and the Shreveport city council had hired experts to review the gas and electric rates and had then been unable to pay them. Long said he then required the utility companies to deposit $10,000 with the commission to pay the consultants' fee, which came to $6,500. The remaining $3,500 of the deposit was returned to the utilities, Long insisted. Answering Thomas' charge that he had received the money in return for support for higher gas rates, Long concluded that "a blacker defamation, nor a more open falsehood was ever told by any human being."

Finally, Long cited Thomas' attempt to secure the endorsement of the New Orleans ring in his bid for governor in the 1928 primary. According to Long, even that group refused to endorse Thomas, and as a result Thomas turned on the ring.[23]

Thus in responding to Thomas' attacks on him, Long usually attempted a rational answer to the charges. However, to an equal degree he employed derision and sarcasm in an effort to ridicule Thomas and to question the man's character.

Long's old adversary, J. Y. Sanders, received mention in at least three speeches. As in his attack on Thomas, Long chose to ridicule Sanders. At Shreveport on September 17, he asked derisively, "Where is the illustrious J. Y. who leads them all?" Continuing his sarcasm, Long suggested that Sanders had asked his followers to follow without telling them where.[24]

In two other speeches Long attacked Sanders for his equivocation. To a Hammond audience, he insisted that Sanders would be satisfied if either Wilson or Simpson were elected and challenged the two opposing candidates to declare which one Sanders supported.[25] Later in the campaign, Long continued to denounce Sanders for his failure to declare himself in favor of Simpson or Wilson. At the same time, Long asserted, Sanders had lieutenants in both camps.[26]

Long used these four individuals in his attempt to polarize his audience. Each man was presented in an uncomplimentary light and was identified in some sense with Long's opponents. The speaker thereby confronted his listeners with an either-or choice: Simpson or Wilson would perpetuate the philosophies reflected in these flag individuals, whereas Long would repudiate those philosophies, offering a new departure in government. Long usually closed his attacks on the flag individuals by placing this very choice before the audience and suggesting that they express their decision by their vote on January 17.

DERISIVE JARGON A third polarization technique that Long used was derisive jargon. The earlier discussion of flag issues and flag individuals made occasional references to Long's use of sarcasm. However, there were so many other instances in the speeches when Long

23. *Ibid.*, November 25, 1927.
24. *Ibid.*, September 18, 1927.
25. *Ibid.*, October 6, 1927.
26. *Ibid.*, November 26, 1927.

ridiculed his opponents that the technique is worth careful analysis.

This technique was exemplified in the Shreveport address on September 17, when Long directed a number of derisive terms at his opponents. A favorite target was the Alexandria convention that nominated Wilson for governor. Using some of his most colorful epithets, Long referred to the participants as the "Lords, Dukes and Earls" of Louisiana and, in mock humility, expressed his pleasure that these "rulers" had permitted the crowd to attend Long's rally. Continuing his ridicule, Long denounced the delegates as "the leading trough-feeders and pie-eaters of this community," and further as "the self-appointed over-lords of finance and political affairs, the self-named rulers of the earth." Later he called them "distinguished and anointed royalists." [27]

He directed derision at other groups as well. In the Shreveport speech he characterized Sanders' followers as "disciples of politics and habitues of the pie-counter" and labeled the state conservation department as the "Coonservation Department," a term he applied over and over during the campaign.

Newspaper accounts indicate that crowds responded warmly to these verbal volleys. As a technique of polarization, the caustic jargon apparently accomplished two results. It portrayed the opposition as pompous, self-important men of ludicrous pretensions, perfect targets for Long's barbs. And like the flag issues and flag individuals, the jargon further served to polarize the audience. In particular the mocking analogy with royalty sharpened the contrast between Long and his opponents. The controlling oligarchy, the ring politicians, represented the interests of the wealthier groups; Long on the other hand became the champion of the common man. By a simple extension, to vote for Long was to vote for the interests of the people, whereas to vote for either of his opponents would favor continuation of the control of the upper classes. It was an effective polarization technique.

Solidification

Of the solidification techniques mentioned by Bowers and Ochs, Long employed only two. First, he created a slogan that became his

27. *Ibid.*, September 18, 1927.

theme throughout his career. Concluding his Shreveport speech on September 17, he declared, "Every man shall be a king, but no one shall wear a crown." Shortened to "Every man a king," the slogan highlighted not only the 1927 campaign, but later campaigns as well.

One other solidification technique is worth mentioning. In his speeches Long used language designed to stress identification in a common cause. In Shreveport, for example, he enlisted his listeners with him in his crusade. He reminded them, "You are your own leader, your own sovereign, you control your own vote, your political rights belong to you. Your command is that element which threatens to destroy every man who fails to follow the dictation." He concluded that "we are fighting a battle of principle."

In other speeches Long stressed that he and his listeners were joined in a common cause, and that it had been his pleasure to be closely associated with most of the people in the audience. Further, he reminded them that what was of benefit to one was of benefit to all. For one to tolerate the squandering of public funds and the other abuses was to injure all.

Conclusions

In his campaign speeches, Long revealed that he was a skillful rhetorician. Conducting a tireless speaking tour that carried him to many parishes of Louisiana and provided him with maximum exposure, Long chose his issues for their persuasiveness. He spoke of concrete, tangible goals, such as better roads and better education. For his specific audiences, he tailored selected themes for maximum rhetorical effect and substituted specific examples and simplified statistics for the generalities provided by most of his opponents. Further enhancing his effectiveness, Long invested his development with strong emotional appeals and ethical dimensions, often turning a problem into a moral issue.

Discussing southern popular leaders, including Long, Thomas D. Clark and Albert D. Kirwan refer to their "ruthless and extravagant" rhetorical methods.[28] Of course, such devices sometimes char-

28. Thomas D. Clark and Albert D. Kirwan, *The South Since Appomattox* (New York: Oxford University Press, 1967), 111.

202 / HAROLD MIXON

acterized Long's speeches. It is true that at times he exploited his listeners, manipulating their prejudices, fears, and frustrations. He attacked the character of his opponents and resorted to namecalling and sarcasm to ridicule them. Adept at shifting ground, he blunted opponents' criticism by reinterpreting the issue to make his case appear stronger.

Long learned these rhetorical techniques from careful study. In his earlier years he studied the speaking techniques of Jeff Davis of Arkansas and James K. Vardaman of Mississippi, both of whom he admired, and Theodore Bilbo, for whom he had less respect.[29] From these men Long learned much about constructing appeals that touched rural, lower economic voters.

However, Long's rhetoric differed from that of most other southern demagogues in two respects. First, he seldom incorporated the southern myths found profusely in most southern oratory. As the previous analysis indicates, among the speeches examined this writer could find only one instance in the 1927 campaign when Long referred to a southern myth. Secondly, Long made little use of racism. Although later in his career he maintained a public stance as a segregationist, Long seldom included racial slurs in his speeches, and when he did, Williams concludes that "he never did it very well."[30] Williams believes that Long "was completely without prejudice in his personal relations" when he dealt with minority groups, and the image he cultivated as a segregationist was a calculated strategy to give him greater latitude in handling racial matters before his Deep South white listeners.[31] For whatever reason, Long rarely employed racebaiting so common among many of the southern demagogues.

Taking his case to the people, he developed a rhetoric uniquely suited to Louisiana. Huey Long's speaking in 1927 contained all the elements that made his later speaking so successful.

29. Williams, *Huey Long*, 69–70.
30. *Ibid.*, 328.
31. *Ibid.*, 704.

9 / CAL M. LOGUE

The Coercive Campaign Prophecy
of Gene Talmadge, 1926–1946

Eugene Talmadge of Georgia won his first statewide campaign in 1926 at the age of forty-one and his last in 1946, the year he died at sixty-one. In each of his campaigns, Talmadge set a "gruelling pace." For example, in his first gubernatorial campaign in 1932, from July 4 to September 13, he spoke "nearly 100 times" to "approximately 175,000 people." In his bid for reelection in 1934, he talked face-to-face to "about 300,000." As he campaigned from "mountain to sea," was Talmadge, as some believed, "the candidate of bigotry, arrogance, and egotism," or rather one who was "fearless and unafraid" to fight "battles with a strong hand," yet had "a heart . . . as tender as a woman's?" Partisan opinions obscured the image of "old 'goose grease' Gene Talmadge." To establish a more reliable perspective of the man and his public discourse, I have studied seven of his campaigns, those of 1926 and 1928 for commissioner of agriculture, and those of 1932, 1934, 1940, 1942, and 1946 for governor. He won all but the 1942 election. By following Talmadge over a twenty-year period, I attempt to make a comprehensive synthesis of his campaign strategies and performance.[1]

Two critical components of a Talmadge campaign become apparent. First, the scene of his speeches was exploited as a spectacle of persuasion, and second, three qualities of his speaking enabled him

1. Atlanta *Constitution*, September 12, July 31, August 30, September 14, 11, 1932, September 12, 1934, July 18, 1940, May 14, 1946, September 9, 1932; Savannah *Morning News*, July 14, 17, June 27, 1946; Augusta *Chronicle*, August 23, 1942.

to win Georgia elections. In addition, Talmadge generated a coercive climate seductive to supporters and intimidating to opponents and nonpartisans.

The Speech Scene

In the towns where he was to speak, Talmadge and his helpers created a scene to condition the people for the coming of Gene. Although these occasions took on an atmosphere of spontaneity, the proceedings were as repetitive and predictable as a high school parade. Even though a "holiday mood" prevailed, these boisterous occasions were intimidating to opponents and nonpartisans. For all citizens were expected to attend and to conform. Disbelievers were not indulged. Differences of opinion concerning issues and candidates were barred by the campaign principals' posture of omniscience. The scene was created to attract people, sanctify Eugene Talmadge, and celebrate his coming victory.

To prepare people for Talmadge's speech, these persuasive productions were given the sounds and strategies of a Fourth of July celebration and traveling tent revival. Music aroused citizens who "began to gather . . . hours before the governor was scheduled to begin his remarks." In Macon a "brass band" played. "Fiddlin' John Carson" and the Cartersville string band "kept the vast throng" in Dalton "more than amused." Carson sang about "Talmadge and his $3 Automobile Tag," a campaign promise, and Professor J. A. Anderson, a Decatur musician, "added to the program." Prior to a speech in Douglas the Harmony Singers from Waycross sang from "a flat trailer truck."[2]

Voters were also baited by barbecue and watermelon. At Bainbridge, the crowd consumed "nine tons of beef," "hundreds of gallons of sauce," and "thousands of loaves of bread." In Louisiville, the twelve thousand plates ran out and "several hundred had to use newspapers or anything else they had to hold their lunch." To entertain citizens of Moultrie, "J. W. Toney's farm hands had fired the big black syrup kettles at dawn," and "all day long the pungent aroma of

2. Atlanta *Constitution*, July 13, 1934, May 23, June 23, 1946, August 5, 1934; Atlanta *Journal*, July 10, 1942.

frying fish was wafted through the pine land" attracting people. "Piled high on makeshift wooden tables were stacks of mullet. 'We got 15,000 pounds from the Gulf Coast,' Mr. Toney said. He figured one pound would feed two folks. Also on the menu were 5,000 pounds of potato chips, 100 gallons of pickles, and 2,000 loaves of bread." However, during the 1946 campaign, Gene, now established as a powerful figure, altered his strategy and courted primarily the politically elite. He provided "no barbecue for the rank and file." Only "a chosen few ate very well at a local roadhouse."[3]

The scene of the speech was carefully staged in such locales as an American Legion Park, courthouse hall or square, high school auditorium, tree grove, "basketball shell," hotel steps, a truck bed, warehouse platform, or hastily constructed stand. A "typical setting" included "a speaker's stand draped profusely with Talmadge-banners" and "Talmadge-henchmen dispensing . . . copies of a campaign song, of the current *Statesman*, Talmadge's weekly newspaper, and other campaign literature." A motorcade headed by a "magnificent 22 piece" band greeted Talmadge, accompanied by "automobile horns, fire sirens," and "mill whistle."

These arrangements attracted people from several surrounding counties and provided Talmadge with large and supportive audiences. Policemen and firemen were recruited to "aid in handling the crowds." Hundreds or thousands of curious citizens came in trucks, buses, cars, wagons, school buses, old-fashioned buggies, "farm conveyances of every description," and on foot. Vehicles "fanned out beyond the crowd." During the several campaigns, the rallies varied in size: 700 at Fort Valley, 1,000 at Danielsville, 1,200 at Toccoa, 3,500 at Elberton, 11,000 at Thomson, 19,000 at Griffin, 25,000 at Bainbridge. Many others listened by radio. "Placards" and "campaign buttons" identified the counties from which citizens came. Among the "sea of faces" were children, women, and men in overalls or white shirts. These campaign congregations were "rustic and vociferous and close-packed," hardly a forum for open debate.[4]

3. Atlanta *Constitution*, July 1, 1934, May 19, 1946; Atlanta *Journal*, July 5, 1942.
4. Atlanta *Constitution*, July 5, 1940, July 27, 20, August 6, 1932, August 16, 1934, July 31, August 2, September 13, 12, 16, 1932, July 1, September 1, 1934, September 2, 1932, July 13, 5, 1934, July 21, August 28, 1932, August 9, 1934, August 23, 1932, Au-

On schedule, thirty minutes late amidst "impatient" calls of "we want Talmadge," the "Sage of Sugar Creek" was greeted by "wild cheering, whistling, and applause." In town after town, Talmadge supporters attempted to crowd the audience inside the courthouse or some other structure, knowing the auditorium would not hold the large throng. Still, all seemed pleased when it was announced that the meeting would *have* to be moved outside, a decision Talmadge bragged about in most of his speeches and supporting newsmen echoed in the press.

The ritual immediately preceding a Talmadge speech was carefully planned to heighten audience interest. Accompanying Talmadge on the platform was a supporting cast of preacher, lawyer, mayor, judge, farmer, and/or a "pretty Miss Sisabelle Woolford" of Atlanta who "tells the crowd she plans to cast her first vote July 17 for 'Eugene Talmadge'." Suddenly the throng became silent when a chief of police, sheriff, newspaper editor, colonel, doctor, mayor, lawyer, or even a team of pollsters gazed seriously about and announced the "official" estimate of the size of the audience, designating the attendance as "the largest crowd ever assembled" in that county. After a "beloved" minister prayed, Talmadge was introduced by a prominent judge, school principal, mayor, university president, woman county superintendent of schools, brick mason, union leader, lawyer, editor, farmer, Speaker of the House, or "blind retired minister." From place to place, this introduction, spoken with great conviction, always sounded strangely similar, and it was contrived to contribute to Talmadge's chosen image. Introducers bragged that this candidate was a "man of courage," a "man with a fighting heart," "a worker and a doer, fearless, and human," a "friend of the farmer," a "champion of the people," "a man who keeps his promises," "one who will fight for the common man."

Another regular ritual was the insistence by the crowd that the introduction be ended prematurely—a part all knew, but one which the listeners persisted in acting out. "Give us Talmadge," they shouted, interrupting the introduction. "The chorus" rose, the introducer

gust 19, 1934, June 23, 1946; Augusta *Chronicle*, July 25, 1942, August 8, July 28, 1940; Macon *Telegraph and News*, July 5, 1942; Marietta (Ga.) *Journal*, July 21, 1932.

gave way to the wishes of the crowd, and the candidate stepped to the microphone amidst "deafening" applause. "A tremendous cheer" went up and "auto horns" honked their approval. Enthusiasm "spread from throat to throat." The result was a scene that appeared "to be a Roman holiday and no scene in the Circus Maximus ever surpassed the fire of its enthusiasm, the intensity of the fervor of the greeting." Promoters programmed this ritual from the first fish fried to the counting of the crowd, priming the audience to perform for Talmadge.[5]

The Speech

Talmadge satisfied audience appetites whetted by the emotional scene. Having debated in college, defended legal clients, and campaigned locally and statewide, he became an experienced persuader. Although he adapted his remarks to each new occasion, during a particular campaign he delivered basically the same speech. The day he inaugurated a campaign Talmadge often prepared a manuscript, but most of the time he spoke extemporaneously. When he did have notes or a manuscript, he made it part of his act to "deviate," "disregard," or "refer" to them "casually on but two or three occasions." A reporter covering his Moultrie speech described how the procedure worked. Talmadge "used his manuscript as an innovation, but only got through two pages of it, when the supporters began as usual to yell at him to 'tell us' about this or that."

Although Talmadge was particularly effective in confronting audiences face-to-face, he also reached listeners by means of radio in all five gubernatorial campaigns. For example, in 1934 he delivered a thirty-minute radio address that "concluded his campaign for re-election . . . summing up the issues." He thus was required to adapt his stump speaking to the medium of radio. Speaking in Rome, Georgia, Talmadge "himself had to quiet the applause in order not to keep

5. Macon *Telegraph*, August 20, 1932; Macon *Telegraph and News*, July 5, 1942; Atlanta *Constitution*, September 5, 6, 1934, August 6, September 1, 1932, June 23, 1946, September 4, 1932; August 16, 19, 1934, July 20, August 14, 28, September 12, August 24, 1932, September 1, July 13, August 28, September 5, 1934, June 2, 1946, July 26, August 21, September 9, July 5, 1934, September 6, 1932; Savannah *Morning News*, June 14, 1946; see also Thomas W. Hardwick's speech in Atlanta *Constitution*, August 14, 1932.

the radio audience waiting." "Thousands . . . heard the address . . . over station WSB" in Atlanta. Colonel Mebane explained the effect that radio had upon the size of the audience assembled to see his candidate: "The crowd would have been far greater had not the address been broadcast, however, all we want is for the people to hear the speech. We do not care whether they are listening here or at home just so they are listening."[6] Nevertheless, one would speculate that persons watching the Talmadge speech show would have been significantly more affected than those merely listening by radio.

In his stump speaking, Talmadge made himself the dominant issue. "Despite all this talking," concluded reporter L. A. Farrell after listening to two months of campaigning, "there is only one major issue with the voters and that is Talmadge. They either like him or they do not."[7] Ironically, this politician claimed to deal "in issues and not men" and to "avoid any petty politics and personalities." Talmadge's manner, however, was his message and his personality his prescription. Following this strategy throughout his political career, he personalized his campaigns into a politics of prophecy. He represented himself metaphorically as the mind of the citizens. "Various candidates," he said, were conspiring to "defeat the will of the people in this next election." But "the end and reward of deception" was "at hand," and he personified his candidacy as the promise of the voters. Choosing religious symbols rooted in the rural South, this Georgian prophesized their "financial salvation." "The people are entitled to the light," he continued, and he alone was free to follow "the faith of the people," the "only man" who could confront successfully "the most critical times that this commonwealth has ever seen." Thus Talmadge nominated himself as the new Moses: "Today I am offering to lead the people of Georgia in this great undertaking."[8] In campaign-

6. Atlanta *Constitution*, July 29, September 6, 13, 1932, July 10, June 16, July 13, 1946, July 1, 13, 5, 26, September 9, 1934, May 17, 19, 1946; Augusta *Chronicle*, July 5, 1940, July 19, 1942; Atlanta *Journal*, July 5, 1942; Macon *Telegraph and News*, July 5, 1942. For accounts of radio speeches see: Atlanta *Constitution*, July 7, 1932, August 22, 28, 29, September 11, 12, 1934, July 20, September 9, 1940, April 28, May 14, 1946, September 9, 1934; Augusta *Chronicle*, July 26, August 31, September 7, 1940, July 11, 30, August 15, July 22, 1942; Atlanta *Journal*, July 10, 18, 1942; Macon *Telegraph*, August 1, 1942.
7. Atlanta *Constitution*, September 9, 1934, August 3, 2, 5, 1932; Marietta *Journal*, July 21, 1932.
8. Atlanta *Constitution*, September 2, 4, July 16, 1932, September 9, 1934, August

ing on a strategy of personal prophecy, Talmadge invented a public discourse characterized by three qualities: familiarity, novelty, and infallibility.

Familiarity

When he entered a town, Talmadge behaved in a manner familiar and acceptable to white Georgians. Although he was college trained and from a successful family, he had lived on a farm; thus, he stressed his credentials as a man of the soil. This schooled lawyer cultivated an image of being one of the masses and disguised himself as a spokesman concerned about both their cruel working conditions and their abuse at the hands of government and business elites. Early in his political life this "Wild Man of the Soil" courted primarily the farm vote: "This is a fight I am making for you farmers." He claimed to understand that "the life of a farmer is filled with drudgery, toil and little pay." Indeed, he said, "I am a farmer." Misrepresenting his own background, Talmadge argued: "We need a man in the governor's chair who knows how a poor man feels. No one knows that except by experience."

Realizing the potential favorable impact of Talmadge's identification with rural voters, political opponents attempted to disrobe "ole' Gene's" farm disguise: "You ought to see him . . . sliding across those polished ballroom floors in Atlanta's hotels," one critic stated. "A carnation stuck in his coat, his fingernails polished and his hair slicked down with goose grease. No Arabian sheik in all his pomp and glory was ever more dolled up. And then, when he gets out of Atlanta, he puts on those old red galluses, pulls his hair down over his eyes, bites off a chew of tobacco and starts spouting about all he is going to do for the farmer. By his shenanigans he has given Georgia a black eye all over the nation. . . . He's an obstructionist who gets power drunk and like a mad bull, just charges all over the place, not caring what he wrecks."[9]

1, 1926, July 23, 1932, July 23, May 30, 1946, August 10, 1926, August 11, July 5, 1932, July 5, 1934; Augusta *Chronicle*, August 25, September 6, August 29, 1940; Americus *Times-Recorder*, September 13, 1932.

9. Dalton (Ga.) *Citizen*, September 15, 1932; Atlanta *Constitution*, July 1, 1926, May 26, 1946, August 17, 1928, Americus *Times-Recorder* August 27, 1928; Savannah *Morning News*, June 26, 1946.

212 / CAL M. LOGUE

Talmadge's strategy of identifying with farmers and disassociating his candidacy from social elites had wide appeal among many white Georgians. Ironically, while campaigning for the poor farmers' votes by blaming the political and business leaders for the farmers' economic problems, Talmadge called upon those same leaders for financial support. As V. O. Key states, although speaking a message pleasing to poor workers, Talmadge practiced policies popular with the business establishment, favoring "a balanced budget, a low tax rate, and not much public regulation of private enterprise." Thus, Talmadge managed to win elections on the back of the poor workers' votes and the businessmen's funding. He exploited the persuasive formula of familiarity in several ways.

Talmadge looked physically the part of a farmer. He was "swarthy" and, for years, a lean, "wiry" man who appeared as if he would be comfortable walking behind a plow and a mule. In his speeches he capitalized upon this appearance, claiming that his dark complexion was farm-earned, although that condition may have resulted from a childhood illness. To further identify with an agricultural image, Talmadge wore suspenders, a symbol of his and the audience's rural pride and rugged independence. Early in each speech, at the request of a member of his audience, Talmadge dramatically removed his coat and revealed "flaming red suspenders." On that cue, many men in the gathering demonstrated their loyalty by removing their coats and showing off their own red galluses. During his speech, Talmadge began "mopping his streaming brow with a red bandanna handkerchief," another badge of the working man. This also brought a loud vocal response.[10]

Later in his political career, aware of the increasing number of "street car city" voters, Talmadge broadened his strategy to include all laborers. Earlier he had ridiculed "city slickers" as a means of entertaining farmers. And because as governor he had not always acted in labor's interest, when campaigning for reelection, he was put on the

10. V. O. Key, Jr., *Southern Politics in State and Nation* (New York: Alfred A. Knopf, 1949), 116–17; Atlanta *Constitution*, August 11, 1932, May 19, 1946, July 10, 1932, July 5, August 24, September 4, 1934, July 5, 12, 1940, May 23, 1946; Americus *Times-Recorder*, August 5, 1926; Augusta *Chronicle*, August 5, 1940; Savannah *Morning News*, July 17, 1946; William Anderson, *The Wild Man from Sugar Creek: The Political Career of Eugene Talmadge* (Baton Rouge: Louisiana State University Press, 1975), 103.

defensive. In 1946, for example, the "Regional Director of the CIO" indicated that "our aim is to defeat Eugene Talmadge for Governor." The form of Talmadge's appeal, however, remained basically the same as the one he used with farmers. He identified the laborers' experiences as his own. "I resent anyone on earth saying that they are closer to labor, or a better friend to labor, than I. I am a laborer myself. You can look at my hands and the color of my skin, and tell it." "You know, after all," he cajoled, "the city fellows are just country boys shaved up and dressed up a little bit." "The first little poem that I ever remember, when I was a small boy," he stated, "went something like this: 'Mother told me; Father showed me; Hard labor makes a man.' When I go over Georgia and see the thousands of people at work at a low, starvation wage, it makes my heart bleed." "The truth is, I want the votes of city people and have always wanted them." [11]

To project an image of a leader working men and women could trust, Talmadge communicated in their verbal vernacular. He "talked . . . to farmers in the language of a farmer." He told a Thomson audience that he modeled his own crusade for the working class after their former hero, Tom Watson, even attempting to employ "the language" Watson used in his "continuous fight for the common people." "When I was a little boy," Talmadge told his audiences, "I would sometimes go to political meetings. I saw a man with red hair, freckled face and flashing eyes who talked to the people in large assemblages in language that brought them to their feet with wild cheers in acclamation of the principles which he espoused. Today . . . I understand the language that Tom Watson used when he said: 'We must have free speech, a free press and freedom of assembly.'" [12]

To enhance his credibility with audiences, Talmadge communicated in a language that was both poetic and understandable. These two communicative strategies enabled him to enter the towns, homes, and hearts of white Georgians triumphantly.

11. Atlanta *Constitution*, August 5, 1934. For Talmadge's appeals to labor see: Atlanta *Constitution*, July 23, August 3, 19, 1932, August 21, September 4, 1934, June 12, 1946, September 6, 1934; Augusta *Chronicle*, August 16, 25, 1942. For examples of how Talmadge increasingly courted the city voters see: Atlanta *Constitution*, July 6, September 1, 1934, September 9, August 9, July 25, 1932, June 10, 1946; Augusta *Chronicle*, July 26, September 3, 1940.
12. Americus *Times-Recorder*, August 27, 1928; Atlanta *Constitution*, July 22, 15, September 10, 16, 1932, August 9, 1934.

Talmadge captured the feelings and aspirations of working people in poetic political speech. He was gifted with words, capable of
proclaiming the plight of farmers and workers in poetic symbols that
created in listeners a sense of pride in who they were and what they
had endured. Employing emotional speech, Talmadge elevated the
daily struggle of white Georgians to a kind of religious celebration of
their lives of sacrifice. This ability to make eloquent their hard experience endeared him to many listeners. Talmadge publicly recognized
feelings and needs that workers believed to have been ignored. He
was particularly adept in evoking vivid images of suffering. Note too
that these emotional appeals carried the implication that he would
prevent the cause of this suffering when elected governor. "There
were tears in the eyes of many when Talmadge dramatically ex-
claimed" to a Homer audience: "What I am preaching to you today is
not all fun and pleasure, for there is sorrow and pathos behind what I
am saying. There are aching backs and blistered hands, discouraged
souls and broken hearts, hungry women and crying children, there
are men able and willing to work walking our streets trying to get
work with which to obtain food for their loved ones, and yet waste,
extravagance and graft still exist at our capitol."[13] Responding to the
charge that he was a "wild man," Talmadge wore proudly the nick-
name, "Wild Man From Sugar Creek," and argued that to see "hundreds and hundreds of homes and farms being sold each month for
taxes, and know that our people, on account of high taxes, are unable
to pay the taxes on their homes, it is enough to make a man wild. If
you could go over the state as I have during the past summer, and see
in the fields of Georgia the ragged women working in the fields, with
a suckling babe underneath the trees, and knowing that that woman
is hungry, and has a hungry family, it is enough to make me wild."[14]

Although there were moments when Talmadge elevated his campaign rhetoric to expressions of near statesmanship, too often his poetic speech languished in inflated phrases of political extravagance,
promising "farmers . . . irrigation, pumps, and lakes" in their "back
yards" so that "when the men come to call on the young ladies, they

13. Atlanta *Constitution*, September 2, 1932.
14. *Ibid.*, September 9, 1932.

can go out on the lake and sit in the moonlight in a beautiful gondola." Although these campaign exaggerations entertained, they had
little relevance to those pressing problems which, ironically, Talmadge articulated so well. Too often he resorted to verbal tactics con-
ceived to distract voters from their oppressed living conditions. His
campaign chicanery disguised his omission of specific policies con-
ceived to solve the workers' problems. "The Atlanta papers," he
beamed, "are going to have a 'crow banquet' at which they will eat
crow over the Talmadge victory. You farmers kill some crows . . . and
send them up to Atlanta." He promised when elected to "fill up those
four or five acres" around the governor's house "with hound dogs,
cows and chickens. I want you all to come see us there and bring me a
ham." [15] There is tragedy in these talks in that one so familiar with the
social problems and so capable of articulating social conditions was so
flippant in his transactions. There is also irony in these rowdy remarks in that Talmadge presented himself as the sole hope of the future and criticized his opponents for having only their selfish interests
to guide them. Unlike others, he yelled in the slang of rural citizens,
"I ain't got no oil company making profits off the pipelines."

Although enough Georgians liked Talmadge's performance to
elect him to state offices numerous times, not all observers were
pleased by his hyperbole. The editor of the Valdosta *Times* stated that
his paper "has never supported former Governor Eugene Talmadge.
He just doesn't talk our language and his performances during his
terms in office were such as to make it utterly impossible for us to consider giving him our support now." [16]

In addition to its poetic quality, Talmadge's campaign language
was characterized by its high intelligibility. Although many disagreed
with the man, few left a Talmadge rally wondering what he intended
to say. Although he omitted long-range solutions from his discourse,
he expressed his thoughts clearly, translating topics into terms understandable to rural and urban audiences. Critics viewed this practice of
oversimplifying complex social and economic problems as being one
of his greatest faults. Still, for many Georgians he spoke "in ringing,

15. *Ibid.*, May 24, June 1, 1946, July 15, 1932; Augusta *Chronicle*, July 29, 1942.
16. Quoted in Augusta *Chronicle*, July 10, 1942; Atlanta *Constitution*, July 6, 1946.

understandable terms of the condition of the state government and the issues" for which he stood.[17]

Talmadge argued that his verbal clarity was proof of his personal honesty, goodwill, and authority. Unlike his opponents, he claimed, he was exacting and unequivocal, a candidate who would confront issues and voters directly. Consequently, early in each campaign Talmadge isolated a few specific issues to be repeated in every speech. In 1932, he maintained that "the three vital things that are in everyone's mind at present are: First—making an honest living. Second—Educating our children. Third—Good roads." In 1942, the candidate argued that "the four principles dear to Americans are white supremacy, states' rights, Jeffersonian Democracy, and old time religion."[18] To be certain listeners could follow his chain of reasoning, Talmadge developed thoughts in "full and specific detail." His addresses were replete with instances familiar to workers. In plain speech he visualized publicly the private thoughts of farmers and workers. At the same time, each example and analogy carried the clear implication that, among the several candidates, only Talmadge was able to solve problems. "The Highway Department," he said, "now has five times as much road machinery as they need. . . . Look at it scattered in the roads, the swamps, bogged down in ditches." Government, he argued, was bloated with "too many engineers, too many linemen, too many supervisors and clerks to eat up the money and no results are shown."[19]

Talmadge not only simplified the causes of high taxes and wasteful officials, but offered general solutions in plain speech. "Instead of reorganization," as his opponents had recommended, "abolishment is the word." He explained this sloganized solution for making government more efficient and less expensive in a homespun analogy. "I can reorganize 12 marbles on a table from now until midnight and still have 12 marbles on the table unless I break some of them. . . . What Georgia needs is a man . . . who will wipe some of the marbles off the table and call it that." After courts ruled that blacks in Georgia

17. Marietta (Ga.) *Journal*, July 21, 1932.
18. Atlanta *Constitution*, May 14, 1946, September 2, July 5, 1932; Augusta *Chronicle*, August 7, 1942.
19. Atlanta *Constitution*, August 28, 1940; Augusta *Chronicle*, August 11, 1940.

could participate in "white primaries," Talmadge increasingly infused his examples and analogies with racist connotations popular with whites. In fact, he frequently captured both the practical experience and the racist attitudes of his audience: "They want the highway department to put on an order for a negro to receive 40 cents per hour for rolling a wheelbarrow or shoveling dirt on our roads," though "practically 75 per cent of the laborers building roads are negroes and build these roads in country communities where white women and girls pick cotton right beside the road, barely making 40 cents per day. Yet, these women help to pay the taxes of this state."[20]

Novelty

The novelty of Talmadge's campaigning attracted audiences and enhanced his popularity. His unusual performance on the stump made him a legendary political figure whom all wanted to see and hear. Persons who witnessed a Talmadge rally departed with something unusual to talk about. Because of his political antics, he drew crowds and reactions with a charisma created today more by rock stars than politicians. At Bainbridge, for example, in 1934,

time and again, although his crowd was with him wholeheartedly, the governor had to appeal for permission to continue, so warmly was his address received. The great throng, which defied all efforts of the police to keep it within bounds, surged about the speaker's stand, pushing women and children and making it impossible for authorities to maintain any semblances of order. From the way Governor Talmadge's address was received it was impossible to determine which, if any, portion of it received wider approval than the others. It all brought satisfaction to the immense throng.

That same year at Sardis Church in Hart County, "Talmadge and members of his family narrowly escaped serious injury . . . as a stampeding crowd which heard the . . . address . . . surged upon the speaker's platform and caused it to collapse just after the chief executive finished his speech."[21]

Two qualities contributed to the novelty of a Talmadge performance and to his ability to attract and hold audiences: he was unin-

20. Atlanta *Constitution*, July 5, 1932, September 1, 1940, August 7, 1932, August 19, 5, 24, 21, 1934.
21. *Ibid.*, July 5, 26, 1934.

hibited and he stocked his speeches with surprises. Unlike most of his opponents, Talmadge was indeed totally uninhibited on the stump. In order to attract crowds, make his candidacy distinctive, and win votes he performed without constraints. He argued that his admittedly radical behavior confirmed his willingness to serve the common man and oppose sissy behaving elites who segregated themselves from Georgia workers. Although his emphasis was upon the entertainment value of his remarks, he linked his insolent language to topics such as jobs, income, and race.

Talmadge pleased many in his rowdy audiences by talking tough. He communicated in a loud, boisterous, and coarse manner, unaffected by social convention or political protocol. Standing before the audience with a noticeable "lock of" hair hanging "over his right eye," he snarled empathetically at his listeners. He pounded with his clenched fist and pointed fearlessly to emphasize one point after another. Talmadge "flayed his opposition" as "crooks," "coupon clippers," "bums and loafers," "profit-sharing henchmen," a "bunch of jackasses," a "gang of hijackers," and a "machine of political farmers." He labeled Ellis Arnall, an opponent, "Little Boy Blue" and "'Benedict' Arnall." Talmadge interpreted the actions of opponents as being "pernicious and corrupt," "arrogant dictation," "bribery," "sinister influence," and a "sweet orgy of robbery." To him, the Atlanta *Journal* was an organ "that's got to be Christianized." When campaigning for governor in 1946, after having been defeated by Arnall in 1942 and after a court ruled that blacks could vote in so-called "white primaries," Talmadge "made negro voting his principal issue," warning against "social equality," "alien influences," and "Moscow Harlem zoot-suiters" who would go "into Atlanta's First Baptist Church" and "try to sit down right there alongside a white lady." [22]

Talmadge also employed the element of surprise in his speeches. Audiences anticipated the unexpected to occur. Many of the candidate's stock acts, however, were repeated from town to town and dis-

22. Augusta *Chronicle*, September 12, 1940, August 16, 1942; Atlanta *Constitution*, July 18, 1946, August 5, 1934, July 5, 1942, September 8, 1932, August 22, 1934, July 4, 1, 7, 1926, May 26, June 2, July 10, 1946; Americus *Times-Recorder*, September 13, 1932; Savannah *Morning News*, July 17, June 14, 4, 1946.

guised as being spontaneous. He enticed his listeners with behavior that shocked and saddened, exploiting emotions ranging from anger to pity. In Macon, he "unloosed" a "sensational charge" by making "public correspondence . . . linking" his opponent with questionable "highway contracts." He "waved the original letters . . . reading them to his audience and inviting anyone . . . to come up and look at them," while "five thousand copies . . . were distributed to the audience." [23] Talmadge dramatized his message by packaging surprises in stories that exploited his familiarity with working people. Each account was communicated dramatically as a means of heightening the credibility of his candidacy. "An old lady," he explained to one audience, had told him "that last year when she was sewing for a living she was only able to keep one light on in the house. She looked at me and said: 'Governor, since January 1, I can have three or four lights burning in my house, and my bill is less than it was last year.' Thank God that I could help light that dark home." During World War II, Talmadge exploited patriotic themes, even using his son's military service as a means of influencing voters: "Where is Herman," a listener asked, and on cue "the Governor exhibited a photograph of his son and said, 'He is in the Navy.'" [24]

Although many of Talmadge's campaign antics were repeated throughout Georgia, he was also skillful in adapting to the sights and sounds surrounding him on a particular occasion. Once, for example, as he "charged that inferior oils and gasoline" were being "dumped into Georgia . . . an automobile passed by making a lot of noise. 'There goes a machine now talking for Talmadge,' the speaker said and the crowd cheered."

Talmadge's uninhibited behavior and his campaign surprises were intensified by the novel form of public discourse he employed at rallies. He generated interest and approval by involving citizens in his performance. "Everything he said brought a halt and a speech of support from one or more of a half dozen sections of the throng," ob-

23. Atlanta *Constitution*, August 20, September 13, 1932; as a novelty in 1934, Talmadge boasted that he would not refer to his "opponents by name . . . during this whole campaign"; see August 26, July 13, August 29, 1934.

24. Atlanta *Constitution*, August 19, 1934, May 23, 1946; Atlanta *Journal*, July 5, 1942; see full-page advertisement in Macon *Telegraph*, August 25, 1942.

served a reporter. "All in all there were two speeches, one by the governor and another by the crowd." Talmadge intentionally aroused his auditors. To stimulate participation, he asked a series of questions:

He asked if they favored his acts in saving the state $7,880,000 in less than two years, and there were shouts of "yes, yes." He asked the multitude if it favored the $2,141,000 reduction in the state deficit without any increase in taxation and the shouts of approval grew louder. He asked his hearers if they favored the reductions in power, light, and telephone rates . . . and the shouts of approval became a rising crescendo which could have been heard for miles. He asked if the crowd wanted reduced passenger fares and reduced freight rates by rail and truck kept in effect and the response became so vociferous that words cannot describe it.[25]

Some audience participants were coached and planted to ask a helpful question at a particular time. Others were obviously impromptu comments resulting from the excitement of the moment. Most comments were friendly. A few were hostile. "'Tell us about that propaganda menace, Gene,' came a husky voice" from one crowd, obviously prematurely. "Which one?," Talmadge replied, confused by the vagueness of the question. "'Jim Cox,' came back the answer, but the governor parried the question, 'I'll get to him later.'" Some persons simply wanted Gene to turn so they could see him: "Talk over this way," they would yell. Others offered encouragement and support in revival fashion: "Tell 'em about it 'Gene." Supporters prompted him with topics they knew would please the audience: "'What will Pittman do if he gets elected?' a voice in the crowd asked. 'Lord only knows,' the governor responded. 'But I'll tell you one thing and that is that he'll never get elected in the world.' The crowd gave the governor a rousing cheer for this reply."

At the close of his speeches, Talmadge "called the roll of counties," polling his contingents' estimation of how well he was doing in those areas: "'How is Appling?,' the governor asked and received a reply that Appling was present and he would carry it. 'How is Baldwin'?" "As Governor Talmadge shouted the name of the counties . . . there were whoops and reports that 'we are for you.'"[26]

---

25. Debate with J. J. Brown, Atlanta *Constitution*, August 4, 1926, July 26, 1934.
26. Anderson, *Wild Man from Sugar Creek*, 73–74; Atlanta *Constitution*, July 5, 1942;

In his public dialogue with audiences, Talmadge exploited hostile questions and comments as a means of creating interest, displaying his rhetorical cleverness, and intimidating opponents. At Macon, when a "man hollered, 'What about Dr. Swing'?" one of Talmadge's appointees who had "been under fire" in his work as superintendent of the state hospital, he replied " 'He's over at Milledgeville doing a good job as far as I know. . . . If you know where he is doing anything wrong I just wish you'd tell me right here.' There came nothing further from the man in the crowd and the throng cheered lustily once more." At Thomaston, when Talmadge called the roll of counties at the end of his speech, "a small group of young men declared themselves for Candidate Jimmie Carmichael. Talmadge exchanged remarks with them" and stated that "he was more interested in 'hand primaries with grown folks' than 'straw ballots with children.'" If a person were too persistent with argumentative reactions he found himself "soon drowned out by the cheers of the crowd for the answers Talmadge gave to his queries."[27]

Infallibility

Talmadge based his campaign upon the infallibility of his candidacy. He attempted to demonstrate this oratorical omniscience in two ways, first by emphasizing the infallibility of his understanding of social problems, and second by stressing that he was the only person with the ability and courage required to implement solutions. He led his audiences to believe that he best understood their problems. When Talmadge discussed economic and racial topics, he allowed no doubt to enter his discourse. To this arrogant man, compromise was a sign of weakness and uncertainty, an abdication of one's convictions. He warned that statements of qualification were proof of a candidate's personal unreliability. "The opposition says that they are in favor of a $2 or $3 tag," Talmadge stated. "Whenever an indefinite statement is made, and too many ifs and ors put in it, you had better not attach too much credence to it."

Savannah *Morning News*, June 21, 1946; Atlanta *Constitution*, September 5, July 13, September 4, 1934.

27. Atlanta *Constitution*, September 4, 1934, May 26, 1946, August 24, 1934.

To depict himself as a man of authority and to prevent open discussion of ideas, Talmadge reasoned in categorical assertions: "Raise Taxes? No!," he screamed. On one occasion, "at the prodding of the crowd" he vehemently declared, "Before God, friends, the 'niggers' will never go to a school which is white while I am governor." Talmadge spoke in a language reeking with professed infallibility. He reduced complex economic and social subjects to simple phrases. For example, choosing a solution to the state's financial problems his audience could easily comprehend, Talmadge promised to implement a "cash and carry" policy. Through these oversimplifications he manufactured aphorisms popular with working Georgians: "It has reached the point in Georgia," he stated, "where the larger a farm a man has, the more land he has, the more people he has working on his land doing honest, intelligent work, the quicker the man goes broke." [28]

In addition to trying to validate his persuasion with rhetorical verities, Talmadge exuded an aura of infallibility in a second way. He claimed that only he had "nerve enough" to change the social order. The person they elected, he argued, was far more important than any issue. "The only yardstick by which the platform of a political candidate may be accurately estimated," he said, "is the integrity of the man behind it." Other candidates, he reminded them, only "tiptoed around the main issue" of cutting expenses. Contrasting his credentials with his opponents', Talmadge insisted that he was not a "soft-handed, lilly-faced" individual who would be "bluffed and bulldozed," "handicapped by timidity," and "afraid to risk a row for his principles." [29]

To demonstrate for his listeners that he could help them, Talmadge assumed at the podium the pose of a courageous fighter. He performed in such a way as to prove himself a doer of deeds. And in molding this image, he looked the part of a fighter. At his rallies, citizens insisted that he "roll up" his "sleeve and tell them about it." Then when he "started speaking with his arms as well as his lips the

28. Atlanta *Constitution*, August 21, 1934, July 5, 1932; Augusta *Chronicle*, July 26, September 5, 1940; Atlanta *Journal*, July 5, 1942.

29. Atlanta *Constitution*, July 15, 17, August 26, 1932, August 26, 29, 1934; Americus *Times-Recorder*, September 13, 1932.

crowd went wild." Assuming a fighting stance, Talmadge moved "back and forth over" the platform and leaned toward the audience, his right fist clenched and raised, then both arms stretched parallel to the ground. He pointed decisively and scowled, creating an attitude of fearlessness. Considerable attention was given in the press and at his rallies to his courage in speaking day after day, even though his "voice was husky from the strenuous campaigning." [30]

To illustrate to voters that he meant what he said, Talmadge "radicalized" his public rhetoric. Defending this aggressive strategy, he contrasted his own courage with the cowardice of his opponents: "This smooth crowd wants to have a stalking horse on which to trade, because the interests need a bridle on them in the governor's chair. . . . My countrymen, you will never get the graft and rottenness out of the state government; you will never get taxes cut down . . . by running things smoothly, but it will take some one who is not afraid to fight to get relief from these things." Talmadge pledged to the voters that he would "fuss," "complain," "agitate," and "keep up the fight until something" was "done." Witnesses reported that he was a "forceful" and "aggressive" campaigner who "stormed" the state "talking with a fervor that brought enthusiasm and prolonged applause." His speeches were "full of flash and fire," "bristling with enthusiasm of purpose, sparkling with bits of wit and cemented with the zeal that has brought Talmadge more hearers in two years than any other public speaker the state has ever had." Employing these aggressive tactics, Talmadge worked his "crowds to a fever pitch." [31]

Throughout Georgia Talmadge contrasted what would happen if he were not elected with what would be accomplished if he were. If

30. Atlanta *Constitution*, August 28, September 6, 1932, July 5, 1934, September 9, 1932, August 26, 1934, July 22, 16, August 31, 6, 1932; Atlanta *Journal*, July 5, 1942; Savannah *Morning News*, June 21, 1946; Americus *Times-Recorder*, September 13, 1932. On occasions he "began talking in what was not more than a hoarse whisper," explaining to his audiences that "his voice would clear up shortly. It did in . . . less than five minutes"; Savannah *Morning News*, June 21, 1946; Atlanta *Constitution*, June 11, 1946, July 5, 1934.

31. Atlanta *Constitution*, August 25, 1932, September 9, 1934, August 17, 1928, August 9, 3, 1932, August 5, 1934, September 2, 1932, May 23, 1946, July 23, 1926; Americus *Times-Recorder*, September 13, 1932. Although Talmadge persuaded incumbent J. J. Brown to debate him during the commissioner of agriculture campaign in 1926, when he was in office he refused to debate challengers; Atlanta *Constitution*, September 6, August 29, 1934.

he were not elected, he warned, laws which required "separation of whites and negroes in schools, hotels, and on trains—even those which prohibit intermarriage" would be repealed. When asked by a listener why something had not been done to remedy problems, Talmadge replied, "Because nobody had the guts to do it." "Every lick that I got at a tax bill in my life I cut it," he insisted. He pledged to "stay on" the "neck" of wrongdoers, to "go into the dark vaults" and expose inequities. He would "use the red pencil to wipe out useless waste and extravagance and to eliminate graft."

After the United States Supreme Court ruled against segregation on public interstate conveyances, blacks were allowed to vote in "white primaries," and the topic of race became even more important to white voters, Talmadge increasingly emphasized the role of blacks in southern society. Although he did not *stress* the topic of race earlier in his career when blacks were less a political force in the state, there was significance in candidate Jimmie Carmichael's 1946 complaint: "Ever since I was 10 years old, Eugene Talmadge has been running for office in Georgia on the race issue. . . . He has played the role of a modern Paul Revere, hollering 'Wake up, wake up, the nigger is coming.'" To prevent the integration of whites and blacks, Talmadge promised "to stop all buses at the State lines and make the passengers walk across the line." As for railroads, he would "put inspectors in at the State line to look into every sleeping car and see that there's no mixing of the races in Georgia." [32] "If any faculty members of any of the state colleges do go insinuating or preaching any doctrines that would mix the races, Talmadge," as he referred to himself, "will fire them." Quite simply, he claimed to be "the white man's candidate" in the race, "the only" one "against nigger voting." He planned to have "'the Nigger' . . . come to the back door with his hat in his hand." In both the 1942 and 1946 campaigns, Talmadge gave his "word as a white man that a Negro never will be a white man's boss in a cotton mill" or be "placed over white women workers." Politicizing what he defined as the threat of blacks to dominance of whites, Talmadge

32. Savannah *Morning News*, June 4, 1946; Atlanta *Constitution*, September 13, 1932, June 5, 1946, July 12, 1940, August 13, 1926, July 14, June 2, 1946; Augusta *Chronicle*, July 26, 1940; Macon *Telegraph*, August 20, 1932; Americus *Times-Recorder*, September 13, 1932.

urged that "White people lay aside . . . petty differences and . . . have a solid march of white people who will go to the polls and save good old Georgia from the carpetbaggers."[33]

After serving as commissioner of agriculture and governor, Talmadge campaigned for reelection on his record of doing what he said he would do. "If I have made life's burdens easier for you," he told a radio audience, "I ask at your hands an endorsement term. If I have tried, and made an honest effort to carry out these campaign pledges, I ask an endorsement term." He "came nearer filling all his campaign pledges than any governor in the past 40 years," he argued. Again assuming the infallibility of his performance, Talmadge indicated that to change one's mind publicly was a sign of personal weakness: "There was no promise that I didn't carry out, and there was no principle that I advocated that I don't advocate now." In his first campaigns Talmadge was cautious to make only concrete promises he could keep. Motivated more by showmanship than statesmanship, he anticipated being able later to remind voters that he had kept his promises. When asked at Statesville, for example, "what he would do about road building if elected," Talmadge replied: "That is a question which, as a candidate for governor I cannot answer." He would "not make any promises to Echols or any other county. Your commissioners will have to discuss that with the proper state authorities."[34]

Having been defeated in his race for governor in 1942, in 1946 Talmadge abandoned all caution and participated in "a promising contest" with E. D. Rivers. He promised the following: "largest" road-building program ever, "hospitals in every county," improved farm-to-market roads, rural electrification, improved rural schools, increased pay for teachers, vocational schools, increased pensions and aid to the veterans, additional power lines, "co-operation between capital and labor," preservation of the county unit system, special license privileges to veterans, and placement of every sheriff in the state on rolls of the Georgia Bureau of Investigation in order "to aid him in 'investigating crime.'" As an added attraction, Talmadge said

33. Macon *Telegraph*, July 29, 1942; Atlanta *Constitution*, May 19, June 11, 1, May 26, 30, 1946; Augusta *Chronicle*, July 5, 24, August 16, 25, 1942; Macon *Telegraph and News*, August 2, 1942.
34. Atlanta *Constitution*, August 29, 1934, August 2, 1932, August 26, 1934, July 17, 1932, July 13, 1934; Augusta *Chronicle*, August 16, 1940, August 28, 1942.

he would provide all these benefits without Georgians having "to pay more taxes to get them."[35]

To combat criticism that his radical campaigning was demagogic, Talmadge exhumed mythic defenders from Georgia's past, including John B. Gordon, Tom Watson, Robert Toombs, Robert E. Johnston, and Alexander Stephens. To promote an image of his own bravery, Talmadge placed himself on this honor roll of Georgians. For example he stated: "I am happy to be in this county, the home of Alexander Stephens, and I pay tribute to his honesty, courage, and patriotism. We need more men of his type in Georgia politics . . . who are willing, fearlessly and courageously, to fight the battles and yet be free from demagogy." Then in Thomson, Talmadge indicated that just as he had done in his own political life, Tom Watson also had gone "to the jailhouse door" for his convictions and for the interest of the people. Talmadge's followers contended that he was "wild" in the tradition of Thomas Jefferson, Abraham Lincoln, Woodrow Wilson, and Tom Watson.[36]

Conclusion

To win political campaigns, Gene Talmadge handily exploited the hardships of working Georgians. Many of these working men and women were caught in the lower levels of the southern socio-economic system and struggling to eke out a living. The social and economic distance between a dirt farmer in debt and the banker, mayor, and governor was virtually insurmountable. Also southerners were taught at home or learned firsthand to either respect or fear bosses, public officials, and others in positions of power. Although they were angry over their arduous situation, many workers were reluctant to complain publicly.

Gene Talmadge spoke for them. He shouted on the stump what many working men and women felt and whispered privately. First he

35. Atlanta *Constitution*, July 14, May 19, 23, 26, 1946; Savannah *Morning News*, June 14, 13, 8, 1946. Talmadge "advocated vocational training so that young folks will not be walking the streets looking for a job after finishing school"; Macon *Telegraph and News*, July 5, 1942; Augusta *Chronicle*, July 24, 1940.

36. Atlanta *Constitution*, September 8, 1932, July 22, 1946, July 22, 1932, August 5, 1934, September 3, 1932.

openly recognized problems that citizens believed had been ignored. In both plain and poetic speech, Talmadge effectively called attention to their needs. Secondly he irreverently criticized business and government officials as being responsible for existing social inequities, and many white Georgians delighted in his radical speaking of disrespect.

On the stump Talmadge accommodated the inflated acclaims and expectations of even his most loyal followers. Totally uninhibited and concocting his ballistic symbols from the barnyard, he entertained, surprised, saddened, and inspired his Georgia audiences. Talmadge's timing and his selection of popular "issues" were uncanny, whether the issue was a three-dollar automobile tag or theme of race. He was a master of the rhetorical act. Employing a style of crusading that was novel in its *ornate lucidity*, Talmadge shrewdly promoted his candidacy in a language working men and women believed.

Although Talmadge expertly manipulated the masses, his campaign discourse was flawed in two ways. First his preoccupation with his own political image often resulted in superficial claims. The campaign stump was admittedly no place for elaborate policy statements, yet instead of rational plans for relieving farmers and city laborers of hardships, Talmadge was content with persuasive theatrics perfected to fill his own campaign coffer. Because he was such an effective talker, many citizens left his speech show having faithfully swallowed his prescription of chicanery. But, after Talmadge's rhetorical act had moved on and reality had set in, what did "'ole Gene" actually offer working men and women?—primarily a magic man's illusion of a gondola in each Georgian's backyard, ham in the governor's mansion, and a heightened pride in a hard way of life. There was merit, then, in his critics' representation of his campaign chicanery as "a Punch and Judy Show," "minstrel," "brag and bandwagon," and "claptrap demagoguery."[37]

Talmadge's rhetorical antics were flawed in a second way. He established a coercive climate that abridged free discussion. Advancing

37. G. C. Adams and Thomas W. Hardwick in Atlanta *Constitution*, July 29, 1928, July 31, August 21, 1932. Whereas in the 1932 campaign, W. T. Anderson, editor of the Macon *Telegraph*, severely rebuked Talmadge, in the 1942 election, Anderson supported Talmadge and recommended him to a Macon audience; Macon *Telegraph and News*, August 28, 1932; Macon *Telegraph*, August 26, 1942.

a public argument of personal infallibility, Talmadge demanded that what he said was right. All others were expected to acquiesce. Consequently, he and his followers exploited supporters, rebuffed nonpartisans, and ran roughshod over opponents.

As early as 1936 an editorial in the Atlanta *Constitution*, a newspaper that opposed Talmadge in some campaigns and supported him in others, warned of the "nazi" methods of "Talmadgeism." In his campaign speeches, Talmadge attempted to frighten blacks away from the polls. Although this Georgian could be subtle and blunt with his threats, few black or white listeners would have misunderstood his meaning. In Statesboro in 1942, he warned that "the two races get along better in the south than in any spot on earth, but if outsiders try to dictate too much, we'll need more of you red-gallused men." These were Talmadge's most aggressive followers, many of whom identified their loyalty by wearing red suspenders like the ones Gene wore. And such men often intimidated persons in the audiences who disagreed with Talmadge or who supported other candidates.

Speaking at Cochran in 1942, Talmadge attempted to frighten whites and blacks: "Maybe it would not be inappropriate to warn some of these fellows to be careful, since one of these days, in the not distant future, there is going to be one of the greatest house-cleanings of bureaucrats the country ever saw. . . . The former Governor . . . also hurled a veiled threat to Negro voters when he said: 'I think it would be extremely wise for Negroes to stay away from the white folks' ballot boxes on July 17, for neither the U.S. Attorneys nor Jimmie Carmichael [Talmadge's opponent] will have a corporal guard to back them up.'" A Kingsland audience in 1946 heard Talmadge advise "that very few Negroes would vote *if 'registrars do their duty.'"*

In addition to threatening black voters, Talmadge also created a mood hostile to opposing candidates and their followers generally. During the 1940 gubernatorial campaign in Warm Springs, "Blood streamed from bashed noses when a head-knocking spree developed between supporters of Eugene Talmadge and Abit Nix." About that conflict Talmadge was quoted as saying, "The Nix crowd got a good whipping." At another of the campaign rallies a group of persons present who spoke out against Talmadge was gassed. After that event, a newsman described how "Eugene Talmadge brought the Palace Guard from Atlanta, one of whom was indicted for throwing cans of mustard gas at a crowd of heckling Georgia State Teachers College students in the courthouse square."[38]

Critics were justified in fearing a candidate who wanted to be governor so, as Talmadge said of his own intentions, he could not be "lawed."[39] In 1934, Ellis Arnall made "a ringing speech for Eugene Talmadge" at Newnan.[40] After observing Talmadge's behavior for eight years, however, Arnall withdrew his support, and during his victorious campaign over Talmadge in 1942, he wisely warned Georgians of Talmadge's alarming appeals "to base passions, hatreds, and intolerances."[41] Because Gene Talmadge exploited a democratic system of decision-making by attempting to monopolize that free process and because he preyed on an already burdened people primarily for personal gain, the "Sage of Sugar Creek" earned the designation of political demagogue.

38. Atlanta *Constitution*, August 23, 1936, July 31, 1940, June 2, July 13, 1946; Augusta *Chronicle*, July 29, 1942, July 28, 1940; Macon *Telegraph*, July 29, 1942.

39. Macon *Telegraph*, August 20, 21, 1932; Atlanta *Constitution*, July 31, 1932.

40. Atlanta *Constitution*, September 7, 1934.

41. Augusta *Chronicle*, July 5, 1942. Talmadge admitted that "possibly I have been a little different. . . . Possibly I have not been so timid, or a little brash in carrying out my campaign pledges"; Atlanta *Constitution*, July 5, 1934.

Contributors

HOWARD DORGAN is professor of communication arts at Appalachian State University and currently serves as editor of the *Southern Speech Communication Journal*. He authored one of the essays that appeared in *Oratory in the New South* and has contributed several articles to speech communication journals.

MARY LOUISE GEHRING, now retired, was associate dean of the College of Arts and Sciences and professor of oral communication at Baylor University. She has served as executive secretary of the Southern Speech Communication Association (1958–1961) and as a member of the Legislative Assembly of the Speech Communication Association for nine years. She is coauthor with Waldo W. Braden of *Speech Practices* (1958).

G. JACK GRAVLEE is professor and chairman of the Department of Speech and Theatre Arts at Colorado State University. He authored "The New Deal" in *America in Controversy*, coedited *Pamphlets and the American Revolution* and *The Whores Rhetorick (1683)*, and has contributed articles to speech, broadcasting, and historical journals.

JERRY A. HENDRIX is professor of communication and director of the Public Communication Program at American University in Washington, D.C.

CAL M. LOGUE is professor of speech communication and director of
the Public Communication Division, University of Georgia. He
has served as president of the Southern Speech Communication
Association (1975–1976) and is presently associate editor of the
Southern Speech Communication Journal. He is author of "Restoration Strategies in Georgia, 1865–1880" in *Oratory in the New
South*, of *Ralph McGill: Editor and Publisher*, and of numerous
articles in communication journals.

M. L. MCCAULEY is on the faculty of the Episcopal School of Dallas.

HAROLD D. MIXON is associate professor of speech at Louisiana State
University. He is former book review editor of the *Southern
Speech Communication Journal* (1972–1975) and has served as
associate editor of the *Speech Teacher, Southern Speech
Communication Journal*, and *Bibliographic Annual*.

ANNETTE N. SHELBY is visiting associate professor in the School of
Business Administration at Georgetown University. Her essay,
"The Southern Lady Becomes an Advocate," published in
Oratory in the New South, received a 1980 SCA Golden
Anniversary Monograph Award.

WILLIAM M. STRICKLAND is assistant professor of speech at the
University of South Carolina and co-ordinator of speech for the
Department of Theater and Speech.

Index

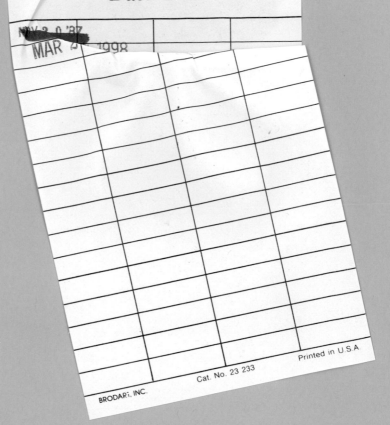

Date Due

NOV 3 0 '87			
MAR ~~3~~ 1998			

BRODART, INC.   Cat. No. 23 233   Printed in U.S.A.